THE DESIGN CO

YOUR ESSENTIAL GUIDE ⌐ ⌐⌐⌐⌐⌐ OPERATIONS

Rachel Posman

John Calhoun

 Rosenfeld

NEW YORK   2024

"If you've been overwhelmed finding your place in the rapidly expanding universe of DesignOps, this book offers the ideal combination of broad perspectives and deep insights to give you direction on your journey."

—Jesse James Garrett
Author of *The Elements of User Experience*

"Bravo! A maestro's manual! Finally, a comprehensive look at how to establish, scale, and mature DesignOps, no matter your org shape. Rachel and John say it loud for everyone in the cheap seats... DesignOps is Design!"

—Dominique Ward
Former head of Design Operations, Atlassian

"In true DesignOps fashion, Posman and Calhoun deliver a practical and inclusive guide, chock-full of practical frameworks, definitions, and tools. This is an incredible resource for practitioners and companies alike!"

—Danielle Barnes
Coauthor of *Present Yourself* and CEO of Women Talk Design

"*The Design Conductors* illustrates how exceptional design teams are also culturally strong and well-supported teams. This is the blueprint for growing small orgs into large ones and transforming them into design powerhouses."

—Chris Risdon
Coauthor of *Orchestrating Experiences*

"Calhoun and Posman provide clear and comprehensive guidance for building a DesignOps program, which, in turn, enables design and research to be their most effective."

—Peter Merholz
Independent consultant and coauthor of *Org Design for Design Orgs: Building and Managing In-House Design Teams*

"Everyone needs this book—how is it possible we've not had anything like this until now? It's well written and exceptionally well-thought-through. I am impressed with how much goodness they manage to pack in. It's an essential guide for everyone!"

—Patrizia Bertini
DesignOps strategist and leader

The Design Conductors

Your Essential Guide to Design Operations

By Rachel Posman and John Calhoun

Rosenfeld Media LLC
125 Maiden Lane
New York, New York 10038
USA

On the Web: www.rosenfeldmedia.com

Please send errata to: errata@rosenfeldmedia.com

Publisher: Louis Rosenfeld

Managing Editor: Marta Justak

Interior Layout: Danielle Foster

Cover Design: Heads of State

Illustrators: Rachel Posman and John Calhoun

Indexer: Marilyn Augst

Proofreader: Sue Boshers

© 2024 Rachel Posman and John Calhoun

All Rights Reserved

ISBN: 1-959029-23-1

ISBN 13: 978-1-959029-23-6

LCCN: 2024943639

In loving memory of my mom, Alise,
and to all the extraordinary women whose brilliance
and resilience ignite stars and balance galaxies.

Rachel Posman

To my family and mentors who've taught me
to find an excuse to say Yes.

John Calhoun

HOW TO USE THIS BOOK

Who Should Read This Book?

If you picked up this book because it said *design* or *Design Operations* on the cover, this book is definitely for you. But we also wrote this book as an essential field guide for project and program managers of all stripes. It's our belief that anyone who works at the chaotic intersection of process and change management (we're looking at you, healthcare, tech, and financial services!) can benefit from learning the design methodologies used by DesignOps practitioners.

Further, anyone who partners with or works adjacent to designers—be they software, hardware, or creative designers—will come away with a thorough understanding of how designers approach their craft and see how the operational complexities of design benefit from dedicated Ops owners. Lastly, we hope design, product, engineering, and business leaders will read this book and be inspired to lead with design, build their *own* DesignOps practice, and create a culture where the teams who build great user experiences can thrive.

What's in This Book?

We did our best to keep this book simple, and only wrote about—well, everything anyone would ever need to know about Design Operations. As we ideated on our topics, interviewed subject matter experts, and (to be honest) learned more about the DesignOps practice *while we were practicing it*, our vision for what should be included in this "essential guide" evolved and grew. In the end, a handful of overarching themes emerged, allowing us to organize this book into the following five acts (or *movements*, if you prefer to play along with the musical motif of this book).

Act One:
Fundamentals of the DesignOps Practice

For readers seeking an overview of the history and fundamental principles of Design Operations, these first two chapters are for you. In Chapter 1, "The First Note," we write about the beginnings of DesignOps—from its design agency roots, through its various implementations in the modern world of software, hardware, and creative design. Chapter 2, "Learning the Score," is our attempt to codify some basic definitions of Design Operations, grounded in the three universal tenets of where DesignOps *focuses*, how its practitioners *act*, and what the practice *delivers*.

Act Two:
Fundamentals of the DesignOps Practitioner

This act shifts from practice to practitioner, bringing readers a comprehensive study of the *individuals* who are employed in (or seeking to be employed by) Design Operations teams. Chapter 3, "Drawn to the Stage," outlines the most common backgrounds from which DesignOps practitioners come, such as "traditional" design fields, program management, business and administration, and more. In Chapter 4, "It's All About Practice," we define the eight career competencies that all DesignOps practitioners share; these are the fundamental abilities that anyone seeking to work in Design Operations would be expected to learn or be skilled in. Looking at these backgrounds and competencies together brings us to Chapter 5, "Composing Your Career," in which we reveal an end-to-end framework that defines the expectations and career ladder for DesignOps professionals and those seeking to build a DesignOps practice. In Chapter 6, "Your DesignOps Crescendo," we interview DesignOps veterans who have found themselves at the top rung of this ladder, and we explore the different paths a DesignOps career can lead to. Finally, Chapter 7, "Playing Your Part," dives into one of the most important individual responsibilities of anyone practicing DesignOps: leading with and operationalizing *values* to effect transformative change in design teams and businesses.

Act Three:
Fundamentals of DesignOps Organizations

In this act, we zoom out from the practitioner and practice, and focus on how DesignOps teams are shaped by the specific organizational contexts in which they appear. Chapter 8, "Shaped by the Orchestra," looks at the relationship between DesignOps and design teams, and how the four most common design org models influence the ways in which Design Operations teams are organized and function. Chapter 9, "Your Performance Partners," examines the network of related roles with whom DesignOps partners and how the maturity and influence of these roles in any given business defines different opportunities and areas of ownership for Design Operations. Finally, Chapter 10, "From Soloist to Symphony." shows how the most complicated organizational context of all—a design team's size and maturity—can end up being the most influential factor in shaping the contours of its DesignOps partners.

Act Four:
Establishing and Growing a DesignOps Practice

Our fourth act takes all the fundamentals discussed thus far and pivots them into the practical application of building, running, and growing a Design Operations team. Chapter 11, "Ready to Take Up the Baton," is for readers who have made it this far and are interested in starting a DesignOps practice from scratch; it includes the basic, tactical steps required to establish a new team's mission and work-streams. Unsurprisingly, Chapter 12, "Maintaining Your Rhythm," focuses on *growing* the DesignOps practice, the organizational signals to tune in to that indicate it's time to grow (and mature), and some of the key factors to consider when a DesignOps team reaches these evolutionary milestones. Finally, Chapter 13, "The Wrong Notes," looks at the messy and unfortunate side effects of growth— namely, the risks and obstacles of growing too quicky (or too slowly), and how to manage the challenges associated with reductions in force and other negative externalities.

Act Five:
Strategies to Improve DesignOps' Impact

The final act will equip readers with methods and frameworks that ensure a DesignOps team is always improving and delivering impact. In Chapter 14, "Tuning Your Instruments," we show how to apply two of the most important tools in the DesignOps toolkit— design strategy and change management—in service of its practice. Chapter 15, "Measure by Measure," turns to the topic of DesignOps value, specifically, frameworks for defining the measures of its value, and how to prioritize and implement them. Lastly, DesignOps' impact would be nothing without the *people* responsible for driving that impact. Chapter 16, "A Symphony of Talent," provides a comprehensive toolkit for individuals seeking to join a DesignOps team through the interview process and a set of guidelines for hiring managers to conduct fair, thorough interviews of prospective talent.

What Comes with This Book?

This book's companion website (rosenfeldmedia.com/books/ design-operations/) contains a blog and additional content. The book's diagrams and other illustrations are available under a Creative Commons license (when possible) for you to download and include in your own presentations. You can find these on Flickr at www.flickr.com/photos/rosenfeldmedia/sets/.

FREQUENTLY ASKED QUESTIONS

What is the most important lesson in this book?

The lesson is easy to summarize but complicated to explain. Hence, we wrote this book to help readers of all backgrounds understand that "DesignOps *is* design."

What's the difference between Design Operations and design program management?

We generally use the term *Design Operations* (commonly shortened to *DesignOps*) as the highest-order label to refer to this practice. The name is inclusive of many aspects of design, such as user experience design, content design, and research; we acknowledge variations and subtleties in this label in Chapter 1, "The First Note." Our position is that the work of design program management is just one component of DesignOps. That said, the role and title of *design program manager* (commonly shortened to *DPM*) is the best descriptor of someone who practices Design Operations, regardless of their skill, level, or day-to-day job responsibilities.

Is this the first book on DesignOps?

Yes! But also—sort of? This is the first book entirely devoted to DesignOps. In recent years, product and design books have started to describe Design Operations in the context of *their* practices. Some authors have dedicated sections and even whole chapters to the topic! But as leaders in this field, we felt it was important to have a book about DesignOps written and informed by those who practice it daily. We know that there is a risk to Design Operations of being defined by other disciplines (which we cover throughout Chapters 8–10) and wanted to provide readers with *our* definitive viewpoint of the practice.

How do I build myself up to become a DesignOps practitioner? How do I build up a DesignOps practice?

This book is ideal for individuals and businesses alike who are "DesignOps curious." We define core career competencies (and mindsets) in Chapter 4, "It's All About Practice," which can be used by prospective DesignOps candidates to focus on areas to skill up or promote on a résumé. Similarly, businesses can use these competencies to articulate career ladders and levels, which we cover in Chapter 5, "Composing Your Career." As far as building out the practice, our journey map of Design Operations teams from small to medium to large (and their relationship to the design maturity or their partner design orgs) is covered exhaustively in Chapter 11, "Ready to Take up the Baton," and Chapter 12, "Maintaining Your Rhythm."

Will AI take over DesignOps jobs?

Our book does not explore too deeply the topic of generative AI and its impact on Design Operations. We share our point of view in the Epilogue and acknowledge that this is a hot topic that (unfortunately) doesn't have a lot of definitive answers. At the time of this writing, we maintain that AI will be an important and valuable *partner* in the design process—one that enhances creative thinking and streamlines workflows. AI, in our view, will be less disruptive to DesignOps and will mostly replace the rote aspects of the role that can and should be delegated anyway.

CONTENTS

FOREWORD

People spend 60% of their time on what they call "work about work," which means trying to figure out who's doing what, when, and why.

—Chris Farinacci, former COO, Asana

As organizations scale and evolve, they often find themselves in a state of inertia. They're unable to move forward toward a holistic strategy, and face too many interdependencies across domains with varied goals and success measures.

Some of the most common issues design teams face—limited time, scarce resources, inconsistent input from the right people, and lack of perceived or proven value—can negatively impact designer happiness and design team success. Individual designer's skills are not to blame. Rather, it is poor coordination of designers' "experience of making" that creates these barriers to success. As teams scale, these issues are exacerbated by departmental silos, increased operational overhead, duplicate efforts, and inconsistent connection of an organization's strategy to its delivery.

Orchestration across people, work, and platforms is an essential activity, yet connecting the dots between vision and strategy, and roadmapping them to the day-to-day activities and output of a team, is hard work. It requires effort and a coordinated focus on structures, accountability, and ownership.

DesignOps does the critical job of figuring out what the work is to be done and then designing the infrastructure to get it done. The field is a reminder that *how teams work is just as important as what they make.*

Cue the Design Conductors!

When I worked with Rachel at Adaptive Path/Capital One (circa 2012), we called this way of working "seeing around corners." This expression captures one of the key principles of how we established and described Design Operations to our colleagues, clients, and community. In those early days of the practice, we sought to collect the overlooked and underappreciated aspects of running a design team. We were not alone in this mission. Across industries, this job emerged with varying names: from design program management, business operations, and producer, to Hootsuite's inventive "Czar of Bad Systems" and Spotify's spot-on "Director of Getting Sh*t Done." Unsurprisingly, many of the problems that existed in our (and others') product and service design teams could be traced back to a lack of communication, coordination, and collaboration. As a result, individuals, teams, and organizations often faced similar challenges across three key areas: people, practice, and platforms. We defined a framework to enable the right people working on the right things at the right time and used it as a lens to identify some of the programs necessary to get to the desired outcomes for each pillar: happier designers, better designers, and more effective teams.

Effective leadership is hard work. Thankfully, Rachel and John's comprehensive guide will equip you with the frameworks and methods needed to navigate the toughest challenges in creating great product and service experiences. Understanding strategy and vision is often the easy part; connecting this strategy to the *work that needs to be done,* and *how it's going to happen,* is the hard part. The chapters that follow demystify this complexity, and will unlock for readers the strategy, planning, and activities necessary to establish, define, evolve, and improve design teams and organizations.

Rachel and John have crafted an invaluable resource with insights drawn from interviews with subject matter experts and years of hands-on experience, providing a solid foundation for how Design Operations contributes to building and managing effective design teams. In these pages, you'll find an extensive collection of definitions, strategies, and best practices that you can put to work right away. Whether you're leading a small design team or managing a large-scale design organization, the principles laid out in this book will help you create a more cohesive, efficient, effective, and well-run team.

It's fitting that the authors chose the "Conductors" metaphor. I see Rachel and John as orchestrators and builders—adept at identifying patterns, envisioning better solutions, forecasting improvements, setting foundations, and blueprinting operating plans for teams and organizations. Using the methods of design, they've demonstrated time and again how to assess business processes and organizational challenges. They imagine, create, and implement novel solutions well-ahead of anyone asking for them; it's almost as if they can see around corners

—Kristin Skinner, founder and chief experience officer at &GSD, an experience design collective, and coauthor *Org Design for Design Orgs: Building and Managing In-House Design Teams*

PROLOGUE: DESIGN IN HARMONY

When we—Rachel and John—first started working together, we met as eight-inch-tall likenesses on a laptop screen, headquartered in (but never having actually stepped *foot* in) the second tallest building on the West Coast. We were frequently talking over each other and pantomiming "You're on mute!" The year was 2020, and like everyone else, we were learning how to conduct ourselves in a workplace suddenly governed by emojis and virtual meetings.

This period marked a profound change for the world. In comparison, the rather prosaic changes we made that year to the DesignOps practice at our company didn't seem particularly significant. Our Design Operations team was growing slowly, responsible for supporting a design organization that was scaling *rapidly*. But then, all of a sudden—it was growing *remotely*, too. And before we knew it, design teams were growing *globally* as well, working across multiple time zones and cultures.

Our DesignOps operating model was showing signs of age before the worldwide pandemic arrived, but the external forces impacting our design org that year really accelerated the need for our DesignOps team to evolve. The changes we made were structural—organizing the team into "horizontal" and "vertical" practices, and also operational—defining how these two groups would work together in (hopefully) force-multiplying ways. Some of our experiments paid off, while others did not. Many existing pain points were solved; several new sources of friction emerged. Under our DesignOps leader and EVP of Design, we kept testing, measuring, and iterating—using the methods our *designers* employed, but in service of designing processes, not pixels.

And as we evolved our operating model, we talked about it—a *lot*—because 2020 was a time when DesignOps practitioners were still discovering one another and building a community. Platforms and events were becoming more accessible (perhaps because of the virtual-first landscape?), connecting the do-it-all design program managers with "mature" DesignOps teams eager to share advice and frameworks. We were plugged in to this scene before it started taking off, and, having missed some of its community during the pandemic, humbly wanted to share our own story with teams that might benefit from our experience.

That year, we presented "Two Sides of the DesignOps Coin" at the Rosenfeld DesignOps Summit, the first online-only megaconference of its kind either of us had spoken at. From our tiny webcams on opposite sides of the Golden Gate Bridge, we chatted with a global audience about our pain points, design org maturity, different operating models, and more. After forty minutes of Google slides and Q&A, we turned off our cameras and returned to the conference as attendees, watching and learning from our fellow presenters. A great day was in the books. That's a wrap!

Or so we thought. As we were presenting, the DesignOps Summit Slack channel was lighting up. Our boss was gracious enough to capture screenshots of the conversation in real time and shared them with us afterward. Many of our favorite comments were in this general vein:

Like, who *wouldn't* love to hear that they had struck DesignOps gold from Kristin Skinner? Other comments were slightly more enthusiastic:

From gold to all the answers of the universe? We'll take it. (So long as we're only talking about the DesignOps universe.) Comments like the following helped us realize that there was a real appetite from novices and veterans alike to hear more candid stories about scaling Design Operations:

daveixd
This is what it means to take a role a turn it into a practice. Bravo Salesforce! this is next level shit! LOVE IT!

👌 9 👏 5 ✌ 1 😊+

But it was this one that really caught our attention:

Bart Renner
hey @louisrosenfeld! Can you make this presentation a book? Take my money!

➕ 9 💰 6 😊+

And So We Did!

...make a book, that is. (Presumably someone else took your money.) The journey to writing this book has taken countless twists and turns—from new children and wildfires to tech industry expansion and contraction; from blockchain and generative AI to obstacles big and small in our personal and professional lives. The hardest part, though, was deciding what aspects of Design Operations most needed to be talked about. So, we settled on the simplest and most obvious path forward: write about *all* of it and create something that could stand up as the "essential field guide" to this practice. You're holding that work in your hands.

The Design Conductors: Your Essential Guide to Design Operations captures our career experience advocating for, building out, and scaling up DesignOps teams. Our mission is to enable cross-functional organizations to prioritize and lead with design, and build a practice that puts its people, products, and processes at the heart of its success. We hope that curious and new DesignOps practitioners will discover how to surface and refine their own operational superpowers and help jumpstart their careers with tested best practices and frameworks. DesignOps veterans will learn how to apply design methodologies to their *own* practice and how to plot a roadmap for sustainable DesignOps growth. And for design and product business leaders, we want to demystify the field of Design Operations and illuminate how this practice *multiplies* the impacts of a design team to the overall business.

Our book is organized into five sections. The first describes the fundamentals of the *practice*—everything that is foundational to DesignOps as a discipline at the highest level. The second section defines the fundamentals of the *practitioner*—the common characteristics and competencies of those currently doing (or being hired into) DesignOps roles. The third section describes DesignOps in various *organizational contexts,* while the fourth section outlines how to take these theoretical foundations and make them practical, by *establishing and growing* a DesignOps practice. Our final section introduces *strategies and frameworks* to measure DesignOps maturity and outcomes, and how these measures can be used to improve the practice's overall impact and success. Lastly, we have included a *toolbox* of templates and guides to inspire teams to action.

Finally, readers will notice a recurring musical motif throughout this book. (It's not subtle.) We are both artists—a musician and a ballerina—and we strongly believe that the process and optimization associated with DesignOps should not disguise the craft and artistry required to do it well. We are also not the only experts and have included perspectives and contributions throughout this book from our fellow practitioners.

DesignOps is a field within the realm of design itself, and its program managers and producers are as much artists as a visual designer or design strategist. What separates the two is merely their respective roles in the performance of their craft. Design Operations' responsibility is, ultimately, to be the conductor of a greater orchestra—one comprised of talented musicians whose performance is unified by a steady hand holding the baton.

The First Note
DesignOps Beginnings

Whatever your taste in music, we would like you to picture an orchestra: bows poised over finely-tuned strings, woodwinds warming up, tympanies thumping away, musicians ready to follow a beautiful score. In front of this ensemble is the conductor—someone who is perhaps also a musician, but in this imagined orchestra has a very different part to play. To the untrained eye, the conductor's role looks like a lot of baton-waving, but behind every reaching arm and flick of the wrist, they are doing something critically important for the orchestra: creating the conditions for the musicians to operate in harmony for the entire performance.

Beautiful music is a product of both roles: the orchestra and the conductor. (Composers and sound engineers, we haven't forgotten about you, but we can only take this metaphor so far.) The musicians and conductor are united by their passion to create beautiful music and move their audience. They achieve this goal in different ways, and their methods and responsibilities are complementary, collaborative, and co-designed to reach the same outcome. Match the passion and creativity of a premier soloist with a conductor who can manage multiple tempos and instrument sections, and the end result is a transcendent musical experience that has the power to inspire audiences.

Design and Design Operations (also called *DesignOps*) share a similar symmetry in roles and outcomes. Designers are invested in and passionate about their creative process. They want to create products that are beautiful and useful, connecting with users on a deep emotional level. Practitioners of Design Operations want the same thing, achieving their goals instead through the design of processes, practices, and cultures where making meaningful user experiences can be achieved.

Design leader Miles Orkin said, "If we want to make great experiences in our products, we have to feel great about the experience of making." This quote neatly summarizes the value of Design Operations, and the impact our practice has on both the designer and the end product: to create the conditions that make great design possible. DesignOps practitioners understand that the "experience of making" is just as important as "making the experience"—a journey and destination so intertwined with each other that they're essentially inseparable, save for a difference in focus on what gets designed versus how it gets designed.

Design and Design Operations

DesignOps practitioners are the conductors of the design orchestra. Just as a conductor must deeply understand the music, the musicians' roles, and how each instrument contributes to a particular score, DesignOps practitioners—designers themselves, of a sort—possess a basic (if not deep) understanding of how designers work and how their roles function within a broader design ecosystem. If DesignOps practitioners are the conductors, then design leaders are composers writing the score. DesignOps helps bring the leader's vision to life.

Design Operations is the team responsible for designing the design team's experience. Focusing on the (mostly) internal aspects of an organization, the work of DesignOps supports better customer and employee experiences. DesignOps practitioners design the systems, processes, tools, and frameworks in service of three specific outcomes, defined by Kristin Skinner and Kamdyn Moore (from their 2019 DesignOps Summit talk) as "better, happier, and more effective design teams." In other words, DesignOps ensures that a design team can produce exceptional products *and* have a fulfilling experience in the process.

At its core, Design Operations exists to amplify the impact and effectiveness of a design organization at scale. Our discipline plays a vital role in shaping the strategy behind how design leaders operate and make decisions (themselves orchestrators, primarily of people rather than processes). DesignOps practitioners are an esteemed partner to their design leaders, trusted as experts for their ability to understand a design team's needs. They provide value to leadership by owning the rails of insights, advocacy, and thought partnership at all levels, from the minutely tactical to the hugely strategic. By building the connective tissue between the design team and design leadership (and design leaders and business partners), DesignOps formalizes and operationalizes the design vision bringing the strategy to fruition. Patrizia Bertini, DesignOps leader at 8x8 (and DesignOps *thought* leader around the globe), describes the practice like this:

> Design operations isn't about tool management, project management, or even program management; it's a strategic discipline focused on making sure that the strategy comes to life.

DesignOps practitioners also act as the intermediaries between different business and product functions, enabling the design team to focus on what they do best: designing. DesignOps' role is to be (and to build) the crucial bridge between HR, legal, procurement, and finance, and to enable strong cross-functional relationships with partners in product and engineering.

With such an outsized part to play, it can be easy to think that design and DesignOps evolved alongside each other from the earliest days of product design. But the fact is that DesignOps is a relatively new and grassroots field—one that emerged organically in many different companies and industries as the need for this kind of role became apparent. In the past, design managers or senior individual contributors found themselves juggling operational tasks alongside design work, prompting the realization of an operational gap. It's been only recently that Design Operations has started to define itself and codify its position.

We'll cover the specifics of this practice in the chapters ahead, but we'll first start by reviewing the foundational elements of DesignOps: its roots, its current state as a practice, and why it is poised for future growth in the years and decades to come.

The Roots of Design Operations

Design Operations emerged in the early 2000s as a way to address the increasing complexity and scale of design work within organizations. During this period, software development practices evolved to address the challenges of deploying and maintaining code in rapidly changing environments. The term *DevOps* emerged to describe the practice of improving collaboration between *development* (*Dev*) and *information technology operations* (*Ops*). In time, DesignOps drew inspiration from DevOps principles, recognizing similar potential benefits for design teams.

As technology evolved in the 2000s, companies began to realize the value of design in creating differentiated products and services. This led to a growing demand for design expertise and services. At the same time, the rise of digital technologies—such as responsive web frameworks, mobile, wearables, cloud computing, and collaborative design software—was transforming the design industry, creating new opportunities and challenges. This disruption created an environment in which larger, legacy companies sought to solve for this "digital revolution" by acquiring smaller design agencies, in order to gain access to their specialized skills and expertise. Before this point, in-house design teams were a rare species.

The mid-2000s was also a period of economic growth and expansion. Big companies that wanted to become design-led had two choices: build or buy. Many had access to large amounts of capital with which to invest, and acquiring design agencies was seen as a way to expand into new markets and grow their businesses and capabilities. Coinciding with this acquisition boom was an increasing recognition of the role of design in business success and the need for design-driven innovation. By the late 2010s, the consolidation of small design agencies and large legacy companies began to taper off, but not before some big moves were completed. Some examples are shown in Table 1.1.

TABLE 1.1   DESIGN AGENCY ACQUISITIONS BY LARGER COMPANIES

Agency	Acquired by	Year
Frog Design	Flextronics	2004
Huge	Interpublic Group	2008
Method	GlobalLogic	2011
Hot Studio	Facebook	2013
Fjord	Accenture	2013
Adaptive Path	Capital One	2014
Lunar	McKinsey & Company	2015
Artefact	Accenture	2017
MATTER	Accenture	2017

While there have always been "accidental" DesignOps practitioners on design teams (see Chapter 2, "Learning the Score," and 3, "Drawn to the Stage," for more on this subject), the formalization of Design Operations as a discipline gained traction in the mid-2010s. In 2015, Lindsay Schweigler (now a DesignOps leader at Apple) was recruited for a chief of staff role at Uber, managing the operations of its 100+ person design team. Having previously led business operations and program management for the design firms, frog and Fjord, she negotiated the retitling of the position to head of Design Operations to better reflect the specific needs and skills required. A few months later, Meredith Black, up for promotion at Pinterest, followed suit after discovering Schweigler's unique title on LinkedIn. Shortly after, the term DesignOps gained steady adoption and recognition for both the role and the discipline.

Producers and program managers have long been an important part of a design agency's core team. These roles oversee the delivery of complex design projects, ensuring that they are completed on time, within budget, and to high quality standards—all while managing client and stakeholder relationships. As design agencies were brought in-house, the value of a "design-focused program manager" was introduced to companies that had never before encountered this role, and it is from these origins that DesignOps took flight.

At the same time, fundamental shifts were happening in tech companies, and especially in the field of user experience (UX). From its early origins in "human computer interaction" (HCI), the UX field began to grow rapidly in the early to mid-2000s, as digital products and services became more widespread. This growth was fueled in part by the rise of smartphones and other mobile and multimedia devices, which created new opportunities for UX designers to design a new category of user-friendly interfaces and experiences. As UX design grew, so, too, did the complexity of design projects and the number of designers involved. This complexity created a demand for more efficient and effective ways of managing the design process. In response, companies like Airbnb, Facebook, Pinterest, and Capital One began to invest in building dedicated DesignOps teams to support their business strategies and design efforts.

The practice of DesignOps continued to codify and gain industry alignment and recognition through community and industry growth. The first dedicated DesignOps conference, the aptly-named *DesignOps Summit,* was organized by Rosenfeld Media in 2017. Here, early DesignOps leaders came together to define the practice of DesignOps and articulate the case for establishing the role and practice in companies where it didn't yet exist. Since that first program, the focus of the DesignOps Summit has evolved from defining DesignOps to scaling DesignOps. Now in its seventh year, this conference attracts attendees globally from hundreds of companies, including a large portion of the Fortune 100.

This time period also saw the birth of DesignOps Assembly (DOA). The year 2017 marked the inception of a close-knit group of DesignOps experts led by Meredith Black and Elyse Eshel, with a shared mission of knowledge exchange and support. DOA's exponential growth since then is a testament to the rapid evolution of the DesignOps industry.

THE RISE OF THE DESIGNOPS COMMUNITY

Meredith Black, director of DesignOps at Figma and founder of DesignOps Assembly

DesignOps Assembly started in 2016 when Elyse Eshel and I were working at Spotify and Pinterest, respectively. We realized we were doing very similar things, and we weren't going to do it alone. Slowly, we kept finding others on LinkedIn with DesignOps titles who are now the the the high priestesses of DesignOps: Rachel Posman, Kristin Skinner, Jacqui Frey, Lindsay Schweigler, Adrienne Allnutt, Diane Gregorio, Kate Battles, Kim Fellman, Candace Myers (and a few others).

We invited them to come hang out with us. We drew our respective org charts on whiteboards at Pinterest while eating Delfina Pizza. We realized we were onto something. Our orgs were all very similar, and we started talking about what was working and what wasn't. Then we were like, "You want to do this more often?" And everyone said yes, so we kept meeting. Things formalized in 2017 when more DesignOps folks were getting hired, and people started offering up their office space for meetups.

Our meetups focused on community building with other DesignOps pioneers, sharing job opportunities, and learning from each other. DesignOps folks are usually the ones with the hard and not-so-fun jobs, so we wanted to make sure our events weren't too serious.

When the pandemic hit in 2020, events weren't possible, so we shifted our focus to our tiny Slack workspace. Fast forward a bit, and we hit 1,000 people and thought, "Whoa—1,000 people want to talk about DesignOps? No way!" We then learned how Zoom and virtual-first events would work and offered up ways for people to connect. At this time, DesignOps was a buzzword in the industry, so we knew that this was a pivotal point in how we defined DesignOps.

The demand for these roles was growing so fast. But the problem was that there weren't enough people in the field and very few "experts." So, Learning Labs emerged to train the next generation of DesignOps practitioners based on real-world learnings and experience. Today, DesignOps Assembly boasts 6,000 members in our Slack channel, 21 global chapters hosting regular events, and a thriving educational program. It's a testament to the growth and recognition of DesignOps in the industry.

In 2015, I embarked on a new journey at Adaptive Path, joining Kristin Skinner's pioneering DesignOps team as a program manager. While I had previous experience in design and program management on design teams, this role felt like the beginning of a new era. We were a small, but growing, team of program managers who had a deep understanding of design, and we were leading the way in a new and important practice. At the time, our team was called *Design Management* since the industry had not yet settled on the term *DesignOps*.

Adaptive Path was still in its early days of acquisition by Capital One, and we functioned like an internal agency hired by business units across the company for service and experience design projects. Our design teams were organized by the skills needed for each project. We might have a couple service designers, a UX designer, a graphic designer, a design lead, and a program manager (me) who would work together on complex and strategic vision work and design end-to-end experiences involving many touchpoints across multiple channels. The work was complicated and exciting, and with our design knowledge and backgrounds, our ownership went well beyond the typical program management tasks like scope, schedule, and budget.

I participated in the design process up until the "making," collaborating on storyboarding, service blueprints, journey mapping, workshops, and more. However, once it was time to design the app, the artifacts, the web pages, etc., my attention turned to figuring out what was needed to make this idea real. I was responsible for navigating the complex financial services regulations, partnering with legal, compliance, brand and marketing, and many more to figure out what was needed to deliver our design innovations to customers or internal teams.

In addition to our day jobs managing these strategic projects, we were tasked with defining, advocating for, and scaling the new DesignOps practice. The practice was not yet fully understood by the business or even within the design industry, so we spent a lot of time showcasing our value and making a case for DesignOps as a strategic practice.

Looking back, those early days were some of the most challenging, but also the most rewarding, of my career. We were pioneers in a rapidly evolving field, and every day brought new opportunities to innovate, push boundaries, and make a real impact. The work we did laid the foundation for what would become the cutting-edge field of DesignOps, and I'm proud to have been a part of such an exciting and transformative journey.

DesignOps practitioners in the early years focused primarily on streamlining design processes and improving design team efficiency. In practice, this meant creating standardized design workflows, tools, and documentation to ensure consistency across design projects and teams. As the field has evolved, DesignOps has come to encompass a broader range of activities, including supporting global/distributed design teams and scaling and integrating design into larger organizational structures.

Today, DesignOps has become an invaluable part of many design organizations, helping to ensure that design and business strategy are intentionally linked, and that the needs of design teams are met in a responsible and sustainable way.

Design Operations Today

Today's design organizations face common challenges organizing, running and scaling their design functions. This is true regardless of the industry, product, or service being delivered. As such, Design Operations teams have emerged across a variety of industries, including software, hardware, and creative fields. Whether they work in-house, at agencies, or as independent consultants, DesignOps practitioners are in high demand.

The field of design has seen steady growth for over a decade, with a hiring surge peaking in 2020. Demand for DesignOps rose alongside it, leading to a global increase in new practitioners. From early 2021 to 2022, 24% of DesignOps practitioners were first-timers who had just entered the field.[1]

Despite tech and design layoffs in 2023 (which also affected DesignOps), 15% of all current DesignOps practitioners joined the field that year.[2] Interestingly, while a quarter of DesignOps teams experienced layoffs during this time, 9% experienced growth, and 31% remained unchanged.[3] This underscores the increasing recognition of how important DesignOps is in helping companies create outstanding products and ensuring that their design teams are effective, efficient, and happy.

---

[1] Angelos Arnis and Adam Fry-Pierce, "State of DesignOps 2022," https://designops.report/

[2] *2023 DesignOps Benchmarking Report* (DesignOps Assembly, 2023), www.designopsassembly.com/2023report

[3] Ibid.

Alongside the evolution of the DesignOps practice came an evolution of the language to describe this discipline. In this book (and as a recognized industry standard), we use the terms *DesignOps* and *Design Operations* as an all-encompassing label to describe our practice in the broadest sense: as a person or team that applies the practice of operations to a design or design-adjacent team. Today, there are more specific DesignOps roles (e.g., design chief of staff) and functional areas (e.g., design systems) that exist under the DesignOps umbrella.

We commonly say *DesignOps practitioner* as a general term to refer to a person who does DesignOps. Today, it's also common to hear *design program manager* (DPM or DPgM) as a standard title. In some organizations, this title is a term for a specific role, which may connote more explicit expectations of the person doing the job; for the purposes of this book, though, we will use DPM or design program manager as an all-inclusive label. Some additional terms to know:

- **Design Operations (DesignOps):** A team or person that applies the practice of operations to a design team. This is the umbrella term used to describe the practice overall. Most often this practice applies to UX and product design teams, but other design disciplines (marketing, creative, etc.) can be included as well. Some horizontally focused DesignOps focused teams are called *DesignOps* to distinguish their work from the delivery-focused DPMs.

- **UX Operations (UX Ops):** This is sometimes used in product organizations that include more than just design teams. For example, if research, content writing, and product design are all part of the user experience (UX) organization, a practitioner may support *all* of these functions. For these people, *UX Ops* can be a more inclusive title. UX Ops may also be used to reflect the name of the organization they sit within, i.e., if the parent org is called *UX* and not *design*.

- **Product (or Delivery) DesignOps:** This is a subset of DesignOps that specifically concentrates on optimizing design delivery for individual product design teams. To avoid any confusion, and to distinguish it from the operational role within product management teams, we recommend including "design" in the name.

- **Central DesignOps:** Also known as *CentralOps*, *TeamOps*, or *PeopleOps*. This is the central pillar of DesignOps that focuses on horizontal programs for the whole design org. Similarly, to avoid confusion with other Ops roles, we recommend including "design" in the name. Sometimes the horizontal function is just simply called *DesignOps*.

- **Research Operations (ResOps):** Used for operational teams focused on research and insights, inclusive of project managers and recruitment specialists. These roles may be included within DesignOps or sit separately, depending on how the user experience team is organized.

- **Creative Operations (CreativeOps):** This relatively recent label is used for roles in creative organizations, such as brand marketing and web design. Experts in digital asset management (DAM) systems, who are accustomed to helping teams produce creative content quickly, are commonly found here.

- **Design Program Manager (DPM or DPgM):** The standard role and job family that DesignOps practitioners hold within a DesignOps or design team. We use this term throughout to include anyone performing a DesignOps role. This role title encompasses a spectrum of levels. More on DesignOps levels and ladders in Chapter 5, "Composing Your Career."

If you remember only two terms, remember *DesignOps* and *design program management*, the two terms used most often in this book.

A Growing Need for DesignOps

Designing and developing products in a fast-paced, complex, and high-stakes environment is no easy feat. With customers having more public platforms to air their grievances, getting the product experience right has become a top priority for most organizations. "Getting it right," however, requires more people and more roles to deliver quality experiences. This in turn means investing in more tools, which are often incompatible with one another, difficult to learn, and expensive to maintain.

To make matters more complicated, today's design and development teams are often global and distributed, making it impossible to rely on traditional methods of alignment. Teams can no longer assume that everyone will be in-person at a stand-up meeting, nor can they track a backlog on an actual wall of traditional stickies. When you multiply the compounding factors of high customer expectations, complex tooling, and distributed teams, the result is unnecessary friction for design and development teams, who just want to do the right thing and make great products.

As those of us in DesignOps know, the operational side of design work needs to get done whether or not there is someone with that job title. And if there is no dedicated DesignOps practitioner, someone else has unofficially stepped into that role. Now, responsibilities are blurred, with designers handling the "what" and "how" aspects of their work, leaving little time to focus on what they do best. This also means that their available time to mentor designers, oversee work, and lead strategic efforts across the organization is compromised.

This is why there is a growing need for DesignOps. On a small team, one designer might take part-time ownership of operations, creating early processes and standards. However, as the team scales up from a design team to a design organization, leadership will be faced with the operational challenges of managing more people. Coordination at an organizational level requires a dedicated DesignOps practitioner— someone who can ensure operations and management processes and systems are adequate, freeing up the design team to focus on their craft.

To be effective in the future, design organizations will require strategic operational leaders who can solve ambiguous problems, anticipate evolving needs, navigate change, and create solutions that adapt to new technologies. Furthermore, designers can build better products when they are happy, energized, supported, and inspired. It is at *this* intersection where DesignOps does its best work—partnering with design leadership to create the environment where designers do their best work.

Coda: The Best Is Yet to Come

Regardless of what the future holds for software and hardware makers, the importance of design is not going anywhere. Users will experience products in exciting and unimaginable ways, but the fundamentals of crafting a "user experience" will be as critical tomorrow as they are today—if not more so.

Design Operations will follow a similar trajectory. As of this writing, our discipline is at an inflection point, passing through a transitional period of being new, to being necessary. (Not to mention weathering a pandemic, economic downturns, and the tidal wave of generative AI.) Recognize where your design organization is on this readiness spectrum and know that if DesignOps still feels novel and untested in your business, it will soon become indispensable and critical to your business success. And for the design program managers along for that journey, we want them to know: the best is yet to come.

Learning the Score
DesignOps Defined

If you're new to the idea of DesignOps, hopefully our overview of the practice and its history struck a chord. Sometimes, we meet people who have never heard the words *design* and *operations* stitched together, but the details and story of how DesignOps came to be will have a familiar ring: "That sounds just like me! That's what *I've* been doing, I just never knew there was a name for it."

Unofficial practitioners of Design Operations are pretty easy to spot. They are always in some design adjacent role, such as designer, producer, programmer, or project manager. The definitions of their "actual" roles are well understood, but for these people, there are poorly defined "other things" they find themselves doing and gravitating toward.

Think of a UX designer who is savvy at creating wonderful user journey diagrams, but also has an acumen for organizing artifacts to make them easy to search and reuse. Or imagine a programmer who implements those user journeys in code—but also has a point-of-view on which design artifacts and team checkpoints are most helpful throughout the delivery cycle. Lastly, picture a producer who coordinates reviews between a studio and client, and *also* concocts new ways of working and learning to make the studio's designers more engaged and enabled.

Each of these people are doing bits and pieces of the DesignOps practice. They're orchestrating small motions of Design Operations, but don't have the official title of DesignOps "conductor." (Nor, for that matter, formal training or even a "score" to follow!) When these unofficial practitioners learn about DesignOps, it's like music to their ears. Suddenly, all those operational side projects and affinities make sense; they're not just "other things" they do, but core elements of an established and well-defined discipline.

Defining the Discipline

To all the unofficial practitioners, unsupported design organizations, and curious businesses new to the concept of Design Operations, we *see* you. Having a shared understanding of the basic DesignOps framework and its underlying details is critical to understanding this practice. Although Design Operations has only been around since the last decade, that's still ample time for core tenets to have evolved and converged. Which begs the question: after all these years, why isn't DesignOps better known?

One of the biggest challenges DesignOps practitioners face is that while its tenets may be innately *understood*, they have not been formally *defined*. To that end, this chapter will cover how we define the basic vocabulary of where Design Operations *focuses*, how it *acts*, and what it *delivers* (Figure 2.1). By grounding our practice in a set of shared definitions, we hope to establish a firm foundation that novice and veteran DesignOps practitioners alike can stand on when communicating about their field and to confidently answer the question: "What does DesignOps *do*?"

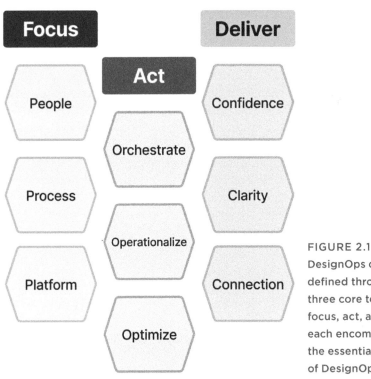

FIGURE 2.1 DesignOps can be defined through its three core tenets: focus, act, and deliver, each encompassing the essential principles of DesignOps.

YOU SAY, I SAY, THEY SAY

Oh man, this is the part where Rachel and I take on the very-easy-and-definitely-not-controversial task of defining Design Operations...For everyone... In a book...

All the sections coming up are how *we* define DesignOps. We prefer certain terms over others and have grouped some areas together that could just as easily have been categorized differently. With just a little bit of searching, you'll find really smart articles by even smarter people that might say DesignOps focuses on *four* domains (not three) or uses the term *practice* in a different way than us. And that's OK!

Truth is, every DesignOps practitioner is defining this discipline in real-time, and doing so in the context of their own organization. We all own this experience, and we all get to decide which terms best describe what we do. So, even though Rachel and I will set out to define a basic vocabulary for DesignOps in this chapter, we hope you'll translate and remix our definitions into your own words.

Where DesignOps Focuses

A common definition of DesignOps' goal is "To cultivate the conditions in which better experiences can be created, not only for end users, but also for the designers making them." This statement alludes to the most visible defining characteristic of our practice: people, process, and platform, the three domains where DesignOps is most frequently focused (Figure 2.2).

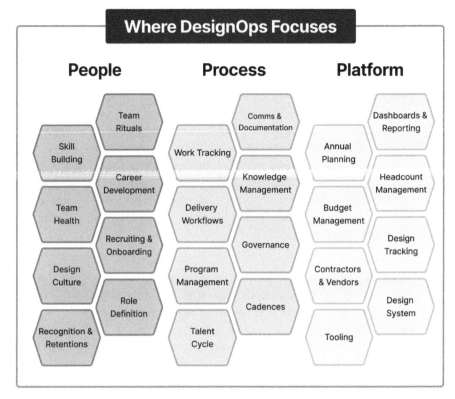

Where DesignOps Focuses

People	Process	Platform
Team Rituals	Comms & Documentation	Dashboards & Reporting
Skill Building	Work Tracking	Annual Planning
Career Development	Knowledge Management	Headcount Management
Team Health	Delivery Workflows	Budget Management
Recruiting & Onboarding	Governance	Design Tracking
Design Culture	Program Management	Contractors & Vendors
Role Definition	Cadences	Design System
Recognition & Retentions	Talent Cycle	Tooling

FIGURE 2.2

The people, process, and platform focus areas encompass a range of tasks and outputs that influence the designer's experience.

People

DesignOps' first domain of focus is the *people* responsible for creating amazing experiences in your organization. These might include software, hardware, and web designers; UI engineers, project managers, and prototypers; artists, writers, researchers; and, of course, their respective people managers and leaders. Whatever the role, these people are bound by their drive to create great user experiences, and they deserve—above all else—the most attention from our discipline.

What's a design org to do with so many role types? Answering this question is one of the most common responsibilities of DesignOps. Indeed, well-defined roles are a necessary function for any healthy design org because they ensure that everybody understands the part they play and how to play well with others. Defining roles is a core aspect of DesignOps, which is responsible for creating and maintaining the artifacts that communicate role boundaries, how roles level up, the responsibilities of a role at various levels, and how roles are expected to collaborate.

DesignOps also focuses on how people perceive a design org as a potential applicant or new hire. When a designer is considering your company, do they associate it with a particular "brand?" A design org's brand is often crafted with a DPM's (design program manager) partnership, messaged through social media, and associated through events and campaigns owned by DesignOps. DesignOps practitioners also have a stake in recruitment, onboarding, retention, performance, and other similar employee experiences for the people in their design orgs.

Lastly, Design Operations focuses on the quality-of-life programs that create community, connection, and up-skilling opportunities for people. We sometimes call this "creating a culture of design"—building rituals that engage and enable designers to feel part of a vibrant design community that will support them for years. This focus has become more complex as design org cultures have expanded locally, regionally, and globally! Culture and quality of life are such defining characteristics of our practice, that some DesignOps teams have multiple DPMs dedicated to just these efforts!

Process

The second domain where DesignOps focuses is the processes that your organization deploys to create their amazing experiences. Great design doesn't just consist of pixels being magically transformed into products. There are a lot of steps that need to happen in between, and it's in this space that many DesignOps practitioners find themselves every day.

Process is an umbrella term for the many levels of workflows and checkpoints that help a design team operate more efficiently and confidently. Teams may sometimes balk at process as unnecessary friction, but the truth is that a little friction is actually a good thing. It creates opportunities to realign and validate decision-making, all of which makes designers happier and more productive in the end. Bob Baxley, design leader and author, describes the purpose of process as "establishing the Path to Yes."

He writes:

> All of you have a process with your team to figure out what
> you're going to build and how you're going to build it. You can't
> *not* have a process, because process defines the rules, the norms,
> and the methods by which you're going to make collective
> decisions. And you can't function as a team without making
> collective decisions. So, I believe the key purpose to process is to
> establish the Path to Yes. Specifically, how are we going to decide
> when something is good enough to go out?

DesignOps practitioners design and implement all manners of
processes. Delivery processes—at a macro level—can outline the full
concept-to-production pipeline: defining the criteria needed to begin
design discovery, the kinds of artifacts to be created, the system of
measuring and scoping work, the review cadences, the kind of specs
necessary to be considered "ready," the definition of "done," and
more. At a micro level, there might be processes and guidelines that
describe each of these steps in even greater detail! A DPM's entire
role could be entirely focused on executing and improving the design
delivery process, a specialty of DesignOps practitioners "embedded"
with product design teams.

Other common processes owned by Design Operations include
onboarding, software licensing, release planning, and promotions.
A design team might need bespoke processes to manage how people
are celebrated and rewarded, how to archive and catalog design
assets, and how to evaluate headcount needs. Basically, if something
requires more than one step, or mentions the word *criteria*, the odds
are high that DesignOps will get involved.

Process is a focus of DesignOps because it aligns to its skills and
mindset. (We'll go into more detail here in Chapter 4, "It's All About
Practice.") But critically, DesignOps' ownership of processes is an
immediate value-add to the creators, because it gives back time and
mental energy to designers, so they can focus on what they do best.
We sometimes tell our design partners that they should focus on
the "what and why" and let DesignOps focus on the "who, how, and
when." Managing the latter is complicated, and having someone
dedicated to the process is a welcome addition to any design team.

Platform

The third domain where DesignOps focuses is creating the platform for design to thrive; by this, we mean managing the design org as a business. This "platform" is where people and process intersect, because both require a solid foundation built on solvency, strategy, and leadership. Having a dedicated practitioner focused on these fundamentals ensures that designers and design teams can grow, change course, and provide business impact over multiple time horizons.

No matter what the size of your design org is, maintaining this platform requires partnership between design leadership and DesignOps. This partnership may be divided along the "what and why" and "who, how, and when" lines described previously, but more often the platform is a co-creation of the two disciplines. Because, at the end of the day, a leader's vision will have to be managed as a business priority—with all the budget, headcount, and policy considerations taken into account.

Some examples of how DesignOps manages this platform include: evaluating which design tools to invest in (or deprecate), what regions to hire in, and when to augment design capacity with external agencies or contractors. Having a single DPM to administer software accounts; manage dashboards, lists, and calendars; and triage budget requests can make the teams that the DPM works with happier and more efficient.

Moreover, Design Operations plays a crucial part in leading with values and scaling those values through a design org's people and processes. By focusing their energy on the platform of design, DesignOps practitioners can imbue values directly into their business at a fundamental level; more on this in Chapter 7, "Playing Your Part."

PEOPLE OVER PROCESS

I have a few professional mantras: one of them is "people over process." Basically, if the process I'm trying to implement isn't being adopted by the people, then I'll change the process. I don't care how clever and streamlined my workflow is—it's not going to accomplish my objectives if it doesn't work for the people using it.

Now, this is a mantra, not a rule. I don't always change my processes. But this mantra reminds me to think like a designer: to do usability research on my workflows, roll them out in stages, and perform occasional retrospectives of how the process is going. Measure, iterate, and repeat.

This is all to say that if I were to stack-rank these three domains, I'd definitely put people over process. But where that leaves platform, I'm not quite sure!

How DesignOps Acts

The three domains described previously are a highly visible way to define DesignOps. DPMs can literally be seen working alongside the people in a design org. Their processes land at the top of your inbox and channels. If the business platform feels shaky, DesignOps is the team you contact to make things right.

Just as important as the ways Design Operations can be defined *visibly*, is how it can be defined *invisibly*. This refers to the intrinsic actions and modalities that describe how DesignOps practitioners think and act, and the frameworks they use to solve problems. While there are many lenses through which DesignOps perceives its problem space, the three actions that most typically define the practice and its practitioners are *orchestrating*, *operationalizing*, and *optimizing* (Figure 2.3).

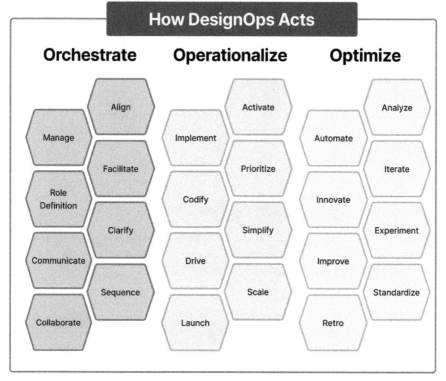

FIGURE 2.3
Many activities support the three primary DesignOps actions: orchestrate, operationalize, and optimize.

Orchestrate

The tendency to orchestrate designers and design teams is a defining characteristic of Design Operations. (So much so, that it inspired this book's title!) Orchestration is often the default way of thinking for a DPM: "These things are not in tune. How can I bring them into harmony?" Whether those "things" are people, projects, or pixels doesn't matter; to the DPM, the desire to orchestrate is one of the first to kick in.

When applied to DesignOps, *orchestrating* is a way of thinking that emphasizes alignment among the players. But DPMs don't achieve alignment by managing directly or telling players what to do. Rather, they orchestrate through the skills of collaboration and communication. DesignOps practitioners excel at bringing the right people together at the right time. They use storytelling and data to communicate shared goals. They improve the signal-to-noise ratio to reduce distractions and clear players' minds. Alignment happens once everyone hears the same tune in their heads, and it's *then* that teams can start moving forward in the same direction—which is music to any DPM's ears.

The tendency to orchestrate shows up elsewhere in the DesignOps practice. A design sprint or workshop, for example, requires multiple pieces to be executed in sequence; a DPM in this example would be likely to create the agenda, facilitate the experience, and make sure that participants don't move too slowly. Organizing community events, coordinating release dependencies, or managing the announcement of major org changes all require the timing and alignment skills that define the DesignOps practice.

Operationalize

This way of thinking should be pretty obvious—it's literally right there in the name *Design Operations*. What's *not* always obvious is what this modality means. For DesignOps practitioners, *operationalizing* is the tendency to make processes easier to repeat. If you tend to think, "Oh, that worked! But if we just made a few changes, it would be so much easier next time," then you're thinking like a DPM. And if you have a bias toward thinking about streamlining workflows and codifying best practices, then you're *really* on the right track.

First, not every process has a "next time." (One of the basic competencies of a design program manager is the ability to recognize when and why something should be repeated—or not.) But identifying the *right* repeatable processes and projects, and then operationalizing those into repeatable programs, is a core tenet of the DesignOps mindset. It's also a key factor in design org growth: complexity scales as teams grow, so having a dedicated DesignOps thinker on board to manage that complexity is necessary for the team to grow healthy and happy.

If one-off things benefit from orchestration, and repeatable things need to be operationalized, what are some common design challenges that benefit the most from an operational thinker? For DPMs closer to the people domain, cadences like performance reviews, development series, and internal events are challenging to scale and ripe for operationalization. On the process side, release planning, design critiques, and design system consumption (and contribution) also need to be operationalized. But wherever your design org's repeatable activities lie, having a DesignOps practitioner on hand to operationalize them will ensure that they can be repeated successfully time and time again.

Optimize

There's one last way DesignOps practitioners tend to think, and that's through the framework of optimization. Yes, DPMs like to orchestrate and align things. Yes, they like to operationalize and make things easier next time. But on top of this, DesignOps practitioners really, *really* like to make things better!

For DesignOps, *optimizing* is the practice of continuous improvement with each iteration. This tendency to incrementally fine-tune work is applied equally across all their focus domains. The cadences that define the "culture of design" for your people? *Let's make them better next season.* The process for archiving design assets each release? *Let's improve the searchability of that archive.* That miscommunicated deliverable with your agency partner? *Let's clarify our expectations the next time the team outsources.*

DPMs who lead with the optimization mindset tend to be both analytical and experimental. They know how to analyze processes and measure outcomes. They also know how to innovate with new techniques and are unafraid to fail when trying a new design process. What's most important to these DesignOps practitioners is to get feedback along the way—through surveys, retrospectives, and interviews—and to ask themselves how they might optimize for better results next time.

What DesignOps Delivers

Thus far, we've defined DesignOps by where it focuses and how its practitioners act. The final defining factor of our discipline is what DesignOps delivers. Not deliverables in the "output" sense of the word, like events, communications, and workflows, but rather in the "outcome" sense: the meaning, impact, and value of the things we produce. The outcomes that DPMs deliver are not unique to DesignOps—many program manager roles deliver "impact," for example. But taken together, the most important outcomes that

DesignOps delivers for its customers comprise a unique trio that distinguishes their operations role from other disciplines. These outcomes are confidence, clarity, and connection (Figure 2.4).

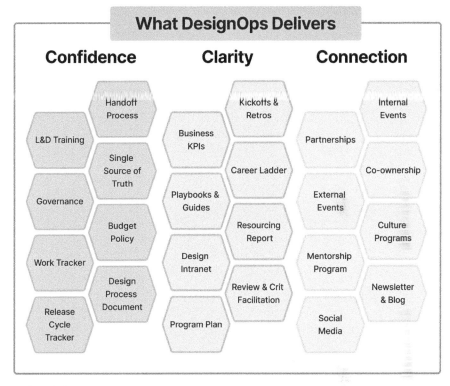

What DesignOps Delivers

Confidence · **Clarity** · **Connection**

Confidence	Clarity	Connection
Handoff Process	Kickoffs & Retros	Internal Events
L&D Training	Business KPIs	Partnerships
Single Source of Truth	Career Ladder	Co-ownership
Governance	Playbooks & Guides	External Events
Budget Policy	Resourcing Report	Culture Programs
Work Tracker	Design Intranet	Mentorship Program
Design Process Document	Review & Crit Facilitation	Newsletter & Blog
Release Cycle Tracker	Program Plan	Social Media

FIGURE 2.4

The outcomes of confidence, clarity and connection are achieved through many core DesignOps deliverables.

Confidence

For DesignOps, delivering confidence means that designers are confident they're working on the right things, at the right time, and with the right tools. It means that design leaders are confident that release commitments are transparent, prioritized, and achievable. And lastly, it means that design teams are confident that their team health and the "business of running the business" are taken care of. This is all accomplished by developing processes that remove friction, align product priorities and design commitments, and solidify the operational rails of tooling and documentation. Some of the ways that DesignOps delivers confidence to design teams and its design org include:

- Defining design governance policies
- Managing a design team's release cycle
- Codifying design review and handoff guidelines
- Curating digital spaces where artifacts are shared
- Spending design budgets in a compliant and responsible way
- Aggregating customer/business needs into a "single source of truth"

Clarity

Delivering clarity means that design stakeholders clearly know who is accountable for delivering design work and by when. It means that designers understand the best practices and what *good* looks like. It means that product and client stakeholders know the design health of their projects and trust that they are resourced appropriately. It means that designers are clear on the expectations and responsibilities of their role. Finally, delivering clarity means that business stakeholders know how their design priorities are tracking for long-term success. Some of the practical ways that DesignOps delivers clarity may include delivering the following:

- Resourcing and capacity reports
- Collaboration models and "ways of working"
- Reports on design milestones, team health, and performance
- Design success measures and impact to key performance indicators (KPIs)
- Playbooks and codified best practices
- Career ladders and promotional cycle support

Connection

The outcome of connection is near and dear to every DPM's heart. For DesignOps, *delivering connection* means connecting designers through programs that cultivate strong relationships and foster a sense of belonging. It means enabling designer growth by providing the opportunities to build skills, grow as leaders, and be supported during their career journeys. Connection means that DesignOps amplifies design contributions through formalized communications, best practices, and shared processes. And connection goes beyond the design team! It includes internal partners like research, marketing, data intelligence, and other peer disciplines. And it extends externally, too, to a design org's network of sdors, contractors, and recruiters. Connection outputs from a DesignOps team might include:

- Design org connection and collaboration events
- Communications that amplify design org happenings
- Programming to promote psychological safety and well-being
- Co-ownership of product roadmaps and long-range plans
- Cross-functional creation of sprint and release milestones
- Mentorship opportunities and collaborative solutioning

Coda: The Defining Notes of DesignOps

Just as a musical genre can be defined by its rhythms and tempo, so, too, can Design Operations be defined by its shared tenets and characteristics. As a practice, DesignOps focuses on the domains of people, processes, and platforms. Its practitioners act and think according to the frameworks of orchestrating, operationalizing, and optimizing. And the discipline delivers the outcomes of confidence, clarity, and connection. *These are the defining notes of Design Operations* (refer to Figure 2.5). They give shape to the practice and its practitioners and constitute the basic vocabulary for how we will talk about DesignOps in the chapters ahead.

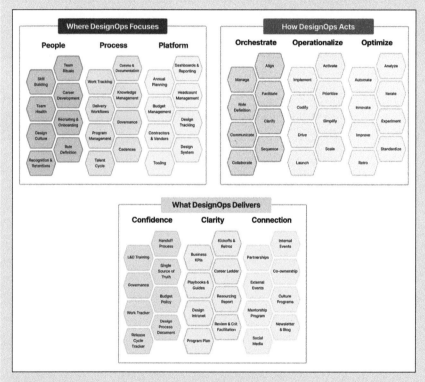

FIGURE 2.5

This comprehensive view of DesignOps provides insight into the extensive scope and significance of the practice, illustrating how DesignOps generates and delivers value within organizations.

CHAPTER 3

Drawn to the Stage

DesignOps Backgrounds and Experiences

In the same way a musician might be drawn to their instrument based on its particular shape or sound, so too are DesignOps practitioners drawn to this discipline for their own personal (and professional) reasons. Perhaps its domains of focus match a practitioner's particular background; maybe the frameworks through which DesignOps acts just *feel* natural and familiar. Whatever the different forces that bring DesignOps players together, the uniting factor is that each one wants to build better, happier, and more effective design teams. If the draw toward the DesignOps stage is what unites our discipline, it follows logically to ask, "Where are these practitioners drawn from?"

There is no Design Operations equivalent of Juilliard, the famous music college. There is no slick boy-band music producer creating DesignOps teams out of thin air, ready to sign to fanatic design orgs. And, unlike product designers or UX researchers, there is no degree program that will prepare you to graduate directly into a DesignOps role (yet). What there *is*, however, are a set of common backgrounds and areas of expertise from which DesignOps practitioners most often enter the field. And it is the skills honed from these shared experiences that have shaped what Design Operations is today.

Further, the jobs many DesignOps practitioners had in the past now form the basis of today's most common Design Operations roles and career paths. In this chapter, we'll explore the backgrounds of practitioners before they were drawn to the DesignOps stage, and how these varied educations and experiences shaped the parts they played once they had arrived.

Backgrounds: From There to Here

When musicians come together, one of the first things they do is warm up. The techniques vary based on their background and training: scales and arpeggios here, tuning and breath control there. Watching DesignOps practitioners "warm up" is a similar experience. Some start a project by gathering customer requirements, others by reaching into the archives for prior research. Is a workshop the default way to kick off? Or a virtual whiteboard? Like musicians, how practitioners approach their craft reflects their training and experience, shaped by the (possibly) long and winding road they have each followed to reach their DesignOps destination.

While every DesignOps path is unique, DPMs often share similar backgrounds that launched their career journey. Whether through formal education or on-the-job training, people in Design Operations typically come from a design, program management, or business background—or some combination of the three (Figure 3.1). Long-term success in DesignOps isn't dependent on which one of these backgrounds you started from, but rather how well you develop expertise from the other two throughout your career journey. Ultimately, the real power and value of the DesignOps role comes from mastering the skills inherent to all three of these backgrounds.

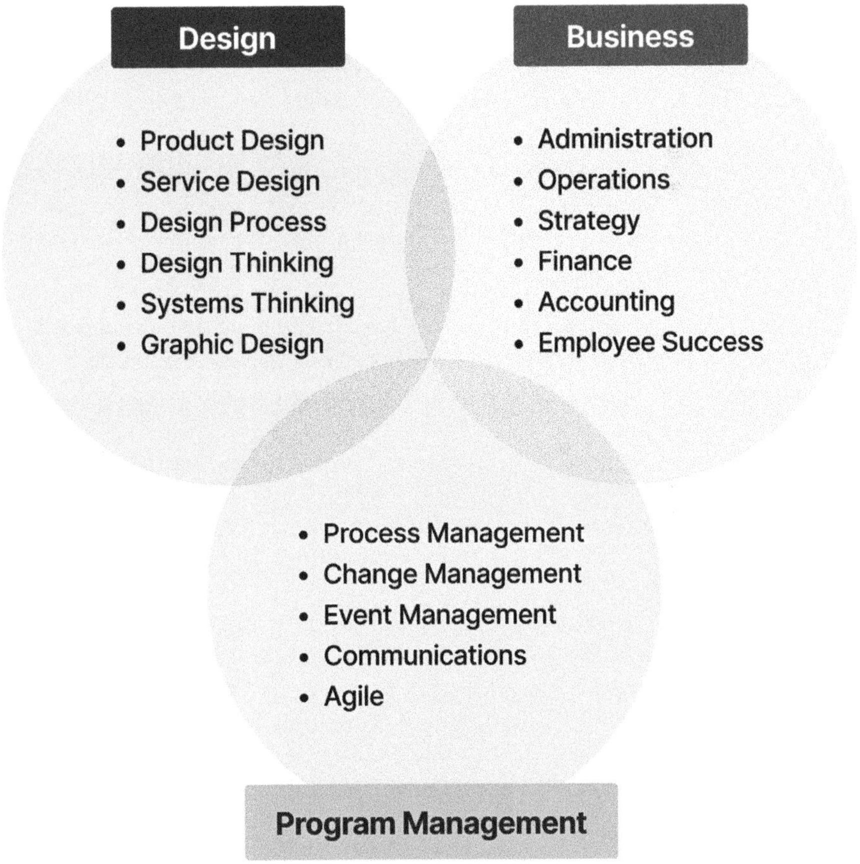

Design
- Product Design
- Service Design
- Design Process
- Design Thinking
- Systems Thinking
- Graphic Design

Business
- Administration
- Operations
- Strategy
- Finance
- Accounting
- Employee Success

Program Management
- Process Management
- Change Management
- Event Management
- Communications
- Agile

FIGURE 3.1

The three most common backgrounds from which DesignOps practitioners come and their areas of expertise.

The Design Background

Many practitioners enter DesignOps with a background rooted in design. Whether learned as part of a formal education, or simply experience gained along the way, a design background is extraordinarily common among DesignOps practitioners. This is because the field of "capital-D Design" is so vast! Whether it's a background in user experience, service design, game design, product design, design strategy, or graphic design, DesignOps practitioners with this background possess a vital skill set that translates into success for DesignOps. We elaborate on these skills in Chapter 4, "It's All About Practice," but they include proficiency in the design process, systems thinking, and familiarity with the language, methodologies, and tools of design—all of which are fundamental components of the DesignOps toolbox.

Designers are increasingly making the transition to DesignOps roles. According to the *2023 DesignOps Benchmarking Report*,[1] 47% of respondents reported transitioning from design (or design leadership) into DesignOps. This report highlighted a growing demand for DesignOps and increasing interest among designers to become DesignOps practitioners.

A designer may shift into DesignOps after finding they are already performing the job of filling the operational gaps of their design teams. For instance, they might be the designer who takes the lead in defining and facilitating their team's design critique processes, or helps fellow designers understand best practices for using their required tools. These "accidental" DPMs might be the ones creating opportunities for connection and celebration on their teams and would like to scale their impact—another competency that ladders up to Design Operations.

The motivation to transition into a DPM role can also stem from the visible impact that DesignOps practitioners make. This impact can be particularly rewarding for those from more strategic design backgrounds—such as service design or design strategy—where being able to witness the direct results of design work is sometimes obfuscated through layers of presentations and analytics.

---

1 *2023 DesignOps Benchmarking Report* (DesignOps Assembly, 2023), www.designopsassembly.com/2023report

FROM PRODUCT DESIGNER TO DESIGNOPS LEAD

Cai Charniga, DesignOps at Figma and licensed tatoo artist

At many tech companies, individual contributors operate using the 80/20 model, where you're meant to spend eighty percent of your time on the core duties of your job and twenty percent of your time on efforts outside of those responsibilities.

In my first decade as a product designer (including roles at Kickstarter and Spotify), I was always fond of the work within that twenty percent. I gravitated toward accessibility working groups, team culture conversations, processes, and systems improvements—and ultimately, anything that aimed to make those experiences sweeter and easier for people at work! I didn't realize it then, but those projects helped me build my DesignOps muscle.

Since starting my new role at Figma, as its first DesignOps hire, many folks have asked me how I knew Design Operations was something I wanted to explore. The truth is that I had never clocked this role as an option for someone with a design background, until I read the Figma job description. All the possible projects listed were similar to what I was already doing for that twenty percent of my time! DesignOps felt almost like this hack for designers like me—something that allowed us to dive deep into the process, culture, community, and beyond.

Changing your career path might feel scary and nebulous, especially when your options have always felt binary. In product design, our industry tells us we can either be "this" or "that"—a manager or an IC—and that we must invest heavily into those paths to grow. I disagree. There's value in exploration and fluidity. Being a "designer" goes beyond what the standard career ladders tell us.

My advice to anyone interested in Design Operations is to find ways to insert yourself and mold your work to work for you. Start a working group around a topic you're passionate about. Talk to your team about implementing a new brainstorming style for the next project on your roadmap. Plan an event. Propose a new critique structure. All these things build operational muscles and, more importantly, help you figure out what you enjoy doing. (I'm also a licensed tattoo artist!) Don't be afraid to switch things up.

Designers seeking to transition from a strict design role to a DesignOps role should prioritize the development of their program management and business skills. These competencies require deliberate effort and training and cannot be mastered through mere improvisation.

The Program Management Background

Another common entry point into Design Operations is via a program management background. Program managers often have formal education or professional certifications in their field. Certifications in Scrum, Agile, the Program Management Professional (PMP), or project management classes (offered at many colleges and some companies) are how these skills are refined.

The common experiences of an agency producer, event organizer, project manager, or program manager all prepare you for essential DesignOps competencies, which are grounded in process management, change management, communication, and organization. Among DesignOps professionals, 16%[2] have formal education in program management; nearly 54% employ Lean, Agile, or Scrum project management into their practice; and 35% employ traditional or PMP program management skills in service of DesignOps. Putting it another way, it should be no surprise that design *program* managers often start out as, well—program managers.

While program management within the tech, product, and consulting space is most applicable to DesignOps, program managers have successfully made the transition into DesignOps from a diverse array of industries, including healthcare, events, nonprofits, and even the military. Exposure to design at some point in the career journey, through educational experiences like a company-led design thinking workshop, can serve as a catalyst for shifting toward design. This shift offers an opportunity to adapt and apply your program management expertise within the context of a design organization or team.

---

2   *2023 DesignOps Benchmarking Report.*

FROM PROJECT MANAGER TO DESIGNOPS PROGRAM DIRECTOR

Kristine Berry, IBM Z DesignOps program director

I began my IBM journey 23 years ago, initially as an editor working on the ThinkPad help system content. Over the years, I transitioned into web design and content within the design and information development organization. This was back when websites were fairly new, and we didn't call it "website design," but it was basically designing the user experience for internal websites. From there, I got into instructional design, and I really got interested in project management. At the time, you had two ways to advance: you could either become a manager, or you could become a project manager.

I've always had a passion for organizing, leading me to choose the project manager path. While working in information development, I earned my master's degree in technical communication. As a project manager, I progressed from overseeing small projects like websites, marketing collateral, and eLearning, to eventually managing projects for 70 people involved in dozens and dozens of design and content development initiatives. Taking my commitment a step further, I became certified by the Project Management Institute (PMI) and pursued and passed IBM's rigorous project manager certification process, which includes an application, nominations, sponsorship, and interview.

Seeking a new challenge, I took on a role as a program manager for the Client Experience Validation program, overseeing user research and feedback integration into product development across the infrastructure offerings. The turning point came with the emergence of design thinking and the arrival of Phil Gilbert at IBM. Intrigued, I volunteered to organize events in my free time, ultimately landing my dream job—driving the adoption of design thinking across a 40,000-strong business unit through facilitation and education.

Concurrently managing projects and initiatives, my role evolved into spearheading a different kind of transformation: Agile. Achieving certification as a SAFe coach, I facilitated Agile workshops and emphasized the integration of design and Agile methodologies. An IBM design executive, familiar with my work, approached me about a new thing called DesignOps saying, "I think you're pretty much doing it." And so, I became a founder of the IBM DesignOps community, laying the groundwork for my eventual role in DesignOps.

The Business Background

A third group of practitioners brings a unique perspective to DesignOps, having entered the field with a solid business foundation. These individuals likely have a business-focused degree and have gained experience in fields such as business administration, accounting, operations, finance, change management, or strategy. This background brings foundational skills to Design Operations such as problem solving, budget management, and a deeper understanding of the broader business context in which design teams operate.

Individuals with a business background possess the ability to solve complex problems effectively, navigate business processes, manage budgets, and strategically enhance the discipline of DesignOps. These skills allow DesignOps practitioners to bridge the gap between design and business objectives, making them valuable contributors to design organizations.

A significant proportion of DesignOps practitioners come from a business background, with 45% falling into this category; of those, one-third hold an MBA.[3] Many MBA programs today recognize the growing significance of design in the business landscape and include design thinking classes as essential coursework. As an example, Stanford's Graduate School of Business has been a pioneer in integrating design thinking principles into its MBA program via the Hasso Plattner Institute of Design (also known as the *d.school*). Design schools have responded by offering business-related classes and programs to *their* curricula, such as the MBA in design strategy at the California College of the Arts. This growing intersection of design and business education highlights the synergy between these disciplines and their impact on their industries.

---

3   *2023 DesignOps Benchmarking Report.*

FROM FINANCE TO DESIGNOPS

Diane Gregorio, engineering chief of staff, Digital Customer Experience at Autodesk and former head of DesignOps at BILL and DocuSign

I've been working since I was 14. I come from a first-generation migrant family with a strong work ethic. I was raised by a single mother of four who cleaned houses for a living. She would come home with cash and would store it in a fine china cabinet that she still has. I would pretend like I was a banker, lining it up and counting it. There was always this banking and finance dream for me.

I graduated with a degree in business with a finance concentration. I worked for many banks but was ultimately affected by the saturated job market in San Francisco. A recruiter reached out about a systems administration role at the Walt Disney Family Museum, meaning I'd have to pivot and stretch my skill set: configure a ticketing system, learn SQL, design front-of-house processes, etc. That's where my introduction to design started. I was doing service design and didn't even know it.

Then I took a leap and joined the California Academy of Sciences as a program manager working with developers, creatives, and designers. I learned more about the design process here, which led me to Advent Financial Software in their Program Management Office. I ended up with a team that none of the other program managers wanted—the design group. My work involved figuring out all things DesignOps, including building relationships with cross-functional peers, defining our end-to-end process, establishing the design review process, and more. We built a strong design culture, and I honed my design and operational skills.

Next, I joined the DesignOps team at Adaptive Path. It felt like a master's degree program in design. Being in the war rooms daily, doing design research and synthesis, taught me so much. The time came to move on, and I took on the challenge of establishing DesignOps teams from the ground up, first at DocuSign, and then at BILL.

My business and finance background has been a huge asset in DesignOps. Designers often get stuck in the design bubble, forgetting the business problems they're solving. Understanding business helps bridge that gap. Plus, I leverage my financial and business skills daily, managing the design budget, headcount, and planning. My advice for anyone transitioning from business into design is to be curious: you definitely have a perspective from the business side and that is valuable.

Surprise! The Specialist Background

In addition to these three common backgrounds, DesignOps practitioners are also entering the field laterally from more specific pathways. This is a function of how Design Operations has evolved in recent years, with emerging opportunities for specialization among larger DesignOps organizations. These new positions challenge the conventional definition of the "design program manager" role, requiring highly specialized skill sets that deviate from the foundational DesignOps competencies (which we will review in Chapter 4). Nearly 25% of DesignOps practitioners consider themselves specialists, versus the 51% who consider themselves generalists.[4]

Some examples of these DesignOps specializations include learning and development, communications, and tooling—all of which are critical to the success of large, global, or distributed design orgs. DesignOps practitioners come to these roles with backgrounds in education, training, corporate messaging, editorial, content management, and engineering. While these practitioners may not (necessarily) have expertise in the three common backgrounds discussed earlier, they *do* bring a valuable perspective to how our discipline thinks about DesignOps and a welcome opportunity to be more inclusive and expansive in how we define our practice.

The Long and Winding Road

Whatever their DesignOps entry point, a DPM must acquire education and experience from each of the three main backgrounds to be successful. But—assuming there are gaps—how do you know where to start? While each of these three backgrounds is foundational to the practice of DesignOps, the most important skills to develop are those that deepen one's understanding of design and the design process. Having "design fluency" helps a DesignOps practitioner speak the language of their designers. More importantly, it teaches you to think in design systems and deploy design methods in service of building processes and cadences that allow great design to flourish. Solving operational challenges using design methodologies is at the heart of our practice; whatever your background, this goal should be the destination at the end of your long and winding DesignOps road.

---

4   *2023 DesignOps Benchmarking Report.*

From Librarian to DesignOps Manager in Tooling and Systems

Brandon Perry, senior operations manager, Tooling Systems and Strategy at Zendesk

I started with aspirations of becoming a librarian. I earned my bachelor's degree in English because I loved being immersed in the world of words. If my path had taken a different turn, I could have become a content designer. The librarian career ladder required getting my master's degree in library and information science. These skills and knowledge can be adapted as a program manager, where you're working closely with people and solving complicated problems.

My early career was in library settings, with plans to specialize in either teen or adult services. My focus was creating engaging programming. At the Alameda County Library, I transformed the library into a dynamic space by introducing video games and promoting technology, which challenged the perception that libraries were only quiet, boring places.

My mentor introduced me to digital asset management, a discipline that leverages a librarian's skills in a digital or corporate environment. As a lifelong gamer, I realized I could do this work at a video game company and landed a role at PlayStation as a digital asset manager. My responsibilities included overseeing finalized design and marketing assets for a variety of games and consoles. I gained a lot of experience with software systems, developing processes, and creating frameworks to enable success for global teams.

I found my way to Zendesk working as a digital asset manager. In 2021, my position evolved into DPM with a focus on tools and systems. Now, I manage all the tools and systems that designers, researchers, and leaders use to be successful in their jobs. This includes overseeing Figma, our DAM system, and tools for design, information, and project management. My wheelhouse includes a strategic component of figuring out how to connect teams with the right tools to drive efficiency. I've developed close partnerships with designers and technical experts, built from a simple approach of asking, "How can I help you solve your problems?" or "How can I partner with you to identify what you need to move forward?"

As someone without a design background, I've relied on my allies on design teams. My focus is to deeply understand their processes, the product, and what's needed to ship. My biggest advice is to be curious and understand the broader context at all times. You can't afford to say "I don't need to know what happens beyond my part," because you'll miss important information to be a successful operator.

Rachel's Very Winding Path

Professional ballet dancer, barista, promotional sign spinner, office assistant, certified diamontologist, receptionist, server, event planner, program manager, design strategist, design manager, design program manager, Design Operations leader...

Nope, that's not a snapshot from the Craigslist gigs section, that's my wildly twisty yet totally valid path to DesignOps. I started dancing ballet when I was five years old, and by the time I was 16, I had moved out and joined a professional company. I decided to retire from dancing in my mid-twenties and made a huge pivot and began to study business. I graduated from the Haas School of Business at UC Berkeley but remained determined to apply this new knowledge in creative and artistic spaces, to bridge my passions.

I began working in design agencies in program management roles working very closely with designers, and I soon realized the importance of gaining hands-on design knowledge. So back to school I went and earned an MBA in Design Strategy from California College of the Arts. In the program, I studied design research, experience design, and service design, all things that Adaptive Path (AP) was leading the way in at the time. So, I joined AP as a design program manager and continued advancing in my DesignOps career at Capital One. Then I moved to Uber Eats to start and define a DesignOps practice and eventually joined Salesforce to define and grow a new central DesignOps practice. The balance I've sought with increasing clarity over the years was guided by a longing to unite my love for the arts and creative spaces with my interest and ability to understand systems, put things in order and into motion, and solve problems. My eclectic mix of roles and education turned out to be exactly the skills and experiences I needed to be successful in my DesignOps roles.

John's (Less) Winding Path

Compared to Rachel's experience, my path to DesignOps looks more like a straight line. Video games to Design Operations. End of story. When you zoom out, that's the entirety of my career journey! (I won't count my time writing obituaries for my hometown newspaper...) So, what was it about making video games that led me to Design Operations?

I was a game designer for many years and then a game producer. My time as a designer checks most of the "design background" boxes—I was a systems designer, a level designer, a narrative designer, a UI designer, and more. I wore many, many hats, and in the process, learned the fundamentals of what I'd now call "experience design"—thinking about how players would interact with my creations across the scales of seconds, minutes, hours, days, and months.

Flipping my role to game producer taught me new skills. How to articulate market viability, pitch to executives, prioritize features, engage a player community, and—most importantly—how to ship a product worldwide and on multiple platforms. It's here where my background in program management and business was built. And, finding that my true passion was for "making great experiences at scale," I eventually left games and entered tech as a DesignOps director.

Also in Common...

What else do DesignOps practitioners tend to have in common? Overwhelmingly, people in our discipline tend to be college-educated and enter the trade with senior-level experience. (We describe DesignOps levels in Chapter 5, "Composing Your Career.") A vast majority of DPMs hold a bachelor's degree (90%), and 31% hold a master's degree or higher.[5] Additionally, people in DesignOps roles have a considerable amount of industry experience under their belt: the average career experience of a DesignOps practitioner today is 10–14 years, meaning many in this discipline hold senior, lead, manager, and director-plus level roles in their organizations.

The majority of DPMs fall within the middle of this spectrum, at a mid to senior level. DPMs are generally not hired below an associate level. While there *are* levels below the associate level for adjacent functions (such as junior designer), the nature of the DesignOps role usually requires experience, maturity, diplomacy, and a mixture of knowledge not found in very junior practitioners. Navigating a complex organization and its processes, engaging effectively with stakeholders across all levels, and operating independently, all demand the confidence that comes from acquired professional experience.

While there *are* shifts happening in the industry that are opening up opportunities for early-career DesignOps practitioners, there are several reasons why DesignOps has historically been suited for more senior-level practitioners.

- **Complexity of the role:** DesignOps teams are often born from a need for an operations-minded leader who can understand design and is capable of partnering with a design leader to solve complicated organizational challenges. As the only (or first) DesignOps practitioner in their space, they need to be highly experienced at navigating the complexities and relationships required.
- **Lateral transfers:** DesignOps requires a blend of skills, behaviors, and traits that takes time to develop. As such, the most common entry into DesignOps is through a lateral transition from other established career paths— particularly the design track.

---

5 *2023 DesignOps Benchmarking Report.*

DesignOps Market Trends

Abbey Smalley,
former head of Design Programs at Amazon

In her 2023 research, Abbey Smalley, former head of design programs at Amazon, dug into more than 100 U.S.-based, DesignOps-related job postings. Her research insights are a toolkit of DesignOps market trends across the industry:

Years of Experience

Entry-level roles requiring zero years of experience were almost non-existent, and there were very few early career roles requiring 3+ years of experience. Mid-level roles typically requested 5+ years of experience, while senior-level roles required 10+ years of experience.

Salaries

The majority of salary ranges for these roles ranged from $140K to $270K with salaries of $80K and $350K at the lowest and highest ends of the spectrum.

Experience Requirements

- 28% required prior DesignOps experience
- 30% required prior design experience
- 40% required prior project management experience
- 14% required product building lifecycle experience
- 10% required communication experience

Top Tools Mentioned

Design	Project Management	General/Collab
Figma	Asana	Google Suite
Sketch	Notion	Adobe Suite
Zeplin	Jira	User Zoom
Abstract	Azure DevOps	Dropbox
	Airtable	Miro

At the date of this research, there were more DesignOps practitioners than open DesignOps roles, contributing to the competitiveness of the landscape.

There are additional similarities between DesignOps practitioners. One is that they largely come from (and are drawn to) technical and software fields. The complexities of software development have given rise to many of the fields that predated and inspired DesignOps— DevOps, digital design, etc.—and thus we see "tech fluency" being a critical experience for anyone seeking a DPM career path. Another similarity is the relative importance that partnerships play in a DPM's past and present career path; overwhelmingly, DesignOps practitioners come from fields where relationship building and maintaining connections across multiple fields are key parts of the job.

Similar Backgrounds, Different Destinations

These shared backgrounds connect to paths that wind and twist, but ultimately lead to the same destination: DesignOps. Well, for *most* people, that is.

There are adjacent operational functions and roles within a design organization that are *not* DesignOps. Despite taking a similar path, these practitioners end up at different yet equally important destinations. These roles are intrinsically linked with Design Operations, their reporting structures and focus areas may overlap, and DPMs often have dependencies and partnerships with them. However, it's essential to clarify the key distinction between these roles and the practice of DesignOps. Some of these adjacent operational areas are the following: ResearchOps, CreativeOps, design chief of staff, and executive assistant.

ResearchOps (ResOps)

Research operations (ResOps) refers to processes and activities that support and facilitate product and UX research. ResOps take on tasks such as project management, resource allocation, data collection, recruiting, and logistical coordination to ensure the efficient and effective execution of research projects. ResOps practitioners are also experts (and often admins) of research-specific tools, and they craft research cadences in a manner similar to how DesignOps develops rhythms and cadences for design orgs.

This function is a mirror image of DesignOps, and it is a common destination for people whose design background is rooted in user research, usability, and strategic insights. Many of the day-to-day activities will look familiar to any DesignOps practitioner, with the exception of test recruiting: a time-intensive and at times challenging function that requires its own specialized skill set. ResOps may or may not be a part of a larger DesignOps or UX Ops team, depending on where researchers are organized within the business.

CreativeOps

Creative operations (CreativeOps) are teams of professionals dedicated to supporting and streamlining *creative* endeavors within an organization. CreativeOps skill sets are similar to DesignOps, and include activities like project management, resource allocation, workflow coordination, and quality assurance. This practice typically partners with marketing, branding, and web teams—groups that traffic in designing high-quality, high-volume assets in all kinds of formats and form factors (particularly those related to audio, video, and print media).

Similar to ResearchOps, CreativeOps functions as a counterpart to DesignOps and often attracts individuals with design backgrounds grounded in creativity, aesthetics, and strategic vision. Many of the day-to-day responsibilities in CreativeOps align with those of DesignOps practitioners, although there are key distinctions, such as managing creative talent and maintaining asset management systems.

Design Chief of Staff

If DesignOps is considered relatively new, the role of design chief of staff is even more niche. A design chief of staff (CoS) acts as the thought partner and enabler for a design leader; this is in contrast to DesignOps, which partners with design teams and their surrounding orgs. In some smaller design teams, the head of DesignOps may also be the chief of staff to the org's design leader, at least until the org gets so big that the role needs to be split. The CoS's responsibilities can vary significantly, depending on the organization's size, structure, and the unique needs of the leader. Additionally, the reporting structure for design chiefs of staff may differ, with some reporting directly to heads of design and others integrated into the DesignOps organization.

Isaac Heyveld, design chief of staff for Customer 360 Platform UX at Salesforce, described this position in his 2022 DesignOps Summit talk, "Expand DesignOps Leadership as a Chief of Staff." In his experience, this role is responsible for the strategic prioritization, scale, and operations of the design leader and their leadership team. The CoS is part of the executive team, acting as an advisor and proxy for the design leader. The CoS supports their executive by operationalizing executive programs, strategic org planning, advising, communications, and presentations. It is a role rooted in people management, relationship and trust building, and may be an attractive path for senior DPMs looking to leverage and expand their skill set in new ways.

Executive Assistant

The executive assistant (EA) plays a crucial role in facilitating the day-to-day operations and responsibilities of a design leader. Their responsibilities include managing the executive's schedule, handling travel logistics, and providing support for meetings, expenses, and office organization. Additionally, they may take on special projects or tasks assigned by the executive, such as research, event planning, or coordinating team-building activities.

It's important to note that the EA role typically doesn't require an in-depth understanding of design. This aspect can make it an appealing pathway for administrative professionals and non-designers who are interested in a future DesignOps pathway, as it offers the potential to work closely with design leaders and DPMs to gain exposure to the design industry and the practice of Design Operations.

Coda: Drawn Together

DesignOps practitioners are drawn together from a variety of similar backgrounds. (Recruiters take note! The best DPM candidates might be working outside the realm of DesignOps, so look far and wide in your search.) Where these practitioners come from is not as important as what they've been drawn to, but it's important to recognize how their shared stories and experiences have shaped the current definition and role differentiations of Design Operations. In the next chapter, we'll turn our attention from the past to the future, looking at the career competencies and mindsets that DesignOps practitioners rely on and develop to advance their careers.

CHAPTER 4

It's All About Practice

DesignOps Competencies and Mindsets

Our last chapter looked at some of the characteristics that draw DesignOps practitioners together: our common backgrounds, similar areas of expertise, and shared career paths. However, if landing a job in Design Operations is like showing up to an audition, then the details advertised to make sure the right candidates apply might be: "Design fluency, program management expertise, and business acumen wanted!"

Now imagine the audition is complete, and everyone is being assigned their role in the orchestra. "You! You'll be lead product DPM. And you—you'll play the second chair part of senior manager, Central DesignOps." If this motley ensemble were to start playing right away, there is a one hundred percent chance that the music they'd make would elicit a rush-toward-the-exit reaction from any listener nearby. And that's because with Design Operations, as with music and other skilled professions, it's not simply enough to be drawn to the stage. In order to succeed, you have to *practice*.

French composer Claude Debussy noted, "Music is the space between the notes." Through practice, we develop muscle memory and transform the mechanics of our work into second nature, allowing us to shift our focus toward creativity. Without consistent practice, attention is fixed on the execution of *individual* notes, missing out on the vital space between them where brilliance and artistry live. In the same vein, design program managers can cultivate their expertise through practice—building a solid foundation that enables them to become more creative and strategic practitioners over time.

But... What to Practice?

The broad areas of practice that design program managers need to be skilled in are what we call the *DesignOps career competencies* and *career mindsets*. *Career competencies* are the underlying abilities that DPMs deploy in their jobs day-to-day. These competencies scale in complexity and priority at different levels of a DPM's career, but they are immutable in that they are critical to a DPM's success.

In contrast to one's abilities, the DesignOps *career mindsets* are ways of thinking and feeling: mental frameworks that guide how teams of practitioners make decisions, handle conflict, and interact with other roles. Just as a musician must know how to read sheet music (a competency) and trust the leadership of their conductor (a mindset), so, too, must a DPM know how to read a product requirement document and exhibit empathy and trust with their stakeholders.

In this chapter, we'll review the eight career competencies and ten mindsets that are critical to a successful DesignOps career. Nobody is expected to be excellent at each of these. (It's a professional path where beginners are welcome!) But every aspiring DPM should know their strengths and opportunities relative to the expectations of a DesignOps role. This allows them to assess their skills well enough to know which qualities they can depend on Day 1, and which need to be improved through regular practice and mentorship by peers and senior leaders.

The Eight DesignOps Career Competencies

Career competencies are the fundamental abilities that all DesignOps practitioners are expected to learn and master. The more competencies you know and the higher your skill level is in some areas indicates that you may be suitable for a higher-level role in a DesignOps organization. But remember that mastery of (or even basic competence in) all of these abilities is not a requirement for a DPM role. Rather, you must be able to know what you don't know and set expectations for yourself—and perhaps your team—about what competencies you will improve. The eight DesignOps career competencies are the following (Figure 4.1):

1. Design and Design Operations
2. Trusted Relationships and Partnerships
3. Program Management Proficiency
4. Problem Solving and Resourcefulness
5. Leadership and Influence
6. Communication and Presentation
7. Company and Business Acumen
8. Values and Culture

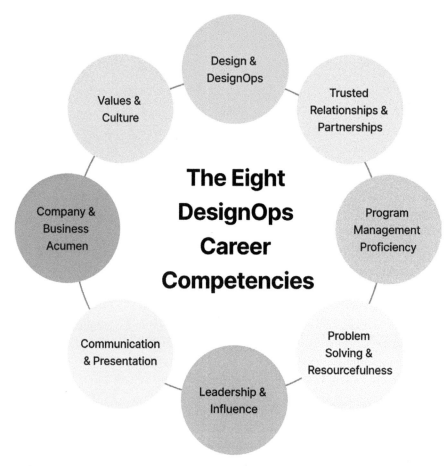

The Eight DesignOps Career Competencies

- Design & DesignOps
- Trusted Relationships & Partnerships
- Program Management Proficiency
- Problem Solving & Resourcefulness
- Leadership & Influence
- Communication & Presentation
- Company & Business Acumen
- Values & Culture

FIGURE 4.1

The Eight DesignOps career competencies encompass a broad range of skills and proficiencies important for navigating the dynamic landscape of DesignOps.

For each of these eight competencies, we'll define the ability in its broadest context, so that the definition is meaningful to practitioners of every level—from total newbie to seasoned veteran. We'll then break down some of the underlying skills of that competency: these are the more tactical traits a DPM might develop and practice to improve in this area. And if you're curious as to how these competencies might be assessed in a DesignOps interview, we cover this topic (and more) in Chapter 16, "A Symphony of Talent."

Competency 1: Design and Design Operations

This competency reflects the ability to think like, reason with, and proxy for a designer as a DesignOps practitioner. Our definition:

> I demonstrate fluency in how design and user experience happens, and I have a solid understanding of the design tool ecosystem. I know the design process well enough to proxy for design leadership. I am adept at applying design methodologies to my own work, and I proactively seek out best practices and thought leadership to improve my DesignOps' processes and programs.

Some of the underlying skills required for design and Design Operations include:

- **Design Fluency:** Has a solid understanding of design tools, principles, and processes (discover, define, develop, deliver). Can confidently measure how design decisions should be scoped and fit into a cycle of continuous delivery.
- **Process Design:** Consistently uses design thinking and design methodologies in pursuit of developing and improving operations, processes, and engagements.
- **Operationalizing Design:** Brings in and applies operational excellence from adjacent disciplines and thought leaders in the DesignOps community. Demonstrates proficiency bringing an operational initiative from idea to delivery.

Competency 2: Trusted Relationships and Partnerships

This competency is all about building bridges to and between the stakeholders in your DesignOps ecosystem. Our definition:

> I build strong, trusted relationships with project partners, stakeholders, customers, and fellow employees and provide the informed guidance that partners need to deliver on strategic initiatives.

Some of the underlying skills required for trusted relationships and partnerships include:

- **Partner Service:** Builds strong, productive relationships and fosters collaboration with partners. Gives project partners the guidance they need to deliver successful projects and programs.

- **Partner Values:** Helps partners lead with values to drive value. Is a trusted advisor who speaks with courage and compassion.

- **Maturity and Diplomacy:** Demonstrates the ownership, consistent communication, and active listening needed to encourage collaboration and dialogue, and develops positive, productive relationships with program leaders.

DESIGNOPS DECODED

THE MOST IMPORTANT SKILL: YOU'VE GOT TO HAVE HEART

Courtney Allison Brown, head of Design Operations at CarMax

The practice of Design Operations relies on championing others and leading with empathy. In diverse design organizations, we play a pivotal role in understanding the needs of our business, the organization, and our customers (which for us, is the design team and its business partners).

Building trust and empathy within teams is vital, especially during complex challenges. Being a champion relies on active listening, assessing organizational issues, and implementing process improvements with a service design mindset to enhance overall effectiveness. Equally important is celebrating successes and embracing failures as learning opportunities.

Ultimately, to succeed as a DesignOps practitioner you have to have genuine compassion and commitment. You've got to have heart.

Competency 3: Program Management Proficiency

This competency captures the project and program management skills that set design program managers apart from their designer peers. Our definition:

> I successfully organize multiple players and activities for complex, large-scale programs, and I prioritize work in relation to broader team commitments.

Some of the underlying skills required for program management proficiency include:

- **Project and Program Fundamentals:** Quickly produces multiple program frameworks, identifying strengths and weaknesses of each. Breaks up complex programs into clear actionable steps that are tracked and communicated.

- **Project and Program Management:** Coordinates and executes a project (or multiple projects within a program) to achieve a business's strategic objectives. Manages resources, risks, and stakeholder expectations.

- **Frameworks:** Adept at implementing and designing for common delivery frameworks (Kanban, Sprint, etc.). Fluent in methods and tools to take in, prioritize, commit, and track work to completion.

- **Impact:** Influences project vision and direction based on planning or organizational variables.

Competency 4: Problem Solving and Resourcefulness

This competency gives shape to the ingenuity DPMs exhibit when confronted with something brand new or without precedent. Our definition:

> I can distill and reframe complex problems, have a bias for action, can navigate through change, and find solutions in ambiguous circumstances. I diagnose, learn from, and iterate on past problems to improve future processes.

Some of the underlying skills required for problem solving and resourcefulness include:

- **Identify and Define:** Is proactive in identifying operational gaps, pain points, and needs for their own team and projects. Crafts quick, effective solutions to stakeholder problems across mediums, environments, and audiences.

- **Resourcefulness:** Explores how other projects and teams have solved similar problems; seeks out existing tools, ideas, and resources with which to address problems. Requests subject matter expert (SME) input and feedback before arriving at a solution.
- **Adapt and Improve:** Through feedback loops and retrospectives with design partners, assesses the impact and effectiveness of operations processes. Uses the resulting insights to improve future engagements.

Competency 5: Leadership and Influence

This competency is critical for all DesignOps practitioners, even those not in formal leadership positions. Our definition:

> I demonstrate behavior, attitudes, actions, and judgment that inspire employees to follow and other leaders to trust.

Some of the underlying skills required for leadership and influence include:

- **Leadership:** Demonstrates stability, trust, respect, and professional confidence. Provides visible and mature leadership, as recognized by direct reports and surveys inside and outside the department. Effectively manages organizational change and iterates on the team's vision, goals, and strategy.
- **Confident People Management:** Confidently manages a growing team of direct reports across multiple focus areas. Can be vulnerable, honest, and authentic with team members. Fosters a culture of cross-team mentoring.
- **Amplification and Advocacy:** Creates opportunities for team members to expand their scope of influence and own strategic initiatives, develops, and helps the team leverage each member's strengths. Advocates for, and receives, appropriate support from stakeholders.

Competency 6: Communication and Presentation

This competency is at the heart of all the successful advocacy DPMs must practice in support of their design teams and new DesignOps programs, from communications and presentations to newsletters and storytelling. Our definition:

THE MOST IMPORTANT SKILL: LEADING WITH INFLUENCE

Changying (Z) Zheng, head of DesignOps at Cloudflare

In my DesignOps role, I have had almost no direct power. Instead, I constantly exercise my expert power, informational power, connection power, and resource power. None of these sources of power are based on position. Over my four years supporting the team as a DesignOps practitioner, I've reported to three different managers. My title has changed three times, and my job function has shifted, too. Regardless, I continue to support the team at the same professional level. Title or no title, my focus remains on leading through influence rather than authority. My most powerful skill is not design, business, change management, facilitation, nor prioritization skills—all of which are important! No, my most powerful skill is the ability to lead with influence.

I have strong verbal, written, and visual communication skills, and I present ideas clearly, confidently, and concisely. I share information in logical, thorough, and easy-to-digest form, telling a clear and compelling story. When presenting, I use tone of voice, inflection, pacing, and related skills to persuade others of the merits of my ideas.

Some of the underlying skills required for communication and presentation include:

- **Collaborative Messaging:** Partners with other disciplines to present a shared narrative, complementing multiple POVs and styles. Leads groups to generate a single message, told through diverse voices, to increase understanding.

- **Voice and View:** Can clearly express the value of design and Design Operations. Confidently presents both their own and existing presentations to known and unfamiliar audiences. Can engage in and direct conversations.

- **Clarity and Confidence:** Conveys work status and other information to stakeholders in clear, compelling, and concise ways, in both presentations and stand-alone communications. Can simplify complex ideas to support discussion.

ADAPTING AND EVOLVING: DESIGNOPS COMMUNICATION STRATEGIES

 Communications have long been a responsibility of DesignOps teams, but as communication volume grows (and the digital workplace becomes noisier), our role in amplifying signals and ensuring quality communications is increasingly vital.

Many of our communications now occur through tools like Slack, evolving our role from mere communicators to community managers. To navigate this landscape effectively, we must be well-versed in the best practices of all the tools we use, from email to Slack, as well as internal platforms like Google Sites and Confluence. Continuously adapting our communication strategies to adapt to new challenges is an essential skill in the ever-changing digital landscape.

A few years ago, it became glaringly clear to me that we needed a comprehensive strategy for all our communications and channels. My team was tasked with reaching a diverse audience across various topics and channels, and managing the workload overwhelmed us. Recognizing this, we established a clear communications plan, akin to those used by official communications teams.

Our communications strategy outlines the why, who, what, how, where, and when of our messaging, as well as message ownership.

First, I outlined why we communicate (as detailed below). Maintaining consistency across all our communications streamlines decision-making, especially in urgent communication scenarios.

Why we communicate:

- **Vision:** DesignOps aims for excellence in all communications, serving to inform, instruct, celebrate, and foster connections across the organization
- **Quality:** Professional, visually polished, on brand
- **Delivery:** Prepared, consistent, timely
- **Content:** Globally relevant, engaging, informative
- **Voice:** Clear, concise, friendly
- **Engagement:** Two-way communications with feedback loops
- **Values:** Inclusion, understanding, simplicity

Who we communicate with:

In this section, we clearly define our audience(s) including, their location, what they do, and what they care about.

What, where and when we communicate:

Here we utilize a table detailing each type of communication, including timing, frequency, audience, channel, fidelity, content, content goal, voice and tone, and links to past examples. Additionally, we ensure that each communication addresses these three questions:

- What's the purpose of the message?
- Why should people care?
- What actions or behavior do we need people to take, and how, and by when?

We also provide avenues for further information where possible.

How we communicate:

This section outlines the specific communication methods and best practices. For instance, we use a custom DesignOps email template and customized banners for each send. In Slack, we utilize our Slack Block Kit templates for consistency and signal boosting. We also established some guidelines, such as limiting "big message" calls-to-action to one per day, avoid sending on Fridays (when India is out of the office), and other organizational considerations.

In addition to this document, we have a communications calendar to coordinate and plan all comms sent by each team member across the organization for their various programs and announcements.

Communication needs within an organization are constantly evolving, alongside the tools we use to convey our messages. Having a clear vision and guide for the DesignOps team serves as an anchor, facilitating smoother navigation through these changes.

Competency 7: Company and Business Acumen

This competency enforces DesignOps' role in leveraging their understanding of their company's product or service and using this knowledge to influence design decision-making. Our definition:

> I have an understanding of how our users do business using the company's products and services. I understand the company's value proposition vs. competitors' corporate messaging and values, as well as the competitive landscape and external trends shaping the industry.

Some of the underlying skills required for company and business acumen include:

- **Product or Service Knowledge:** Understands how the product (or service) meets customer needs and solves their problems. Proficiently explains product (or service) value to clients and stakeholders. Adapts and stays updated as the product (or service) evolves over time.

- **Industry Knowledge:** Stays aware of industry trends, market dynamics, and the competitive landscape. Analyzes industry data and insights to help design leaders make informed design decisions.

- **Company Navigation:** Confidently navigates the company's organizational structure and knows key departments and roles. Locates internal resources and information. Aligns actions to the company's mission, vision, and values.

Competency 8: Values and Culture

This competency reflects a DPM's outsized role in leading with and modeling the values that guide a design org. (This competency is so important that all of Chapter 7, "Playing Your Part," is dedicated to it!) Our definition:

> I ensure that the design org's core values are not just words on paper but are actively integrated into daily operations and decision-making processes. I promote a culture of inclusivity and diversity. I recognize and celebrate the unique perspectives and backgrounds of team members.

Uncovering Designops Superpowers

Brennan Hartich, director, Design & Research Operations at LinkedIn

What are DesignOps superpowers? The first, which I learned well into my career, is what my boss called *entrepreneurial spirit*. Because 90% of the time a DPM's role is not clearly defined, you need someone who can go figure out what their job should be. They need to proactively identify problems and navigate their role amidst others. Initial clarity about their responsibilities is often temporary; once early issues are resolved, you can move onto the next thing. You need to be open to discovering challenges with a "go-getter attitude." (I hate that expression, but it's true!)

You also need the superpower of being able to read the room. That skill leads to earning trust from others, enabling these "others" to be honest with you in a way they ordinarily can't. Those two things are particularly unique to this role. It's about having the pulse of the team and being able to maintain objectivity and detachment, which makes it less personal.

Another superpower is the ability to straddle the line between understanding design and understanding the business. For this, I use the technical program manager (TPM) analogy. TPMs are assumed to have technical expertise in their field; in DesignOps, DPMs are not always expected to be experts in design, which I think is an issue. There's a difference between a program manager and a design program manager.

If we look at UX as a base, the discipline encompasses interaction design, product design, research, content, and more. Many DPMs lack these essential skills. They don't have interaction design capabilities, or they've never worked with UX before, and that's fine. But I think there's a messiness that raises the question: Are you a program manager, who happens to be working with designers? Or are you a genuine design expert, who can do program management? This ambiguity can become an issue. For instance, in a tool like Figma, it's not essential for DPMs to create product prototypes, but familiarity with the tool is essential for doing your job. Similarly, during a design critique, DPMs should be able to contribute meaningfully.

This doesn't only apply to design tools and tactics, but also to design methods and strategies. Design program managers should actively incorporate design methodologies in their own work.

Some of the underlying skills required for values and culture include:

- **Operationalizing Values:** Builds processes and programs with an inclusive mindset and commitment to diversity and equity.

- **Courageous Communication:** Builds meaningful relationships on a foundation of trust and authenticity; gives and receives feedback with both courage and empathy.

- **Motivate and Champion:** Supports and inspires others to drive maximum impact, demonstrate curiosity, and unleash potential. Recognizes and celebrates others in meaningful ways.

And there you have it! The eight DesignOps career competencies that DPMs will practice throughout their career. Although your reliance on these abilities may wax and wane depending on a particular project or business cycle, at no point will you ever need to stop refining and skilling up your competency in these areas. Their complexity and priority to your role's success will only grow as you advance through your career, and it's a good habit to check in with yourself (and your manager, and your team) to assess how well you are performing each competency relative to your level.

The Ten DesignOps Career Mindsets

If the DesignOps competencies are the skills an individual must develop to succeed, then DesignOps mindsets are the *frameworks* one must cultivate for their practice to be successful. Another way of understanding this distinction is that competencies are the "what" for DesignOps, and mindsets are the "how." They inform how Design Operations orients to new challenges and navigates conflict. They are the common patterns of thinking, feeling, and behaving that keep DesignOps practitioners stable and consistent across projects and organizational change.

These mindsets are not unique to DesignOps, but they *are* ours. Unlike our competencies, some of which must be learned and honed through on-the-job practice, it is possible to realize the DesignOps mindsets from Day 1, and fully bake them into everything DPMs do. What's required here is less keeping them refined, and more keeping them relevant—making sure that you return to the common frameworks of Design Operations at all points throughout your career. The ten mindsets are the following:

Mindset 1: We are designers.

We design systems, processes, organizations, services, and experiences for our design team.

Mindset 2: We are leaders.

We step in to manage design projects and programs and help execute strategic priorities for our design leadership.

Mindset 3: We are dot connectors.

We love building relationships, think in systems, and thrive at collaborating with multiple teams and cross-functional disciplines.

Mindset 4: We know how design gets done.

We speak the language of design and understand what happens when and why, what natural dependencies exist, and how to mitigate risks.

Mindset 5: We are problem solvers.

We know how to navigate complex organizations and processes. We act like detectives to find or create solutions if they don't exist.

Mindset 6: We are biased for action.

We are able to bring ambiguous ideas to life by creating actionable steps and carving out a clear path to delivery. We mobilize and operationalize.

Mindset 7: We are good communicators.

We understand the intricacies of advocating and gaining followership for a project or program and know how to tailor communications to different audiences.

Mindset 8: We are always listening.

We are plugged into the pulse of our business. We hear what design teams need, and what other teams need from design. We are tapped into the trends shaping our industry.

Mindset 9: We help teams navigate.

We steer teams through the design process, connect people to the right answers, and help design get the most out of our company's resources.

Mindset 10: We think at scale.

We zoom in and out on the daily and flex between big-picture strategic thinking and detail-oriented tactical thinking.

Coda: Practice Makes Progress

DesignOps practitioners are not unicorns—despite what grateful design teams and leaders may tell us. Unicorns are unique; people in DesignOps roles are actually quite similar, especially in the competencies they lean on daily to do their jobs, and in the mindsets they draw from to tackle unknown challenges. As a practice, DPMs are thinkers and tinkerers, solvers and doers, united by the skills and frameworks required to be successful in their discipline. And like the designers they work with, DPMs are also deeply empathetic, caring, and filled with heart. There's a strong service mindset to DesignOps practitioners that cannot be easily quantified in a competency or mindset.

The goal here is progress, not perfection. By practicing both the DesignOps competencies and mindsets in harmony, you can create a comprehensive and effective foundation for a successful DesignOps career. And for design leaders and recruiters, understanding these fundamentals can help empower you to better hire, support, and grow a DesignOps practice. In the next chapter, we'll look more closely at what that success looks like year-over-year: the levels and role differentiation you can expect to navigate as you grow your DesignOps career.

CHAPTER 5

Composing Your Career
The DesignOps Role

Whether you play in an orchestra or lead a DesignOps program, success in your role is dependent on developing the core competencies and mindsets of your discipline. To be fair, it's not *just* about practice; for musicians and DPMs alike, having a passion for your craft goes a long way, too!

Musicians and DPMs are similar in another way: very few of us are born maestros of our profession. Refinement of the necessary skills requires both time and some way to measure your progress. Fortunately, Design Operations has an established framework of career levels that codifies what is expected and required at different stages. For musicians, this framework sees one graduate from third chair to second chair to first chair; in DesignOps, the concept is similar, but the numbering is reversed: DPMs progress from Level 1 to Level 2 to Level 3, and so on.

Having a DesignOps Career Framework gives novice and veteran DPMs a foundation to grow and advance in their careers. Just as important, *understanding* the career framework is a good check against so-called "imposter syndrome"—that creeping feeling that somehow you don't know what you're doing, despite doing it. (And doing it *well*, we might add!) The DesignOps Career Framework provides perspective about where you are in your career journey and gives DPMs a permission structure to see that the way they sometimes feel about *how* and with *whom* they work shouldn't be perceived as obstacles, but rather as rest stops along their path to DesignOps proficiency.

In this chapter, we will explore the building blocks that serve as the foundation for growth and advancement in your DesignOps career.

Why a Framework Matters

A well-defined career framework acts as a cornerstone for shared success. It empowers individuals to navigate their career paths with clarity and purpose. It also enables organizations to attract, retain, and develop top talent. Understanding how different roles rely on and use career frameworks provides important context for why they exist and what outcomes they need to accomplish. Here we'll show how the basic concept of a career framework has different meanings and use cases for three different types of roles.

Design managers need to:

- **Empower their team's career development journey** by ensuring fair compensation, effective coaching, and clear growth opportunities.
- **Conduct unbiased and structured conversations** throughout the hiring process, ensuring fair evaluation of all job candidates.
- **Lead courageous career conversations with confidence and clarity** and ensure fair and transparent allocation of rewards and opportunities.

Individual contributors need to:

- **Access clearly defined expectations** to gain insight into their strengths and opportunity areas, effectively track their progress, and plan a clear career trajectory.
- **Take ownership of their career growth** by actively measuring their progress against established benchmarks and taking targeted steps to advance.
- **Navigate their career with confidence** and ensure that their efforts are aligned with expectations, enabling them to focus on continuous growth and exploration of new opportunities.

Recruiters need to:

- **Champion fairness and transparency** by utilizing a structured framework that ensures objective evaluation and consistent communication of career paths and opportunities to all candidates.
- **Streamline their evaluation process** by leveraging established levels and roles to assess candidates efficiently against specific competencies and expectations.
- **Foster collaboration by partnering with managers and DPMs** to ensure a smooth and efficient hiring process that benefits both the organization and potential candidates.

No matter what brings you into DesignOps—whether it's your first job or you're transitioning laterally from an established career outside of DesignOps—this framework can inform your starting point, as well as your target destination in your DesignOps journey. Ultimately, what matters most is that you pursue a career where you feel successful and fulfilled, regardless of level or skill mastery.

The DesignOps Career Framework

Our DesignOps Career Framework is a tool that clarifies the role expectations at different levels of Design Operations. For simplicity, we focus on the design program manager (DPM) role at four different levels: associate, senior, lead, and principal. Our framework is shaped by years of experience in different companies and input from our peers; it is a solid tool by which to measure your own career progression and that of your DesignOps team. That said, levels and roles are dependent on the maturity, values, and needs of each particular organization; consequently, the expectations for different levels at your company might vary from what we have defined here.

Our DesignOps Career Framework identifies five factors that differentiate the different levels of Design Operations and maps out the career progression a DesignOps practitioner can expect to experience during their career journey. These are:

1. **Scope of Work:** Your breadth and depth of program ownership
2. **Sphere of Influence:** The stakeholder ecosystem your work impacts
3. **Time Horizon:** Your balance of near-term vs long-range work
4. **Skill Proficiency:** Your proficiency in the DesignOps competencies
5. **Driving Theme:** What you are accountable for and expected to do

A LEVEL IS A LEVEL IS A LEVEL—OR IS IT?

Levels within an organization serve to bring alignment and consistency to the growth path of all role types in an organization. Whether using three levels or ten, the purpose is to ensure that the roles in every discipline are evaluated against a similar set of expectations, ensuring progression and advancement in harmony with one another. They also serve to provide a clear growth path for each role type. Consider the scenario of transitioning from one company as a director to another as a lead; the leveling structures of companies don't neatly align. In fact, there is a whole website (www.levels.fyi) dedicated to comparing companies' leveling structures to aid in career planning.

Expectations for each level within the DesignOps practice can vary across different companies. While your DesignOps organization may look a little different, we hope our DesignOps Career Framework serves as a foundation to bring clarity to your own career path and to your DesignOps team.

Factor 1: Scope of Work

Scope of work (Figure 5.1) refers to the breadth and depth of responsibilities within a design practice. It encompasses the specific areas of focus defined in Chapter 2, "Learning the Score" (people, process, and platform), that DPMs are accountable for, and how much risk they oversee.

	Associate	Senior	Lead	Principal
Scope	Project	Program	Portfolio	Organization

FIGURE 5.1
Scope of work.

In our framework, design program managers can operate at four distinct levels, similar to the different levels of zoom on a camera: project, program, portfolio, and organization. Each level comes with increasing responsibilities and scope; these levels often correlate with DPM job titles and seniority, although exceptions exist. Here is how we define these levels of scope:

- **Project Level:** At this level, DPMs focus on the execution and management of individual design projects. They partner primarily with designers, and are responsible for overseeing the planning, coordination, and delivery of specific design initiatives. Their outcome is the successful completion of project milestones, as measured by adherence to timelines and achieving project-specific goals.

- **Program Level:** DPMs operating at this level handle related, repeatable projects and initiatives. They coordinate and align multiple projects within a broader structure, ensuring that the underlying projects work together harmoniously to achieve strategic objectives. They partner with design managers to lead their programs and are responsible for program execution, managing dependencies, and driving cohesion across projects.

- **Portfolio Level:** At this level, DPMs have ownership over a range of programs and projects—typically within a specific product space or domain. They partner with design leaders to oversee the strategic direction, resource allocation, and performance of the portfolio, aligning it with the overall business objectives. They provide high-level oversight, identify synergies, prioritize initiatives, and manage trade-offs between different programs and projects.

- **Organization Level:** DPMs operating at this level have the broadest scope of work. They partner with a head of design and manage the business and operations of a design org or team, operating much like a design COO (chief operating officer). They set an operational vision and are responsible for shaping the DesignOps strategy and best practices. They drive organizational excellence, ensuring alignment with business goals, and influence the overall design culture within an organization.

While DPM career progression generally aligns with level of scope, it's important to note that this may not *always* be the case: responsibilities *can* and *will* vary depending on the organization's structure and specific needs. Additionally, as scope grows, so too does the likelihood of becoming a manager and overseeing a team. People management comes with additional responsibilities like hiring, talent reviews, and team strategy—even if the actual level does not change. Understanding the scope at which one operates provides clarity on the expectations, requirements, and impact of one's level as a design program manager.

Factor 2: Sphere of Influence

Scope of work is tightly coupled with sphere of influence (Figure 5.2), which represents the borders of a DPM's authority and influence. This sphere of influence extends beyond immediate DesignOps boundaries, and it includes the stakeholders, functions, and teams with whom DPMs collaborate and engage on a regular basis. As one's career progresses, their sphere of influence expands, too.

	Associate	Senior	Lead	Principal
Scope	Project	Program	Portfolio	Organization
Sphere of Influence	Functional	Cross-Functional	Workstream/ Product	Cross-Org

FIGURE 5.2
Sphere of influence.

To illustrate the expanding spheres of influence, our framework defines four different levels: functional, cross-functional, workstream/product, and cross-organization:

- **Functional:** At the functional level, DPMs partner and collaborate primarily within the design team. They influence and contribute to the design processes, methodologies, and culture within the immediate team environment.

- **Cross-Functional:** At the cross-functional level, DPMs partner and collaborate across functions like product management, engineering, research, and technical program management (and perhaps support roles such as finance, HR, and recruiting). They work with these functions to align goals, integrate design practices, and drive cross-functional collaboration to deliver successful products.

- **Workstream/Product:** At the cross-workstream/product level, DPMs partner with functional leads from *multiple* workstreams or products. They collaborate on strategic initiatives, synchronize efforts, and ensure consistency across different teams and projects. This level of influence requires aligning diverse stakeholders and balancing priorities across workstreams or products.

- **Cross-Organization:** This highest level of influence encompasses business units and disciplines *outside of* product development functions. DPMs collaborate with teams in marketing, sales, customer success, and other disciplines. They contribute to strategic planning, champion and share user-centric practices throughout the organization, and drive alignment to achieve overall business objectives.

As a DPM's career progresses, their sphere of influence expands to encompass broader and more strategic areas, enabling them to make an impact across the organization. At more senior levels, DPMs not only actively influence to drive impact, but they also passively foster followership to drive impact. Learning how to partner with the different spheres of influence at their current level can help them navigate their career and meaningfully drive the success of the people, processes, and products within their purview.

Factor 3: Time Horizon

The third aspect of our DesignOps Career Framework is the time horizon (Figure 5.3) that a DPM's work is focused on. It defines the spectrum between "here and now" vs. "there and then" that their work impacts.

	Associate	Senior	Lead	Principal
Scope	Project	Program	Portfolio	Organization
Sphere of Influence	Functional	Cross-Functional	Workstream/ Product	Cross-Org
Time Horizon	90% Near-term 10% Long-range	70% Near-term 30% Long-range	50% Near-term 50% Long-range	30% Near-term 70% Long-range

FIGURE 5.3
Time horizon.

In our definition, the time horizon spans a range from near-term to long-range, with near-term work being more tactical and immediate, and long-range work more strategic and future-oriented.

- **Near-term:** This work typically includes managing day-to-day tasks and delivering projects and programs with a focus on immediate impact and outcomes. We define *near-term work* as that which includes the next two to three release roadmaps, or the next two to three quarters.

- **Long-range:** This work encompasses strategic planning, funding resources for the future of DesignOps and Design, and aligning DesignOps work with the organization and company's strategic goals. This work includes measuring DesignOps impact, researching emerging trends, and holding conversations with leadership partners about roadmaps and priorities. We don't typically think about the long-range focus in terms of product or fiscal cycles (i.e., releases or quarters), but in years, with one year being the minimum time horizon.

DesignOps work always involves a mix of near-term and long-range considerations, but the ratio of the two is rarely 50:50. There is typically an inverse relationship between a DPM's experience and the amount of near-term work they focus on. As their career progresses, involvement in long-range and strategic work increases, too, along with their ability to think strategically and to consider the broader impact of design and DesignOps on their organization's goals. Balancing near-term and long-range work is crucial for DPMs. It requires the ability to switch between tactical execution and strategic planning, ensuring that immediate needs are met while also setting the stage for long-term success.

Factor 4: Skill Proficiency

The fourth factor that differentiates the different levels of our DesignOps Career Framework is a DPM's skill proficiency. In the previous chapter, we defined the eight DesignOps Career competencies upon which our discipline is founded:

1. Design and Design Operations
2. Trusted Relationships and Partnerships
3. Program Management Proficiency
4. Problem Solving and Resourcefulness
5. Leadership and Influence
6. Communication and Presentation
7. Company and Business Acumen
8. Values and Culture

The skills underlying these competencies are required at *all* levels of DesignOps; however, the expectations of skill proficiency (what a DPM needs to know and have mastered; Figure 5.4) will necessarily vary depending on their own level of experience and the DesignOps team's maturity.

	Associate	Senior	Lead	Principal
Scope	Project	Program	Portfolio	Organization
Sphere of Influence	Functional	Cross-Functional	Workstream/ Product	Cross-Org
Time Horizon	90% Near-term 10% Long-range	70% Near-term 30% Long-range	50% Near-term 50% Long-range	30% Near-term 70% Long-range
Skill Proficiency	Novice	Competent	Advanced	Expert

FIGURE 5.4
Skill proficiency.

Regardless of the competency, our framework assesses skill proficiency along a spectrum that ranges from novice to competent and advanced to expert. Here is how we define these levels of proficiency:

- **Novice:** At this level, DPMs are in the early stages of competency development. They have a basic understanding of the concepts and practices of the underlying skills, and they are just starting to gain hands-on experience and may require guidance and support to perform tasks effectively.

- **Competent:** DPMs have acquired a solid foundation of the competency's underlying skills. They can execute their tasks and responsibilities proficiently, and are familiar with standard processes, tools, and methodologies that allow them to contribute effectively to DesignOps initiatives.

- **Advanced:** At this level, DPMs are highly proficient in a competency. They possess an in-depth understanding of complex concepts, best practices, and emerging trends in the field. They can tackle sophisticated challenges, develop and implement strategies, and provide guidance and mentorship to others in the organization.

- **Expert:** DPMs have mastered the competency and are recognized as the go-to expert for the competency's underlying skills. They have extensive experience and a deep understanding of the DesignOps practice, including its strategic implications and impact on organizational success. They can drive transformative initiatives, lead large-scale projects, and shape the direction of DesignOps practices at a tactical and strategic level.

It's important to note that these skill proficiency levels are not fixed milestones, nor are they rigidly defined. Rather, they represent a continuum of growth and development, and are heavily influenced by contextual factors.

The expectations for skill proficiency can vary based on a DPM's specific role and their organization's needs and maturity. Different DPM roles prioritize some skills over others, based on their focus and responsibilities. For example, a DPM specializing in event management in central DesignOps may have different expectations compared to a DPM focused on delivery in product DesignOps. Furthermore, organizational maturity plays a role in determining skill proficiency expectations. Different companies may have varying levels of sophistication and maturity in their DesignOps practices.

As a result, the expectations for skill proficiency by level will differ between organizations.

Factor 5: Driving Theme

The final factor of our DesignOps Career Framework gives definition to the motivations and expectations that drive how a DPM acts, and what they deliver at different levels of their career progression. We call this factor the *driving theme* of their role (Figure 5.5).

	Associate	Senior	Lead	Principal
Scope	Project	Program	Portfolio	Organization
Sphere of Influence	Functional	Cross-Functional	Workstream/ Product	Cross-Org
Time Horizon	90% Near-term 10% Long-range	70% Near-term 30% Long-range	50% Near-term 50% Long-range	30% Near-term 70% Long-range
Skill Proficiency	Novice	Competent	Advanced	Expert
Driving Theme	Delivering	Driving	Orchestrating	Strategizing

FIGURE 5.5
Driving theme.

Being rooted in how DPMs "act" and "deliver," you can probably deduce that the driving theme is intrinsically tied to the core DesignOps vocabulary laid out in Chapter 2. We use this driving theme to capture which of those tenets most neatly defines the overarching objective for which DPMs are accountable at each level within their DesignOps organization. These are delivering, driving, orchestrating, and strategizing. Looking at these factors by role, we see that:

- **Associates deliver:** At this level, *delivering* means ensuring successful execution of tasks and projects. An associate responds to pre-identified needs and is growing their core DesignOps skills.

- **Seniors drive:** *Driving* means taking ownership of initiatives and actively contributing to the advancement of DesignOps programs. A senior DPM is self-directed, requiring minimal oversight and support.

- **Leads orchestrate:** At this level, *orchestrating* means overseeing and leading others to drive complex, multifaceted, multistakeholder initiatives forward. Lead DPMs actively identify new opportunities and design solutions to operational gaps that they uncover.

- **Principals strategize:** *Strategizing* means vision setting and high-level decision-making. A DesignOps principal is in a leadership role, influencing and defining the DesignOps roadmap, gaining buy-in, and influencing roadmaps outside of DesignOps.

Putting It All Together

Our DesignOps Career Framework is a simplified tool for assessing and measuring your own career progression. More advanced frameworks are available for specific Design Operations practices (like software design, hardware design, and agency design), but for generalized and common use cases, this framework can be used by any DPM to quickly gut-check where you are—and where you *should* be—on your journey.

The correlation between career progression and competencies is strong. We obviously believe that the eight DesignOps career competencies from Chapter 4, "It's All About Practice," are relevant at all stages of your career (even if your early proficiency in the underlying skills is at a novice level). Your maturity with any set of skills may vary considerably—this is completely natural. Don't be alarmed to find that some skills are strong at the expected level, while others might be weaker than expected.

But, regardless of your proficiency, we see that some competencies are relied on more than others at different levels (Figure 5.6). While all competencies are critical to success at all levels of your career journey, it's helpful to know which you're likely to use most often, so that you might focus your own personal training and growth.

	Associate	Senior	Lead	Principal
Scope	Project	Program	Portfolio	Organization
Sphere of Influence	Functional	Cross-Functional	Workstream/Product	Cross-Org
Time Horizon	90% Near-term 10% Long-range	70% Near-term 30% Long-range	50% Near-term 50% Long-range	30% Near-term 70% Long-range
Skill Proficiency	Novice	Competent	Advanced	Expert
Driving Theme	Delivering	Driving	Orchestrating	Strategizing

Competencies and Skill Proficiency

		Associate	Senior	Lead	Principal
Design & Design Operations	Design Fluency	Novice	Competent		Advanced
	Process Design	Novice		Advanced	Expert
	Operationalizing Design	Novice	Competent	Advanced	Expert
Trusted Relationships & Partnerships	Partner Service	Competent		Advanced	Expert
	Partner Values		Competent	Advanced	Expert
	Maturity and Diplomacy	Novice	Competent	Advanced	Expert
Program Management Proficiency	Projects & Programs	Novice	Competent	Advanced	Expert
	Frameworks		Competent	Advanced	Expert
	Impact	Novice	Competent	Advanced	Expert
Problem Solving & Resourcefulness	Identify and Define	Novice	Competent	Advanced	Expert
	Resourcefulness	Novice		Competent	Advanced
	Adapt and Improve		Competent	Advanced	Expert
Leadership & Influence	Leadership		Novice	Competent	Advanced
	Confident People Management			Competent	Advanced
	Amplification and Advocacy	Novice		Competent	Advanced
Communication & Presentation	Collaborative Messaging	Novice	Competent	Expert	
	Voice and View	Competent	Advanced		Expert
	Clarity and Confidence	Novice		Advanced	Expert
Company & Business Acumen	Product or Service Knowledge	Novice		Competent	Advanced
	Industry Knowledge		Novice	Competent	Advanced
	Company Navigation		Competent	Advanced	Expert
Values & Culture	Operationalizing Values		Competent	Advanced	Expert
	Courageous Communication	Competent	Advanced		Expert
	Motivate and Champion	Competent	Advanced	Expert	

FIGURE 5.6
DesignOps Career Framework.

DesignOps Titles and Tracks

As we've observed throughout this chapter, there is significant variation in DesignOps roles at different levels. And as the field of DesignOps has grown, so, too, has the diversity of titles associated with it.

Head to LinkedIn to look for a Design Operations job, and your head might spin. You may find yourself confronted with multiple variations of the *design program manager* theme, or versions that include both the words *design* and *operations* in the title but don't mention *program manager* or *DesignOps* at all. (The idea that these two terms should be joined together isn't universally understood by job boards quite yet!) Titles like *DesignOps producer, DesignOps strategist,* or *DesignOps coordinator* might leave you questioning if these roles are the same or different, or how they are related to the design program manager role.

What are DesignOps practitioners called? If politics is practiced by politicians, and surgery is practiced by surgeons, who practices Design Operations? The DesignOps discipline has, for the most part, aligned on the *design program manager* (DPM) title as the universal descriptor for the folks doing this work. This statement might be controversial to some—especially those who don't identify as program managers—but we believe it is the broadest, most generally acceptable term to refer to all practitioners of DesignOps. (A notable exception to this rule would be for those in research roles, where *research program manager* is common.) Ultimately, our practitioners are all DPMs; everyone, regardless of their role, level, or specialty, can and should embrace the common banner of *design program manager* as their common title.

But DPMs are not just "common;" they are also differentiated by their experience. In the DesignOps Career Framework, we use the titles *associate, senior, lead,* and *principal* for the sake of simplicity, and as a proxy for different levels of expertise. But this list of four titles is incomplete and certainly not universal. Out in the real world, you may encounter different titles for the same level, or the same title being used for different levels. To further complicate this, Design Operations titles need to distinguish between their two career tracks: the Independent Contributor (IC) and People Management tracks.

This matrix of levels, titles, and tracks is not as confusing as it may sound. The chart in Figure 5.7 defines the most common, accepted titles you will encounter in Design Operations.

Levels	Individual Contributor Titles	People Manager Titles
L4	Associate DPM	n/a
L5	Senior DPM	Manager, DesignOps
L6	Lead DPM	Senior Manager, DesignOps
L7	Principal DPM	Director, DesignOps
L8	DesignOps Architect	Senior Director, DesignOps
L9	DesignOps Principal Architect	Vice President (VP), DesignOps

FIGURE 5.7
DesignOps titles for IC and manager tracks.

These titles are common but not yet universal. The best titling practice is to follow your company's naming conventions; that said, we believe the titles defined in Figure 5.7 should be the preferred terms used when talking about Design Operations generally, or when starting a new DesignOps practice from scratch.

One of the most common points of confusion in this titling matrix is the frequent use of the word *manager*. A novice job hunter might scratch their head after seeing titles like *design program manager* and *manager, DesignOps*, and wonder which of these positions involves people management responsibilities and which is an individual contributor. To solve this, DesignOps titles are inspired by the adjacent disciplines of product management and technical program management, both of which have a similar "manager" conundrum in their titles. In short, the people management track titles use a "Title, Discipline" format, whereas the individual contributor titles generally use a "Level, DPM" format. (To put it simply: "Don't use DPM in a people manager's title.") That said, as this is not yet a universal practice, you should always rely on the job description itself to grasp the responsibilities, level, and track of any particular role.

We advocate for the adoption of standardized titles within the industry to bring greater consistency and clarity to DesignOps roles. And specifically (and maybe most importantly), we hold that differentiation in titles should be made to disambiguate the individual contributor and people manager tracks.

Many large organizations use the concept of a "job family," which serves as the broadest categorization of a role. Forget titles like lead DPM or senior manager, DesignOps; in the world of job families, all our roles get lumped into a single large bucket.

Why should you care? Because critically, job families are used to determine pay bands and starting salaries for each level. Suddenly, which bucket DesignOps belongs to is a serious question! Should DesignOps practitioners be classified as general program or project managers? As designers? As operations? As something else? (Sadly, DesignOps is usually not big enough to have its own job family.)

My unequivocal response (and maybe a hot take) is to advocate for the same classification, or at least equal categorization, as designers. Every time. *DesignOps practitioners are designers.* Okay, louder now for the people in the back.

100%. Look, one of this book's main themes is that "DesignOps is design." Our practitioners must be fluent in design, use design methods, scope design projects... So, what if we design with processes, not pixels? Our specialized skills are the same as those that designers use on a regular basis. Ipso facto, bingo bango: DesignOps should be categorized under the design job family.

Exactly. The tech industry understands that a technical program manager must have in-depth engineering knowledge and thus is invariably categorized in a technical job family. It only makes sense for DesignOps to be considered in a similar way.

The Individual Contributor Track

The individual contributor track includes *design program manager* in the title because it's the most common descriptor for these roles; it reflects a DPM's primary responsibility of managing design programs. We advise against using descriptors like "coordinator" or "assistant" to describe individual contributor roles, as these titles align more closely with the responsibilities of an executive assistant.

Although "entry-level" in the DesignOps sense, associates are valuable contributors to the field, and possess skills and expertise that are not typically associated with entry-level positions in the broader corporate landscape. That is why associate level DPMs typically start at a Level 4 or 5 in a company's career laddering framework. However, associate level roles are few and far between in most DesignOps organizations. It's important to note that 5.7% of DesignOps roles held are at entry-level, an increase from the 1% reported in 2021 but still low.[1] As the practice of DesignOps grows, there is an opportunity to provide space for more early-career DesignOps roles, especially in larger DesignOps organizations that have room for more narrowly scoped roles and more access to DesignOps mentors.

On the more experienced levels of the IC track, we find DesignOps architects (sometimes referred to as *staff DesignOps*) and DesignOps principal architects. These designations signify a deep and extensive level of expertise and experience in the domain of DesignOps, making these practitioners recognized authorities in their field. They are often sought after for their specialized knowledge and ability to solve complex DesignOps problems.

The "DPM" signifier drops from these titles for two reasons: one is that individual contributors at this level are uncommonly rare (with most practitioners having taken on the people manager track), and thus more bespoke, academic titles are used to signal the practitioner's level. The second reason is that architects and principal architects tend to work nearly 100% in the long-range time horizon and often on exclusively strategic work. There is very little pure "program management" to be done, because the programs have yet to be invented!

---

1   *2023 DesignOps Benchmarking Report* (DesignOps Assembly, 2023), www.designopsassembly.com/2023report

Between associate and architect are the bulk of individual contributor roles—senior, lead, and principal—that DesignOps practitioners hold. These design program managers are at the heart of the DesignOps practice, playing essential roles in design organizations and representing the largest segment of professionals within the field.

The People Manager Track

The people manager track drops the *DPM* label and picks up the *DesignOps* moniker in its place. This subtle difference reflects a people manager's shift in focus, from directly managing programs to managing the people who run those programs. It is through this indirect influence that DesignOps people managers affect change in a design organization, doing so at scale through the coaching and championing of teams of individual contributors.

The entry-level role in this track, "manager, DesignOps" is equivalent to a senior DPM. To effectively manage people and teams, managers must be competent in the senior role expectations outlined in our DesignOps Career Framework. That is, they must be able to handle work at the program level of scope and liaise with cross-functional stakeholders. They must manage people working on near-term and long-range projects, and they need to have achieved skill proficiency across all eight of the DesignOps competencies, such that they can credibly coach and train their direct reports as-needed.

In the middle of this track are the senior managers, directors, and senior directors of DesignOps. These roles are the most common in Design Operations, owing to the relative seniority of DPMs compared to other design and program manager roles. At these levels, DesignOps people managers may be responsible for managing other people managers, a complex yet rewarding dynamic that stretches a practitioner's skill at leading through influence. It is at these senior levels where people managers are more directly involved in business and organizational decisions, such as how, when, and where to grow a design team, which tools to invest in, and product roadmapping.

At the furthest end of the people management spectrum is the vice president (VP) of Design Operations. On the one hand, this is just the logical career progression from senior director; on the other, this is an exceptionally rare level for DesignOps practitioners to hold. While some organizations have a vice president of DesignOps (or higher), these roles have not yet become as widespread as other leadership positions within design orgs, such as VP of design or chief design officer.

Only 4% of DesignOps practitioners report holding a VP or higher-level DesignOps position.[2] In large design organizations, it's common to have multiple VPs of design in addition to a chief design officer, but it's still uncommon to have more than one VP of DesignOps.

It is more common to find someone who is considered the "head of DesignOps" at the director or senior director level, than to find a VP of DesignOps. The rare VP is just as rooted in the DesignOps competencies as any other manager or individual contributor, but also requires advanced skills often associated with a chief operating officer (COO). In fact, VP's of DesignOps are sometimes synonymous with design COO's, responsible for running a global design org the same way a COO might manage a global business.

One reason for the VP of DesignOps' rarified status is the relative infancy of Design Operations in most organizations; there simply hasn't been enough longevity in the org to promote or hire someone at this level. Another reason VPs of DesignOps are so uncommon is because of the hierarchical requirements many businesses have as a prerequisite for the vice president level; that is, there is an expectation that this person would manage a certain number of senior directors (and in turn, directors and senior managers under them), along with an appropriate number of individual contributor DPMs. The size of such a DesignOps team is extraordinarily rare outside a handful of big tech companies.

In addition to the DesignOps competencies, people managers of all levels need to be skilled in basic leadership competencies, too. Plenty of books have been published on this topic, and we believe that effective leadership skills are universal—there is nothing unique about managing individual contributors in Design Operations vs. other disciplines. For readers unfamiliar with some of the basic competencies of people management, we recommend *Liftoff! Practical Design Leadership to Elevate Your Team, Your Organization, and You.*[3]

2   *2023 DesignOps Benchmarking Report* (DesignOps Assembly, 2023).

3   Chris Avore and Russ Unger, *Liftoff! Practical Design Leadership to Elevate Your Team, Your Organization, and You* (New York: Rosenfeld Media, 2020).

Coda: On Solid Ground

The eight DesignOps career competencies in Chapter 4, articulate which skills DPMs need to practice to be successful. The DesignOps Career Framework in this chapter grounds these competencies in context of the different levels in your DPM career journey, from novice to expert. Moreover, this framework sets expectations for you (and your manager, and your team) for what level of proficiency you are expected to have at each level, the scope of work you are capable of completing, the types of stakeholders you are ready to partner with, and more. Having solid expectations is critical for having meaningful conversations about your career growth and identifying at which point in your journey you may be ready (or not) to change tracks to people management or an individual contribution. In the next chapters, we'll explore how these fundamentals show up even further down your career path.

CHAPTER 6

Your DesignOps Crescendo
Advancing Up, Out, and Diagonally

In Chapter 3, "Drawn to the Stage," we discussed some of the most common routes to *enter* DesignOps. But what do the pathways *out* of Design Operations look like?

For every hundred stories about someone who found themselves practicing Design Operations, there's the overlooked tale (or two) about the individual whose DesignOps path eventually led them someplace else. Chapter 5, "Composing Your Career," revealed that executive level roles in design organizations are uncommon, which is why we see the career trajectory of experienced practitioners as a bit of uncharted territory. Nevertheless, DPMs and DesignOps leaders *are* pursuing these paths, charting courses that ultimately twist and wind in a direction that takes their careers up, out, and diagonally across the field of design—and elsewhere. Some of the most common paths include:

- **The Executive:** Ascending to VP+ DesignOps leadership
- **Design Leadership:** Sliding over to lead design
- **Going Solo:** Launching a design or DesignOps consultancy
- **The Rising IC:** Making impact as an individual contributor
- **Beyond Design:** Leading other operational areas

This chapter explores the career trajectories of individuals who have achieved the position of director and senior director of DesignOps and leveraged their experience to pursue new challenges in pursuit of professional growth. We want to underscore that any practitioner who has reached these levels has accomplished something significant. A DesignOps leadership role demands a high level of expertise, a multifaceted skill set, experience that goes beyond the walls of design, and a depth of knowledge that is applicable across multiple functions within an organization. Seasoned DesignOps professionals do *not* need to move up, out, or diagonally to have a long, meaningful career, nor to make an impact!

The Executive Path

For some seasoned DesignOps leaders, their destination is to reach the highest levels of DesignOps leadership within an organization. These roles, often titled *Vice President of DesignOps, Head of DesignOps,* or even *COO of Design,* offer significant influence and strategic oversight. Victor Corral, director of DesignOps at Silicon Valley Bank and two-time interim head of design, advocates for design leaders to recognize DesignOps as potential successors:

> Senior leaders in Design Operations are well positioned to take on head of design roles because we know the ins and outs of our organizations: the systems, processes, people, what's working and what's not. We are often culture carriers, advocates, and servant leaders committed to the success of the team. My wish is for heads of design out there to recognize that their DesignOps leaders are potential successors, and for DesignOps leaders to aspire to and prepare for when that opportunity appears and accept that awesome responsibility when it's offered.

These executive positions provide a platform to make a lasting impact on the entire organization. DesignOps executives become architects of the future, shaping both the strategic direction of DesignOps and influencing the evolution of design practices across the entire organization. Their decisions directly impact how design fuels innovation, fosters user satisfaction, and drives business success.

For some, the appeal of the executive path lies in the intellectual challenge and complexity of these roles. VP+ DesignOps leaders navigate complex business landscapes, balance strategic vision with operational excellence, and manage large, diverse teams. They are constantly learning, adapting, and innovating to ensure that DesignOps remains a critical driver of success in a rapidly evolving business environment. Jason Kriese is one such leader.

THE EXECUTIVE PATH

Jason Kriese, former VP, DesignOps at Salesforce

As a self-described elder in DesignOps, I saw the discipline come into being and forming with its own unique focus, purpose, and practitioners. What was originally a loose community of doers became a defined discipline of experts.

Although my first assignment focused on a single product vertical, the role rapidly evolved to support all of our design leaders. When my peers saw what DesignOps made possible, I set out to establish dependable design workflows, organizational policies, financial rhythms, and more. My leadership at this time required me to focus on defining and defending our ops approach, even as I delivered our tangible work.

It's becoming easier to recognize the unique skills of DesignOps. We are design thinkers, planners, and connectors. We craft visions, build enablement, and invest to deliver. The result is that DesignOps prepares us to excel in every aspect of leadership. We're ready to run teams, lead disciplines, and drive entire organizations to success.

As importantly, a career in DesignOps affords us an opportunity to infuse our values into everything we do. When we own and set agendas, we prioritize inclusion, accessibility, and generosity. When we celebrate our teams, we champion fairness, visibility, and equity. Whatever work we do, we align with our leaders to deliver values-driven results.

As I look beyond DesignOps, I'm embracing my years of operational leadership alongside some of the industry's best practitioners. I'm leaning confidently on my experience in software delivery and what it means to succeed in tech. And I'm challenging myself to go further with my values-driven work. I'm looking for areas where design thinking, process innovation, and operational leadership can deliver new and surprising impacts. I'm looking beyond traditional tech, aiming for the edges and communities who don't know that leaders like us exist: places where empathy, leadership, and operational experience can change people's lives.

My values are leading me toward social work. I want to find places where people are experiencing pain, or where life has left them underserved or brushed aside. There are many organizations and dedicated leaders in these spaces, but I'm sure my contributions will be a welcome addition. I'm convinced that DesignOps skills and experiences can drive innovation in all types of industries, but it's our values-driven leadership that will ultimately show each of us where to go next.

The Design Leadership Path

Another path for senior DesignOps leaders is to transition into design leadership roles, such as design manager, VP of design, or VP of UX. These positions place them at the helm of design teams, where they set strategic vision and creative direction. Their deep understanding of DesignOps allows them to bridge the gap between strategy and execution, fostering design excellence in a tangible way. These leaders leverage their expertise to manage talented design teams, directly impacting the creation of exceptional user experiences. They also forge strong partnerships with product delivery teams, ensuring seamless collaboration throughout the development process. Alana Washington took this path in her career.

DESIGNOPS DECODED

THE DESIGN LEADERSHIP PATH

Alana Washington, head of design, Platform at Rippling

My master's degree is in Industrial/Organizational Psychology—the field that helps organizations be better for their workforce and humans thrive within their organizations.

I interned at HBO on the Organizational Effectiveness team. Here, I fine-tuned soft skills training (for topics like emotional intelligence, team effectiveness, and presentation design), and also inadvertently started a few design practices: service design for organizational development and information design on course materials.

My trajectory shifted alongside a growing demand for data visualization, a field that combines my knowledge of data analysis with communication, storytelling, and designing for user intent. I joined the data visualization team at market research firm, GfK. I grew from designer to the first product designer working on real-time data products, to a leadership role that strategically framed our client's data storytelling needs. An uptick in RfPs (Request for Proposal) for experience maps and blueprints led me to Adaptive Path. I learned that these gorgeous artifacts—simplifications of processes and systems (that were anything other than simple)—were the output of something called *Design Operations*.

continues

DesignOps combined the skills I'd been honing over the years—org design (how work gets done), designing (the output of work), and strategic alignment (work supporting a product, a vertical, or something beyond). I joined Adaptive Path when my assignment changed over the years from service design to growing the data experience design team.

I began itching for a new challenge. Uber Freight was looking for a DesignOps person to scale their design org. Upon arrival, I was unexpectedly asked to lead the design team for a period. After we found a permanent leader, I focused my efforts on the shipper side of the business, which I've been leading for the past four years.

I will always need the "org design, designing, and strategic alignment" trifecta present in my work. I'm open to the idea that there might be a future DesignOps role that offers this mix, but for now, I'm finding these attributes most present leading a product design team. As a design director, I need fluency in organizing people to achieve a goal. DesignOps is the GPS of the organization: building, organizing, and sharing a collective unconscious that designers, managers, and leaders can tap into to turbocharge their work. And working alongside really talented DesignOps folks allows you to scale your operational fluency in areas that you might not work in day-to-day.

Going the Solo Path

Senior DesignOps leaders can also leverage their expertise into a solo venture, launching their own design or DesignOps consulting practice. This path offers a unique blend of autonomy, challenge, and impact. It allows leaders to apply their honed skills and deep knowledge of products and industries for the benefit of small (and large) clients.

For some, the entrepreneurial spirit calls them to start their own practice. Building a consultancy provides the freedom to craft their ideal work environment, shape their client portfolio, and directly set the strategic direction of the practice. Others may be drawn to the collaborative nature of established consultancies. These firms offer the opportunity to learn from a wider pool of experts, share best practices, and contribute to a larger team dynamic. Kristin Skinner followed this path.

GOING THE SOLO PATH

Kristin Skinner, coauthor of Org Design *for Design Orgs and founder of &GSD, Executive Leadership Advisory*

When I first started out in my design career, I was designing and developing websites for women-owned small businesses. My first role in a technology company was at an early-stage startup as a UX designer and developer. In 2006, I joined Microsoft as a lead UX program manager focusing on designing and developing experiences for System Center. I then moved to Microsoft's Pioneer Studio, an innovation studio founded to create new connected experiences and devices for consumers. As studio manager, I shifted focus toward team leadership with an emphasis on the managerial and operational aspects of design and development.

Following Microsoft, I joined Adaptive Path for one of the most pivotal experiences of my career. We were consultants in experience and service design for global clients across retail, healthcare, financial services, and travel industries around the world. But we also were champions for the design community, designing and delivering conferences and workshops, and sharing knowledge through new methods and frameworks we were creating with our clients. I seized the opportunity to establish not just the design program manager role, but also defined and built a practice and team around it.

My role grew to managing projects and accounts, and later leading product design, people, and teams. I was responsible for leadership, management, and operations for the company, including account management, business development, strategy, ways of working, hiring, learning and development, event curation, and design program management. My time at Pioneer Studios and Adaptive Path felt like my bespoke, hands-on version of a dMBA, defining and developing my sense of Design Operations as a practice.

continues

DESIGNOPS DECODED (continued)

After Adaptive Path's acquisition by Capital One, my charter was clear: scale and mature the experience and service design practices. I expanded the design function from 60 to 450 within three years and established a centralized partnership that organized design into one function but distributed its practice across lines of business. I also defined a DesignOps practice. During this time, I coauthored the first book on design management and operations, *Org Design for Design Orgs: Building and Managing In-House Design Teams*, began to apply DesignOps across Capital One's lines of business, and co-founded the DesignOps Summit conference series and community.

I continued working in executive design leadership roles, building and leading experience design and Design Operations organizations at Chase and then at Expedia Group, where I served as its first Global VP of Design Operations.

But I was becoming more and more curious about how DesignOps would work when applied in different contexts, scales, and industries. I also wanted more autonomy over my time and energy. In 2023, I left Expedia Group, and I started my advisory business, &GSD ("and get sh*t done"), where I use my expertise in organization design, management, and operations to help teams of all sizes become more effective.

The Rising IC Path

A growing trend is emerging: senior DesignOps leaders who transition into high-level individual contributor (IC) tracks. This shift is reflected in the *2023 DesignOps Benchmarking Report*, where 26% of respondents hold senior staff or principal IC positions. These high-level, non-leadership roles offer seasoned DesignOps leaders the opportunity to leverage their deep expertise and influence in service of the work and craft. They can directly shape DesignOps practices within their organization, tackling complex problems and implementing strategic initiatives.

For some leaders, this shift allows them to trade the responsibilities of people management for a closer connection to the core design work they may have once enjoyed, albeit at a more strategic and impactful level. One leader who pursued a staff IC role is Michelle Morrison.

THE RISING IC PATH

Michelle Morrison, sr. staff UX program manager at Google

My entry into Design Operations was unexpected. I was an early employee at Square and loved working there. I would do anything asked of me, which meant that my role changed as the business matured. I was working as a product marketing manager, which included responsibilities like managing the website and brand architecture, and finding ways to get new users to consider Square.

I partnered closely with the brand team and loved working with that crew. Together, anything felt possible. The brand team's design director approached me about a creative strategy and operations lead role. A quick reorg later, I had the opportunity to manage our brand producers and lead the team on all things focused on new user acquisition. That was the start of my budding DesignOps career.

From there, I went back to Facebook (as an IC) overseeing the learning and community portfolio for design; later, at Dropbox, I led design and research operations (returning to management). My next move was Twitter, where I led a strategy and operations org of 30 program managers across UX, research, and biz ops. And now I'm at Google, as a senior staff program manager (IC again!), who is responsible for the generative AI portfolio in Search.

When you are a program manager, you are in a leadership position whether you are an IC or a manager. As I've oscillated between the two, I've found that my top priority has always been addressing and adapting to the highest business needs. At Google, I've had to lean into my scrappy 0–1 space, working together with my engineering partners to get new products and technologies into market at a rapid pace. In past roles like Twitter, I leaned into management skills like organizational design and change management because that was what was needed at the time.

My career has been quite dynamic. When you work in innovation, change is a constant. The industry changes, the technology changes, and the needs of the business constantly change; therefore, it's important to be adaptable in your skill and role type if you want to stay at the frontier of new things. After 15 years in this field, I'm still learning, building, and growing. I'm always looking for collective problems to solve, to get things done, and to make them nice.

The Beyond Design Path

While DesignOps offers a fulfilling career path, some senior leaders may crave challenges beyond this discipline. Their cross-functional skills and experience make them strong candidates for leadership roles in other operational areas. The field of roles that match DesignOps skills is vast: human resources (championing employee engagement), strategy (shaping long-term goals), product management (collaborating on user-centric solutions), people operations (streamlining workflows), or even general business management (operations) to name a few!

These ventures allow former DesignOps leaders to leverage their design-centric thinking and problem-solving skills in new ways, to gain exposure to different facets of the business, to broaden their leadership experience, and to continue to make a significant impact on the organization's success. This is the path that Jose Coronado took.

THE BEYOND DESIGN PATH

Jose Coronado, sr. director, Strategic Planning & Operations at Target

As a global design leader with a background in enterprise technology and management consulting, I had direct experience with all things DesignOps before this was a recognized practice. It's a complex domain: hiring and firing; growing and developing talent; creating design systems; defining reusable templates and processes; scaling and supporting the team; negotiating with leaders across product, engineering, HR, finance, and more. After a few years, I had the opportunity to build a Design Operations team from the ground up at one of the largest banks in the world.

My design leadership saw DesignOps as a silver bullet, the place where all process, people, and operations problems could get solved. As a team of just two, our first year was a colossal failure. We started many tracks of work and did not complete almost any of them. Over the next few years, I secured the support to expand the Design Operations practice, delivering business value to executives, and supporting culture and growth across the team. I advocated for the team's growth and secured promotions for the team. Three questions kept coming to mind: So, what? Now what? And, then what?

A Fortune 50 retailer in the U.S. came looking to hire a head of strategic planning & operations role. I thought, "Why me?" since I did not have consumer or retail experience. The opportunity to learn a new industry, take on an expanded role, working in a positive, caring culture with strong UX, product, and digital leadership motivated me to take on the challenge.

Some key transferable skills from Design Operations include:

- Delivering business results and articulating impact
- Developing cross-functional partnerships and proactively expanding your network across the organization
- Scaling teams through experimentation and learning, with new ways of working, processes, and tooling
- Building new teams and expanding existing ones, hiring leaders and practitioners, and galvanizing distributed teams
- Putting structure where there is none

Our paths in and out of Design Operations traverse across industries and disciplines. We come from different backgrounds, and our roles present opportunities that open many doors.

Coda: You *Can* Take It with You

There are many paths that might lead people into Design Operations. As you've examined in this chapter, there are just a few that lead you out (with plenty more to be discovered). DesignOps does not need to be a career stepping stone; many practitioners will discover that this career will be or has always been their destination. For those whose journey winds through, back, around, and out of Design Operations, we believe that they have a bright future ahead. Ours is a discipline whose core competencies (see Chapter 4, "It's All About Practice") are in demand in nearly every field, and the primary DesignOps experience of thinking strategically, while executing tactically, is applicable to any leadership role.

Playing Your Part
Leading with Values

The past few chapters have been a detailed look at the fundamentals of the DesignOps role: the common backgrounds, the shared competencies and mindsets, and its many levels and specializations. There is one last foundational component of the DPM role that makes DesignOps practitioners special, and that is the outsized part that Design Operations plays in driving meaningful, transformational change by operationalizing your (and your organization's) core values.

When the people and practice of a design org are aligned on a shared set of core values, DesignOps can achieve much more than delivering confidence, clarity, and community. DesignOps work can bring about real human and systemic change, by shaping the experiences created (and *how* they are created) by designers and DPMs. This can be accomplished the hard way, through trial, error, and accident; or, it can be done the better way, through values-grounded programs and values-driven leadership. And it's in this capacity that Design Operations' full potential is realized: in its responsibility to transcend the tactical contributions of design delivery and process improvement, to becoming the catalyst for strategic pivots and radical change for both the design org and those whom that org serves.

In their book *Changemakers*, Maria Giudice and Christopher Ireland discuss the crucial role that values play in driving trust as well as transformation:

> Values can and should develop as you learn and grow. But even as they evolve, they need to remain consistent with your actions to be believable and steadfast. We are not saying that changemakers need to conform to select values or demonstrate some level of goodness. We are saying that values represent a significant aspect of a changemaker's appeal and influence, and they can't be easily ignored when it's inconvenient to follow them. Most transformations led by changemakers will be dependent on values in one way or another.

DesignOps is set up to be transformative; this discipline uses design processes to build the ecosystem that enables creation and innovation. And to do that, their practitioners must be grounded and steadfast in their values.

The Value of Values

Values is a loaded word. In English, it has over a dozen meanings, but for our purposes, we'll say that values are the qualities that one holds in high esteem and believes in. For DesignOps specifically, values are the "qualities that guide us in the absence of any other direction." When faced with the unknown (which—let's be honest—happens a lot in Design Operations), DPMs turn to their values to move forward. Even if they're unsure which way to go or what to do next, a DPM knows that allowing their values to guide and inform their decisions ensures that they'll move forward in a consistent, principled way. Values are less of a map and more like a compass, keeping DesignOps headed confidently in a single direction when it doesn't otherwise know where it's going, or how it's going to get there.

Moving things forward and providing direction is a fundamental part of the DesignOps role, which is why understanding how to lead with and be grounded in values is so critical to the discipline's success. Furthermore, when those values are aligned end-to-end in your design org, from the person to the program to the practice, those values can be harnessed to create real, meaningful change.

Don't be daunted by the fact that "transformative change" is a fundamental part of the DPM's role. It may not be in the job description, but it's certainly part of the job. To navigate values-driven leadership in Design Operations, aspiring and seasoned DesignOps practitioners must first know how to identify their design org's core values; interpret and define them at a personal, program, and practice level; and finally, operationalize them into their organization's work. Repeatedly applying these steps in bigger and bolder ways is the key to leading with values and unlocking DesignOps' potential to drive systemic changes inside and outside the design org.

Identifying Your Design Org Values

A design organization should define its organizational values as early as possible in its development. Ideally, this should be done during the initial stages of forming the organization or during a significant period of growth or change. By defining values early on, the organization can establish a clear direction, set expectations for behavior and decision-making, and create a cohesive culture. However, it's never too late to define or refine organizational values, so if they haven't been established yet, it's important to prioritize this process as soon as possible.

The first step to leading with values is identifying those values and to whom those values apply. The latter part is both easy and hard, as values are inherently personal. (More on this in the next section.) But for the purposes of design orgs, it's correct to say that the org's values apply to everyone. So then, how does a large, creative, diverse, and probably distributed design org begin to identify its core values? With the help of DesignOps, of course! And luckily, it all starts with a skill that comes naturally to most DPMs: affinity-mapping.

Think of identifying your org values as a brainstorming exercise, complete with colored stickies. DesignOps' first task is to facilitate a workshop to generate an initial set of values to encourage the org into generating more. One way to start this list is to look at the top. Does your company operate by a set of published values? What about the unit or organization into which your design team reports—what are their values? What about your design leaders? They will likely have a set of personal values that they bring into their professional practice.

The outcome of this generative activity is not to arrive at a final list of values, but an initial list—one that will be added to, reordered, upvoted, and culled over time. Use this list to inspire additional contributions from the design team. What values are missing? What's another way to describe the qualities of the values already captured? How might folks disambiguate values that have multiple meanings? What values reinforce your decision-making and actions at home and at work?

A shortcut to this exercise is to simply begin with a list of core values that are common globally. One such list follows in Table 7.1.

From whatever list the team generates, DesignOps should lead design org representatives to upvote and cull a smaller set—say,

25%—of values that they feel might best guide them and their team. The primary criteria in this selection process should be that the values don't change over time and could be applicable at all scales of the design org, from person to practice.

From this smaller set, upvote and cull again. Try to reduce your list of core values by half. Then do this again and again until your workshop group arrives at a set of no more than three to four values that, through the process of elimination, best articulate the qualities that the design org holds in high esteem, believes in, and can guide them during times of uncertainty. The reductive process of this exercise is challenging and provocative—intentionally so. It's uncomfortable to look at a list of shared values that might contain qualities like "well-being" and "joy" and be asked to eliminate one. But if values are to be your design org's compass, it's important to triangulate around as few points as possible to help navigate forward clearly.

TABLE 7.1 CORE VALUES FROM SALESFORCE'S "KNOW YOUR VALUES" EXERCISE

Balance	Courage	Family	Impact
Growth	Inclusion	Sustainability	Influence
Efficiency	Trust	Belonging	Empowerment
Peace	Responsibility	Accomplishment	Commitment
Creativity	Forgiveness	Individuality	Learning
Development	Security	Adventure	Compassion
Determination	Harmony	Respect	Resilience
Diversity	Freedom	Scale	Love
Power	Spirituality	Affection	Competence
Equality	Fun	Innovation	Loyalty
Recognition	Teaching	Altruism	Competition
Excitement	Clarity	Integrity	Order
Relationships	Well-being	Ambition	Cooperation
Fairness	Helpfulness	Intellect	Passion
Curiosity	Wisdom	Joy	Transparency

FAMILY VALUES

I was a participant in a version of the exercise described earlier, but for a workshop scoped to *just* personal values. For this workshop, groups of six were randomly seated together, were asked to refine their personal values (starting from a similar list as above), and then had to share their top three personal values with their group.

I had the awkward privilege of being seated with our chief design officer and four design leaders, and as a relatively new employee, my immediate core value at that table was "extremely nervous." What would my personal values say about me in front of the people who had just hired me? Would I be judged for choosing "balance" over "innovation?" Was this some test of my ability to stay cool under pressure?

Of course, there are no right or wrong answers when it comes to personal values. (Mine were "balance," "integrity," and "security," by the way.) But what I remember most from that exercise is not what I shared as my *own* values, but what our design leaders shared as *theirs*. Each had "family" as a core value. Moreover, they had each interpreted "family" mostly the same (think "home life," primarily), but with enough nuances in definitions that no two "family" values were entirely alike. "Family" consisted of life partners, parents, children, communities, and—for some—coworkers, but always the value was with whom you chose to share your highs and lows at the end of the day. That our design leaders so unanimously valued "family" helped me understand how *they* thought and operated, and it changed my own relationship with how I chose to balance my own work and life.

It's OK to revisit your design org's core values from time to time, but only do so as part of a planned or recurring cadence (for example, annual roadmap planning) and *not* as a reaction to an unexpected change or emergency. The org's core values are intended to help teams find direction amidst uncertainty—nobody can navigate forward if their compass keeps changing direction!

Interpreting and Defining Your Design Org Values

Congratulations! With your design org's core values identified, your designers and DPMs now have a set of three or four words that look *amazing* on motivational posters, but perhaps are also a little too abstract to put into use. (Hang in there, kitty.) To give focus to your core values, the next step is to interpret and define those values for the different levels of scale in your company, from person to team to practice. Defining values is especially important for individuals and teams, because *values* and *actions* are linked: our personal values influence our behavior and postures toward the teams we are a part of, which, in turn, influence our design practice. How a single designer or DPM interprets their org's core values can very well impact business outcomes, for good or bad.

DesignOps is a key player in this step, which begins with defining the design org's core values. Taking the values identified earlier, DesignOps must collaborate with design leaders to give those values meaning; moreover, it should connect those values with business and human experience outcomes that can be directly driven by the design org. Take, as an example, the following set of hypothetical core values (Table 7.2):

TABLE 7.2 HYPOTHETICAL DESIGN ORG VALUES

Values:	Inclusion	Innovation	Sustainability

DesignOps should collaborate with design leaders to mutually interpret those values through the lens of the design org's business and experience objectives. Likely via another workshop or some async collaboration, a DPM might drive their design leaders to agree upon the following definitions (Table 7.3):

TABLE 7.3 DEFINITIONS OF CORE VALUES AT THE DESIGN ORG LEVEL

	Inclusion	Innovation	Sustainability
Design Org	We make accessible products built by teams that reflect the diversity of our customers.	We experiment and test new features to always be leading our product category.	We minimize our impact on the environment and maximize our work-life balance.

This process should then be repeated at different levels of the organization. For design teams that have a dedicated DPM, he or she might organize this conversation. For the DesignOps team itself, all DPMs should collaborate equally to interpret and define what their org's core values mean specifically for the practice of Design Operations (Table 7.4). For example:

TABLE 7.4 DEFINITIONS OF CORE VALUES AT THE DESIGNOPS LEVEL

	Inclusion	Innovation	Sustainability
Design Org	We make accessible products built by teams that reflect the diversity of our customers.	We experiment and test new features to always be leading our product category.	We minimize our impact on the environment and maximize our work-life balance.
DesignOps	We build programs that are welcoming to all roles, levels, regions, and abilities.	We invest in new ideas, tools, and ways of working that adapt to our design org's needs.	We create processes that are easily adopted and executed with minimal effort.

Lastly, recalling that an individual's actions and values are linked, it's important for each designer and DPM to reflect on and interpret what their org's values mean for *them*. This necessary step ensures that the design org's compass is aligned with theirs, personally, to guide their decisions, deliverables, and actions (Table 7.5). For instance:

TABLE 7.5 DEFINITIONS OF CORE VALUES AT THE DPM LEVEL

	Inclusion	Innovation	Sustainability
Design Org	We make accessible products built by teams that reflect the diversity of our customers.	We experiment and test new features to always be leading our product category.	We minimize our impact on the environment and maximize our work-life balance.
DesignOps	We build programs that are welcoming to all roles, levels, regions, and abilities.	We invest in new ideas, tools, and ways of working that adapt to our design org's needs.	We create processes that are easily adopted and executed with minimal effort.
DPM	I design programs that welcome and accommodate the greatest needs of our design org.	I learn and test new tools, pilot my processes, and learn from failures and feedback.	I optimize processes to succeed initially and over the long-term.

Ultimately, the important thing is for everyone in a design org not to just share a core set of values, but to understand how to put those values into practice for themselves and their design teams, such that the same values can be used to align everyone and move forward in the same direction.

Operationalizing Your Design Org Values

With your design org's values identified and defined in ways that are relevant top-to-bottom among your design teams, the "values exercise" described previously is mostly done. Well, for individual designers and leaders, that is; not so for DPMs. For DesignOps, the values work is just beginning. This is because Design Operations is uniquely tasked with bringing a design org's values to life—to make these values visible and actionable in ways that can be measured and improved.

DesignOps is responsible for living up to its name, by operationalizing your design org's values internally and externally. This can be done with these three steps:

1. Codify and reinforce best practices.

2. Reinforce with intention.

3. Enable learning and awareness.

Operationalizing values starts by codifying what *good* looks like. A lot of this work will be in context to your organization, but two domains where DesignOps commonly codifies best practices are in product-focused activities (what to create) and organizationally-focused activities (how to create).

DESIGNOPS DECODED

THE POWER OF DESIGNOPS

Spencer Stultz, Group PgM 2 Product Equity, Adobe Inc.

You are a professional designer, who is designing policies, practices, protocols, and systems that affect your design org, and that is a form of power. It is imperative to be intentional with the power you hold. You design how creatives within your company are able to navigate the company. If systems are designed to only suit folks with specific identities, your work likely reinforces problematic power structures. DesignOps has the power to recognize these harmful systems and redesign new ones. It's your job to design for all people to thrive.

Consider a design org's hypothetical value of "inclusion," which this org (hypothetically) defined as, "We make accessible products built by teams that reflect the diversity of our customers." Codifying this value as a set of product-focused best practices may include the promotion of accessibility standards, inclusive design principles, and guidelines to ensure that products are designed with diverse user groups in mind. Codifying "inclusion" as a set of organizationally-focused best practices may include things like establishing inclusive hiring best practices, vendor sustainability standards, or an inclusive design process to review and remove biases that may prevent outcomes that are not aligned to your values.

With your design org's values grounded in guidelines and frameworks, the next step is to *reinforce* your design teams' understanding of and access to these resources. Through status updates, design newsletters, and design leader communications, DesignOps practitioners can use their powers of communication and organization to help design teams connect with their org's values-driven best practices.

Enablement is the final step to operationalizing values (or any effort, for that matter). DesignOps plays a critical role in fostering a culture of continuous learning and growth, by owning and delivering learning programs that help teams expand their skills and expertise. DPMs can bridge the gap between awareness and application of their company's values by offering targeted learning and growth programs and maintaining these programs season-over-season.

Taking "inclusivity" again as an example, DesignOps can develop training sessions, collaboration workshops, or arrange for subject matter experts to speak on topics related to accessibility. Or take the hypothetical core value of "innovation," DesignOps can create skill-building programs centered around Agile processes and design vision work. By aligning learning opportunities with core values, Design Operations can help connect the dots between documenting and doing, by enabling a design teams' ability to actually "practice what we preach" in a meaningful and practical sense.

In July of 2020, a lot was changing in the world. For my team in DesignOps, we were hyper-focused on enabling the team to work in a new remote world. We were also tuning into how we, as an organization, could be more inclusive in this new context.

So, I set out to create a best practices guide, the *UX Inclusive Meetings & Events Playbook*, that could be applied to the org-wide events that my DesignOps team owned but could also be used by anyone in UX who was planning, facilitating, hosting, or presenting at an event or meeting (see Figure 7.1).

UX Inclusive Meetings & Events Playbook

Best practices to create meetings and events that honor the full diversity of our teams.

CREATED AND MANAGED BY
DesignOps

Accessibility
Ways to ensure meetings & events are digitally and physically accessible.

Inclusivity
Ways to ensure we are inclusive in our language presentations and interactions.

Respect
Ways to ensure we respect each other's time and different cultures.

FIGURE 7.1
The cover image from our UX Inclusive Meetings & Events Playbook.

My commitment was to create meetings and events that represented our value of inclusivity and honored the full diversity of our team to ensure that everyone felt:

1. A sense of belonging
2. A sense of representation
3. A path to greater visibility for their work and themselves
4. A sense of pride and excitement in connecting with the broader UX community

This included a diverse representation of speakers, topics, and ways to engage with content and one another.

The 16-page guide that I created had sections with actionable tips, resources, and advice asking the team to consider accessibility and inclusive interactions, word choice and language, global considerations and representation, and how to respectfully engage attendees.

This guide acts as a commitment: a way to live our values and have meaningful discussions as an organization. The best practices within the guide have become part of our everyday rituals, and the guide has grown legs beyond our team. This is an example of the impact and value that DesignOps can create by operationalizing and codifying their values into best practice guides that can be applied directly and consistently, changing the fabric of the organization for the better.

Leading with Values

For a topic as human as "values," this chapter might feel overly-indexed on items like workshops, definitions, and guidelines. To put all this into motion in ways that can really drive transformational change in your design org, DesignOps practitioners must take the final, most important step—leading with values.

Leading with values is the practice of constantly checking in with yourself about how you show up, act, and deliver in accordance with your organizational values. This comes naturally to some people, but everyone could benefit from some tips and reminders for how to lead better with values. One way to do this is to create a ritual before starting any new DesignOps project and ask yourself the following questions:

- What values align to this project?
- How will my audience recognize and receive our values in this project?
- How should we interpret these values for this project?
- How are my project's outcomes aligned to our values?

Design Operations can also lead with values by taking advantage of its uniquely visible place in the design org. As the communicators, facilitators, and leaders for many design initiatives, it's hard to argue that DPMs are not seen. So, when DPMs lead with values, designers take notice. DesignOps practitioners are also uniquely positioned to "lead from the front" because of how they design the ways in which the design team works; this practice has the opportunity—and responsibility—to intentionally weave values into the fabric of everything it creates. Once values are defined, it's equally important to ensure that they are integrated throughout your process and are visible to all stakeholders.

Lastly, DesignOps should play a role in holding its design organization accountable to how it leads with and lives up to its values. When DPMs codify their values into best practices, they have the opportunity to also define how to measure whether or not those practices have been applied properly. DesignOps can and should measure what it can, and report to design leadership on where the org is succeeding—and failing—to live up to its values. This is especially true when values such as diversity, equity, inclusion, and belonging (DEIB) are codified into the products and practices of the organization. Jason Kriese, a former VP of DesignOps, puts it this way:

> You should not be rolling anything out without knowing what values you are trying to infuse in your work up front. Whether you are organizing an event, establishing a program, or implementing a new tool or process, you must identify the values that will act as guiding principles and aid in decision-making. If you're uncertain about the values or lack clarity, you should not move forward with the initiative. Full stop. If you aren't holding yourself accountable to this, you're missing a fundamental step. To put it simply, the work is the value, it's the purpose, and it's the outcome. Why are we doing what we are doing? That's values.

Putting It All Together

Here's a thought exercise that considers the scenario of failing to incorporate values into your work. As an example, take a program like a design town hall, which serves as a monthly gathering for the design organization. If this event is not organized in a values-led way, you may end up designing an experience that lacks purpose and direction. "Sure, the town hall was nice, but how did spending 90 minutes in that meeting move the needle forward for your practice?"

In the best-case scenario, you might deliver an experience that is moderately useful, but falls short of its true potential. In a worst-case scenario, you might have unintentionally created something with harmful consequences, or completely missed the intended outcomes of getting your design org together in the first place. Failing to connect how your org's values relate to a town hall event can result in delivering an "anti-value"—the opposite of what you intended to achieve. Worse, the ramifications of getting it wrong again in the future could be significant.

Now, run that scenario again from a values-led perspective. Your design town hall should connect with your org's (hypothetical) values of inclusion, innovation, and sustainability. These three values will serve as your decision-making criteria—they will "guide you in the absence of any other direction." Let's explore where that direction might lead you.

After first checking in with your org's guidelines for inclusive meetings, you design an agenda that intentionally brings diverse voices of the team to the stage; you also ensure that the global team is represented in the content presented and during moments of celebration. (Inclusion—check!). You experiment with a new presentation tool that provides a novel experience for your audience and use this to highlight content focused on product innovations. (Innovation—check!) And, of course, you make the town hall a hybrid event, so folks don't have to drive in to attend; after consulting your vendor guide, you cater the in-person meeting with an ethically-sourced caterer. (Sustainability—check!) Oh, and your org approves a small lunch purchase for all online attendees, too. (Inclusion again—check!)

In the end, the values-led design town hall was not only better for the attendees, but it was also easier for the DesignOps practitioners who organized it. With frameworks to start from, guidelines to drive decision-making, and a relevant purpose baked into the event, everyone benefited from this project being led with values from the beginning.

Coda: Your Values Are a Catalyst

Leading with values is not difficult, but it does take intention. While everyone—not just designers or DPMs—should practice values-driven leadership, it's critically important that your DesignOps practice does so intentionally and visibly and holds others to account when they lose focus. DPMs do this both because it's the right thing to do as human beings and because it's the right thing to do for your business. Along with your common background, mutual mindsets, and shared competencies, knowing how to ground programs and leadership in a shared set of core values is a fundamental part of the DesignOps role. In the next few chapters, we'll explore beyond the foundational elements of our practice the many ways in which DesignOps shapes—and is shaped by—the unique contexts of your organization.

CHAPTER 8

Shaped by the Orchestra
DesignOps in Organizational Context

Our previous chapters detailed two of the core fundamentals that are universal about DesignOps: the scope and domains of the *practice*, and the mindsets and competencies of its *practitioners*. These constants are critical for understanding the value that DesignOps can bring to a business and identifying the foundational characteristics in people (yourself included) that are needed to deliver operational success to a design org. Over the next few chapters, we'll explore the three dimensions that shape how DesignOps operates inside a business: the first is the design org's own organizational model, the second is the network of roles with whom DesignOps partners the most, and the third dimension is the intertwined developmental stages of design and DesignOps.

The first dimension, and the focus of this chapter, looks at how DesignOps is shaped and influenced by the specific organizational quirks, structural nuances, and maturity levels of the business in which it sits. This Design Operations constant is a bit of a contradiction: that the one thing that's the *same* across all DesignOps practices is how *different* they end up looking in the context of their specific companies!

Speak with DPMs from two different companies, and you'll come away with two very different visions of Design Operations. Expand your net further, and you'll be surprised at just how different this practice can seem. Even on a single team, you can compare the "day in the life" of two different DesignOps practitioners and convince yourself that they work at completely different companies.

So what makes this variability a fundamental trait of Design Operations? It's because DesignOps, as a practice rooted in relationships and partnerships, must adapt in the context of the different roles and functions that designers inhabit in their space. Zooming out further, DesignOps is shaped by how and where design teams sit in their organization. And at the highest level, DesignOps conforms to how design is set up as a discipline in each company or business.

Take all those organizational variables into account, and the end result is that the DesignOps practice look *less* like a set of machine-stamped gears, perfectly uniform across all companies, and instead something more like *machine oil*, occupying the unique crevices and negative spaces of a specific engine, making the internal components operate smoothly and efficiently.

So if you were wondering if a DesignOps team is just another cog in the machine, trust us—nothing could be further from the truth!

Design in the Broader Landscape

To appreciate the different ways DesignOps teams are organized and shaped by their design orgs, it's first necessary to understand the fundamentals of how design teams are organized within their business. Sabine Junginger, an academic researcher and educator in the field of design management and design leadership, has a model that describes the multifaceted relationship between design and larger organizations. Her research identifies four different orientations (Figure 8.1) that design teams can assume within their org: *separate, peripheral, central,* and *integrated.*

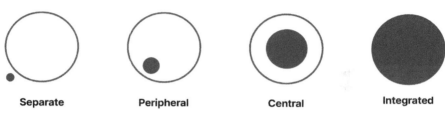

Separate   Peripheral   Central   Integrated

FIGURE 8.1
Sabine Junginger's theory of the four different orientations among small and large organizations.

- **Separate:** This model sees design as an isolated entity, operating as an external resource with no continuous presence in the organization (like an agency).
- **Peripheral:** Here, design plays a role on the fringes, contributing to specific projects and products, but is not deeply integrated into the larger org.
- **Central:** In this case, design plays a core role, where design is recognized and valued but may still operate somewhat independently from its peer disciplines.
- **Integrated:** This model represents a seamless fusion of design into the organization's DNA, where design thinking and practices are woven into the overall business strategy.

These models describe how close (or far) a design org sits from the central core of its organization, and thus the level of impact that design can have. Another factor that affects how design teams are organized is: who sits at that core? Design teams are often situated within or adjacent to core departments, such as marketing, engineering, operations, sales, IT, and more. But by far, the most common "core" in which you are likely to find a design team is *product management* (27%.)[1]

Whether integrated with, central to, or peripheral to a product management (PM) org, the proximity to this discipline heavily influences the ways design orgs function. Here are three common ways that PM teams are organized, which, in turn, impacts design org models, reporting structures, and operations:

- **By product/product suite:** Microsoft organizes its product organization around its product suites, such as Microsoft Office, Windows, Azure, and Xbox. Each suite has dedicated teams (including design) responsible for its development and success.

- **By feature:** Spotify's product organization is known for its "feature squads" structure. Six- to twelve-person squads are organized around specific features (or similar parts of the product), and each squad has autonomy to develop and improve those features.

- **By market segment:** Amazon organizes some of its product teams by market segments and customer groups. For example, they have separate teams and strategies for Amazon Web Services (AWS), which serves enterprise customers, and Amazon Retail, which serves consumers.

It's important to understand how design teams are directly shaped by their broader business landscape. (And how, in turn, this *indirectly* shapes the DesignOps team.) But design and DesignOps teams need not be a copy-paste of the orgs they report into. Conway's law warning against "designing systems that mirror your communication structure," as well as Steven Sinofsky's adage, "Don't ship the org chart," serve as important reminders that organizational structures should *not* dictate how products and services are designed and delivered. So, as we dive deeper into design org fundamentals and explore their impacts on DesignOps, be mindful that these organizational models merely *shape* DesignOps—they do not *harden* it.

---

1   Kate Kaplan, "The State of Design Teams: Structure, Alignment, and Impact," Nielsen Norman Group, January 3, 2021, www.nngroup.com/articles/design-team-statistics

DesignOps Decoded

One Org > Three Orgs

Kristin Skinner, coauthor of Org Design for Design Orgs *and founder of &GSD, Executive Leadership Advisory*

So, this statement may raise some eyebrows, but I believe that teams should operate as one cohesive org. When our teams are trying to come together and deliver a product to our customers, why do we have product managers, engineers, and designers—all with different incentives, and each reporting to different leaders with distinct goals? In today's landscape, I find this approach fundamentally flawed. Instead, I advocate for a unified structure with a single leader at the helm. The title is not nearly as important as the intent. They are the leader of this multiskilled organization. Yes, we need a variety of expertise and specialization, but I feel strongly that it should all roll up to one leader. And I think the evolution of Design Operations could be that leader or a key partner to that leader.

Design Org Fundamentals: Four Models

With this understanding of how design fits into the broader organizational landscape, we can now explore how design *orgs* are most commonly structured. While there are numerous examples out there, DesignOps practitioners are most likely to encounter just a handful of popular organizational models. These go by many names, but we refer to these common design org models as *centralized, embedded, hybrid,* and *agency* (Figure 8.2).[2]

Each model has different origins, strengths, and weaknesses. And as a business matures, its design org model may evolve into something new, only to then later return to some familiar shape. But it's critical for DesignOps practitioners to recognize how these models shape the ways DesignOps teams are organized to deliver.

---

2   Kaplan, "The State of Design Teams."

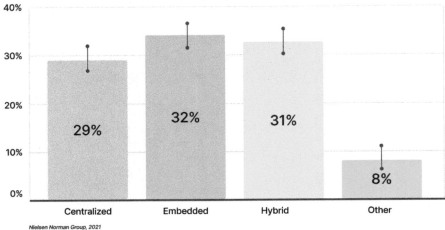

Nielsen Norman Group, 2021
Error bars represent 95% confidence intervals

FIGURE 8.2

The distribution of design org models across all companies shows a roughly even distribution across the three main types.

Distribution among these first three design org models is fairly equal: centralized (29%), embedded (32%), and hybrid (31%). As companies grow, they tend to transition from a centralized to a hybrid model; beyond this, there is little that predicts how a design org will be structured.[3] *Why* a business chooses one design org model over another is a decision informed by the structural advantages (and disadvantages) that each model provides. In the following sections, we'll take a deeper look at each model, and how these structures end up shaping the way a Design Operations team is shaped and functions.

Centralized Design Orgs

As you've seen, these design org models are more-or-less equally common, but the centralized design org is certainly the easiest to spot. They are all designers in a business working together, as a central unit, organized under a single design leader or leadership team, contributing to product and creative teams in the style of a shared service (Figure 8.3):

---

3   Kaplan, "The State of Design Teams."

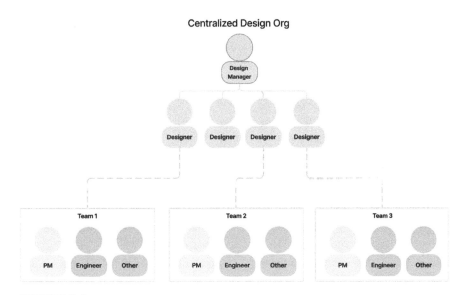

FIGURE 8.3

A centralized design org, where the designers are organized together, separate from their delivery teams.

There are advantages to a centralized design org. For one, the inputs and outputs of design decision-making are vastly streamlined; because all of design is under one roof (literally and figuratively), there are fewer barriers to collaboration. Communication is simpler, access to design collateral is easier to navigate, and tool stacks are more likely to be standardized. The experience of designing in this model may be slightly more homogenous, but the outcomes certainly aren't. A centralized design org is just as likely to produce original and visionary work as any other model—it just gets those results done in a more uniform way.

Companies that choose or tend to have centralized design orgs are often ones where capital-D *Design* is at the core of their business model. Think of any "design-led" company from the past ten years or so, and chances are their design org is centralized (or was, at some earlier point). Here, design strategy *is* product strategy. A consistent user experience is a key differentiator; research insights and product roadmaps are in total harmony.

For a product designer, this may sound like an ideal organizational model, but the centralized design org benefits user experience roles of *all* kinds: UI engineers, motion designers, illustrators, service designers, content writers, graphics designers, researchers, and more. If it's a specialized function in service of a design-led product strategy, chances are it will find a home in the centralized design org model. A potential risk here, though, is that the design org is seen over time as a service to the company and not a full contributor to its success.

All these different user experience roles speak to another common characteristic of this model, which is that centralized design orgs are often responsible for building the "core design" functions on which the rest of the business relies. For many companies, the biggest, and sometimes *only*, function in this regard is maintaining a business's design system. Entire books exist on this subject, so, briefly, a design system is the organization and standardization of composable elements (typography, color palettes, icons, UI components like buttons and fields, etc.), *and* the corresponding guidelines for how these elements should (and should not) be used to create a consistent user experience.

With a robust and durable design system, product teams can experiment and develop with confidence, knowing that both their UI and user journeys are adhering to common principles and best practices. Other "core design" functions in this model might include designing and maintaining brand assets (digital asset management) and creating collateral for presentations and internal or external communications. However, while having a centralized design system team is undoubtedly great for the user experience, the team itself might be challenged in this org model due to lack of governance or oversight to the development teams for whom the design system was created.

DesignOps in a Centralized Design Org

DesignOps plays a critical role in the centralized design org model. When you see DPMs in this context, the DesignOps team are often specialists in very specific design domains (tools, communications, contractor management, etc.). But these specialists all share the same trait: their exceptional project management skills, and their ability to plan, execute, and monitor for high design standards. At senior levels, this skill manifests in excellent program management—the ability to deliver multiple design projects and outcomes simultaneously. As discussed in Chapters 4, "It's All About Practice," and 5, "Composing Your Career," project and program management are a core competency of DesignOps, but these skills are especially in demand in centralized design orgs, where organizational boundaries may wall off designers from PMs or TPMs who manage this role in other parts of the business.

In the centralized model, design frequently sets the tempo for product decision-making and roadmapping. In turn, Design Operations is responsible for organizing those cadences and rituals in the first place. We call these crucial milestones the *rhythms of business*. Among other things, this includes owning quarterly reviews, release roadmapping, prioritization, integrating research insights, organizing retrospectives, and defining (and holding teams accountable) to their success metrics.

To match the variety of user experience functions around them, DPMs in centralized design orgs tend to bring specialized skills to the projects they manage. A creative branding team, for example, will need DesignOps practitioners skilled in content management systems and triaging marketing requests. A design systems team will need a DPM who is experienced working with engineers, savvy in governance practice, and excellent with versioning and documentation. This DPM can also manage the challenges associated with product teams unwilling to concede new feature development at the expense of design system consistency; to this end, the DesignOps skills of advocacy, enablement, and measurement can all be put to good use (Table 8.1).

TABLE 8.1   CENTRALIZED DESIGN ORG OPPORTUNITIES AND CHALLENGES FOR DESIGNOPS TO CONSIDER

Opportunities	Challenges
• Streamlined decision-making • Low barriers to collaboration • Communication is simpler • Efficiencies in navigating systems, resources. and knowledge • Standardized tool stacks • Broad range of skills on the team • Diversity of opportunities for designers • Clear career paths • Clear reporting lines • Consistent User Experience • Strong design culture	• Making the case and asking for design headcount • Design seen as a "service," not part of the team • Designer's lack of ownership and visibility • Designer's shallow depth of experience in a product space • Friction with product that lacks oversight • Staffing challenges

Embedded Design Orgs

Embedded design orgs are those in which designers are embedded directly inside a product or functional team. Most embedded design teams are aligned to products (43%) or internal departments and lines of business (27%).[4] This style of design org could be considered the opposite of a centralized design org, but it would be a mistake to call them *decentralized*. Rather than having *no* central authority, embedded design orgs have *many*, each suited to the specific needs of the team or function they align to (Figure 8.4).

Embedded Design Org

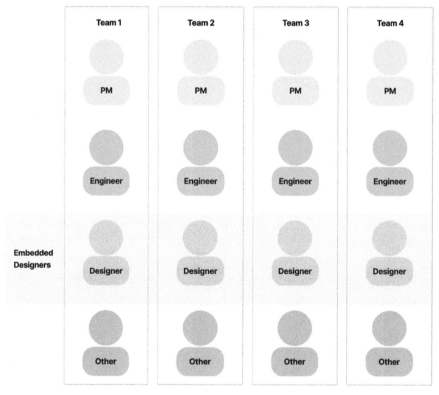

FIGURE 8.4

An embedded design org, where designers are organized directly inside their respective delivery teams.

---

4   Kaplan, "The State of Design Teams."

The advantage of an embedded design org is its proximity to the design team's partners (Figure 8.4). Designers work side-by-side with all functions—engineers, marketers, writers, QA (quality assurance), etc.—increasing these designers' agility and decreasing decision-making time. Need some placeholder copy for a feature you're prototyping? Turn to your left. Want to push an A-B test into production? Turn to your right. These scenarios are vastly oversimplified (and not always as easy to execute in practice), but the promise and possibility of these kinds of interactions are made easier when designers are embedded with their teams.

Another advantage of embedded teams is that designers get hired for their specific skills. This makes sense at a basic level, such as "mobile teams need mobile designers." But given the full spectrum of skills and abilities that designers bring to the table, this advantage becomes more acute. Maybe your product has a desperate need for a data-visualization prototyper? Well, the odds are good that there's a designer out there who matches that description. What about a graphic designer who can code? A service designer who writes copy? A medical hardware designer with gamification experience? Sure, why not! Designers (and contractors) with bespoke skills or an unusual combination of talents are more likely to find a home in embedded design orgs.

We find that embedded design orgs are often found in companies with "small but scrappy" roots. Small teams that need to move fast, hire for specific talents, and deliver uncommon solutions are typically founded with different roles embedded and working closely together. As these teams grow, the DNA of the embedded org gets passed on, and may evolve slightly, but the basic principles remain the same. Even very large companies, which may be comprised of multiple acquired teams or businesses, can be home to the embedded design org model.

The embedded design org's advantages of agility and specialization are sometimes neutralized when multiple design teams need to work together. It's great to work with fellow designers, but what happens when two teams discover they use different tools, delivery processes, or timelines? One solution to this dilemma is to evolve into a hybrid design org (more on this in the next section). But change of this magnitude takes time. A more common solution is for embedded design orgs to create temporary working groups or "councils" as a first step, to define project-based working models and make decisions on basic needs, like tools and communication channels. This approach models the "small-but-scrappy" principles of embedded design orgs, and can even be quite successful long-term.

DesignOps in an Embedded Design Org

Recall that in a centralized design org, DesignOps roles tend to be *specialized*. Befitting the contrasting style of the embedded design org, DPMs in this model tend to be *generalists*—proficient in many Design Operations skills, unafraid of ambiguity, and masters of bringing order to chaos.

There's a reason that embedded design orgs tend to need a "jack-of-all-trades" DPM. Specialized designers working with great agility are the *most* likely to need some process management and logistical oversight. Think of it this way: a team formed to go *fast* needs a design program manager to ensure they can also go *far*. And a design team composed of bespoke skills and specialties is the most likely to have unusual and untested operational gaps to fill, meaning a DPM generalist (who can plug *any* gap) can be the perfect fit.

Lastly, the working groups and "councils" that embedded design orgs rely on to work across teams are where DesignOps skills are most needed. It's hard to predict when two embedded design teams will need to collaborate; it's even harder to anticipate the problems and operational solutions they'll need to be successful.

Smashing two design teams together creates the conditions where DesignOps generalists shine. DPMs in embedded design orgs can serve as the first point of contact between teams. They assess the roles and abilities of their teams, map them to the short-term needs of a project, and identify lanes for everybody to work in to ensure a good outcome. In a way, each opportunity for embedded design teams to work together is itself a design challenge, requiring some discovery and definition to be in place before starting. Having DPMs on staff who can drop in and adapt to unpredictable operational needs is exactly why generalist skills are most needed in embedded design orgs (Table 8.2).

TABLE 8.2 EMBEDDED DESIGN ORG OPPORTUNITIES AND
CHALLENGES FOR DESIGNOPS TO CONSIDER

Opportunities	Challenges
• Agility and speed of delivery • Proximity to and trust with partners • Specialized skills • Empowered designers • Ownership • Deeper understanding of product space • End-to-end involvement as full team members	• Process and quality inconsistencies across teams • Friction with collaboration • Lack of diversity of opportunities and product spaces • Designers disconnected from other designers • Weak design culture • Inconsistency in process and quality consistency • Duplicated efforts

Hybrid Design Orgs

There's no surprise how this model is defined: the *hybrid* design org (also called a *matrixed* org) is literally just a hybrid of the centralized and embedded design org models, taking successful elements of each and mixing them together.

Hybrid design orgs are typically organized under a central authority, such as a head of design or chief design officer. The majority of (if not all) designers in the company report to this person's organization, regardless of their team, and have their career growth and performance managed by design leaders. But these designers may also report in a dotted-line capacity to a product or functional leader, who is responsible for setting the vision and design priorities of their specific domain (Figure 8.5).

Hybrid design orgs also feature "this-and-that" team structures. This model may have some centralized units, such as a design system team, and some embedded units, such as those organized to support specific products or business functions. The designers are all part of a single community, but they may also identify with a certain "tribe" for their day-to-day work.

Hybrid Design Org

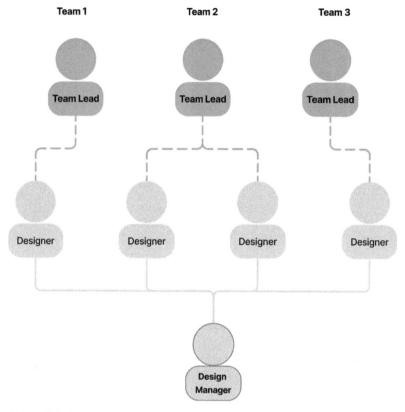

FIGURE 8.5

A hybrid design org, where designers report to centralized design leadership and are matrixed to support various delivery teams.

Designers in a hybrid org model need to manage their responsibilities in a matrixed way. Allocation is one way this challenge manifests itself, with designers required to manage what percentage of their work (or time) is dedicated to different priorities of the design org. This simple feat is complicated by the fact that allocations change regularly. Imagine a designer who is 100% dedicated to a product in Quarter 1 (her embedded team), then spending Quarter 2 documenting those new components and patterns for the design system (her centralized team), and then spending Quarter 3 split between enablement of those new components and new feature work (both teams).

It's not just a designer's work or time that is matrixed. Tools, communication channels, and processes may all be dependent on what the designer is focused on at any given time: their community, their tribe, or a mix of both. If this all sounds a bit confusing, you'd be right—to a certain extent.

Hybrid design orgs do add some friction to the design process, but we contend that this necessary friction is a feature, not a bug, of the hybrid model. Embedded teams optimized for agility can benefit from some centralized checks and balances; for example, a governance model to ensure that smaller teams are taking advantage of existing components or have completed accessibility reviews. Similarly, the centralized parts of the org can take advantage of the experimentation and innovation that is afforded when embedded teams have some leeway in what and how they work. It takes a lot of operational energy to keep a hybrid design org on track, which perfectly explains why Design Operations is such a welcome discipline in this model.

DesignOps in a Hybrid Design Org

Who manages the messy matrices of tools, comms, and processes for a hybrid design org? DesignOps, of course! Chaos control is just one of the many functions that DPMs own for this kind of design org. In fact, we believe that hybrid design orgs create the best conditions (and the most opportunities) for DesignOps growth and success, relative to the previous two models.

Every operational function of both models still needs DPM ownership. The kind of needs that fall under "the business of running a business"—like controlling budgets, managing shared tools and licenses, and sourcing contractors—are all improved when organized centrally. DesignOps in hybrid orgs will likely also manage the rhythms of business, like shared design org KPIs and performance reviews, in one consistent manner.

Release roadmapping and design program management for specific products are likely owned by DPMs closest to those areas. So, too, are the bridge-building and first point of contact roles that DPMs play, whenever adjacent teams find themselves working together. Perhaps in a previous world, these DPMs were "embedded" with their products; in a hybrid model, these DPMs are more accurately described as "affiliated," since they are both members of a specific product or function *and* a unified design org. (Everyone wears a few different hats in a hybrid org.)

A DesignOps team "organized centrally" and also "affiliated with teams" may sound like no team at all. We admit that making DesignOps work in a hybrid design org is hard! For this reason, Design Operations in *this* model is likely organized under a formal head of DesignOps. Having a single leader, a single vision, and a shared mission statement are all first steps to making hybrid Design Operations successful.

Another step is having a well-defined operating model for the DesignOps team to follow. Most operating models in this type of org are "federated," which is an oversimplified way of describing the complex governance of managing Design Operations both centrally *and* locally. (For U.S. readers, think how citizens have both federal and state rules.) Federated DesignOps teams need to have a team agreement, or "way of working" document, which gives shape to the operational boundaries and collaborative spaces for each DPM. Creating shared knowledge bases, curating forums for DPMs to show and bring work to their peers, and building mutual DesignOps competencies for *all* DPMs to build and aspire to, are steps that hybrid DesignOps teams need to take to ensure that they are working together, even when the work sometimes pulls them apart (Table 8.3).

TABLE 8.3 HYBRID DESIGN ORG OPPORTUNITIES AND CHALLENGES FOR DESIGNOPS TO CONSIDER

Opportunities	Challenges
• The best of both the embedded and centralized models • UX oversight comes from both design and product • Adaptable	• Increased complexity causes confusion • More checks and balances needed • High need for operations

Agency Design Orgs and DesignOps

The last common design org model DPMs may find themselves in is the agency model. One way to recognize this model is if your company is, in fact, an agency! Agencies are focused on customers or clients who need creative services from experts outside their own practice. For design agencies, these services can range from service design consulting, to visual design and branding, to creating design artifacts like icons, wireframes, and prototypes. A design agency typically has a fixed amount of time to deliver, and managing customer expectations and satisfaction is paramount.

While it's easy to think about the agency design org in the sense of an independent, third-party agency, the truth is this model can appear and function successfully inside any large company or business. Agency design orgs are typically centralized, but in contrast to a central design org—which often leads product strategy—internal agency orgs are responsible for taking in, triaging, and prioritizing work that originates elsewhere in the company. Designers in this model may not always decide why certain tracks of work come their way, but they certainly have a say in what work is worthy of their time and how that work will get done. In other words, the company's strategy is not as important as the internal agency's ability to control the quality, accessibility, and cohesiveness of the final experience.

Above all else, DesignOps in an agency design org requires excellent project management skills. "Taking in, triaging, and prioritizing work" is just the beginning. So is breaking down deliverables, managing design resources, and keeping track of time spent (or hours billed). A DPM in this model often has the title of *producer*, and may be aligned as a peer to their design leads; one is responsible for the "what and why" of the project, the other owns the "how and when" logistics. Agency DPMs also likely have excellent communication skills, owing to the proximity of working with customers and clients. If the DPM (or producer) recognizes obstacles in the timeline, or an increase in scope, it's often their responsibility to communicate this back to the client, with trade-offs and solutions already mapped out as mitigation steps.

DESIGNOPS DECODED

THE FUTURE OF DESIGNOPS VS. DESIGN MANAGEMENT: A PREDICTION

Adrienne Allnutt, head of Design Operations and Program Management at ServiceNow

As we see design rise to the C Suite and become vital to a corporation's competitive advantage, the future will include further specialization of labor within the design organization. Design management roles will evolve back to the core essentials and specialization of the craft—creative direction, experience strategy, design innovation, and storytelling. If we consider the design organization as a business within the corporation with customers across engineering, product management, marketing, and the executive suite, we need to run it like a business. DesignOps roles will run the labor of the business and ensure that our business is successful.

Coda: Design Orgs and DesignOps

Are there other design org models out there? Absolutely! The four described in this chapter are just the most common ones we've encountered. And even the basic definitions we give to each are mutable and not always applicable to every org, even if they fit the basic description.

Further, organizational models are not static—they evolve over time in response to internal and external forces like changes in leadership, shifts in market dynamics, advancements in technology, or changes in regulatory environments. One common disruptor is when companies merge or acquire another business, forcing different design org models to adapt to each other, or change completely. The hybrid model is a common post-M&A (mergers and acquisitions) structure because it can accommodate multiple cultures and operational philosophies. Given that 60% of CEOs plan to make at least one acquisition in the next three years, this may very well be something you experience yourself.[5]

The takeaway, though, is not to be able to define *every* type of design org. Rather, it's to underscore one of the foundational elements of DesignOps, which is that DesignOps teams are always shaped and influenced by the org they support, not the other way around. Being able to recognize and appreciate different design org models is critical to your DesignOps team's success, because it can help your team grow on its proper path, one carved out by the edges and contours of the overall design org. Trying to operate *against* your design org's model is counterproductive and wasteful. But building a DesignOps practice that is in harmony with your design org's structure? Well, that's music to our ears.

---

5 PwC's 27th Annual Global CEO Survey, www.pwc.com/gx/en/issues/
   c-suite-insights/ceo-survey.html

CHAPTER 9

Your Performance Partners
The Ecosystem of Partners

The organizational factors that shape and influence DesignOps teams are complex and multidimensional. In the previous chapter, we covered the different ways in which design orgs are structured within a business and the second-order effects these models have on Design Operations teams. Sticking to our musical metaphor, this is like examining how an orchestra's *internal* organization impacts the role of the conductor.

But in music (as in business), *external* factors shape this relationship as well, and the actual performance—the thing your audience is paying to experience—is not just a function of the conductor and orchestra, but of *all* the partners that contribute to putting on the show. From sound technicians and ushers to stage managers and roadies, a performance is shaped by the ways these roles work together, and a successful conductor needs to know how all these different functions work together to get the best sound out of their orchestra.

DesignOps teams are shaped and run by a similar relationship: the ecosystem of adjacent roles within the business with whom DPMs directly (or indirectly) partner to accomplish their goals. The maturity—or even *existence*—of roles like technical program manager, corporate messaging, or talent development will create opportunities and negative spaces of different sizes and importance that could be filled or co-owned by Design Operations. In other words, your team's mission will be partly shaped in context of the different roles and disciplines orbiting DesignOps at your company. Therefore, having a baseline knowledge of the roles with whom Design Operations most works, and the ways in which these roles do (and do not) contribute to design success, is critical to building long-term DesignOps success.

Your DesignOps Partners in Context

Design Operations is rooted in relationships and partnerships, so it's no surprise that DesignOps practitioners partner with a lot of disciplines outside of design. But because no two businesses are alike, context is important: how these roles are organized internally, their size and influence in a company, and their relationship to design (and DesignOps) can vary tremendously from company to company. With all these variables, it's nearly impossible to state definitively how a design program manager (DPM) partners with an adjacent role like a technical program manager (TPM). So, in this chapter, we'll simplify the conversation by focusing on DesignOps partnerships in the following contexts:

- **Definitions and differences:** In a world with only one DPM and one adjacent role, how do you define and clarify the differences between the two disciplines?
- **Shared opportunities:** What are the most common ways these two disciplines work together?
- **Role ratios:** What does the size or growth of an adjacent role signal for the Design Operations role?

The Product Trio: PM, Engineering, and Design

At the center of most DesignOps partnerships are the core disciplines that form the *product trio:* product management (PM), engineering, and design (Figure 9.1). Each has a specific function in service of creating digital experiences, and each might have an outsized influence in how those experiences are made, depending on a company's unique culture. For many DesignOps practitioners, defining ways of working that bring the product trio roles together in a design-centered or user-first way is the biggest (and sometimes sole) responsibility for which they are hired.

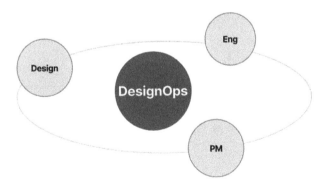

FIGURE 9.1
Successful companies recognize that the product trio are not isolated departments but interconnected functions driving overall business success. DesignOps is often at the center of all three.

Product Managers (PMs)

In many teams, the product manager (PM) is responsible for establishing product viability, vision, and strategy. This can be true at the broadest level (like an entire product line or product suite) and at the micro-level (say, a specific feature or product initiative), depending on the PM's grade and skillset. In PM-led organizations, this role might steer the product trio throughout the development lifecycle, defining the product roadmap, prioritizing features, and connecting cross-functional teams. They may complement a research team's insights by proxying as the voice of the customer, connecting the dots between the product's value to the end user and its alignment to the company's overall strategy.

In PM-led orgs, there is a symbiotic relationship between DesignOps practitioners and product managers. Both roles are invested in ensuring that product requirements are defined, technical constraints are surfaced, and end user needs are understood. The key difference is that DPMs desire these outcomes so that designers have the right inputs (and time in their schedule) to do their jobs properly; this is in contrast to product managers, who gather and articulate these details in service of the business hitting its goals properly. A common collaboration path for PMs and DPMs is to ensure that the design team is included in product roadmap decisions, that design dependencies are called out alongside technical dependencies, and that design complexity is assessed for each feature to measure the required design resources adequately.

Product manager roles are typically ratioed to the product itself, with a single PM responsible for a specific business investment: for example, a feature, a vertical, or an outcome. While PM staffing is complicated, ideal PM:designer ratios are not—we believe that, on average, organizations should strive for no more than a 2:1 (PM:designer) ratio. Organizing around this goal effectively means that a designer coordinates with at most two teams, on two product areas—splitting time between each according to design complexity. In product-led teams, an official DesignOps practitioner should be introduced as soon as possible, but certainly no later than when there are at most 30 PMs in the organization (spanning all levels, including management).

DESIGNOPS DECODED

OWN YOUR DESIGNOPS ROLE

Anel Muller, director of Design Operations, PayPal

DesignOps is like a design team's secret weapon, but rollout can be a battlefield. Getting everyone on board (from execs to designers) requires clear wins; for example, focus on a pain point like design handoff delays, and showcase the efficiency boost that DesignOps brings. Embrace the chaos, the ambiguity, and speak up! DesignOps leaders cannot afford to be flies on the wall. They are often the lone design voice in many rooms. Understand your team's design process and be ready to advocate for them. Push back on engineering deadlines that negatively impact the customer experience. DesignOps can never be just about the design; you are the web that connects product and engineering. Build strong bridges and celebrate wins together.

Engineers

While product managers concern themselves about commercial viability and business outcomes, engineers think about *feasibility* and *technical capabilities*. Within the product trio, engineers are responsible for actually building the product with the company's current technology, surfacing advantages and trade-offs—time, budget, performance—to their partners so that everyone is aligned to what is likely to be produced at the end of development. Given their semi-omniscient point of view of how projects might succeed (or fail), engineering-led organizations are quite common in all sectors (digital goods, finance, automotive, and more), and have created some of the greatest products and services of our generation.

Engineers are often the largest and most well-supported team in the product trio. Supported by their own technical program managers, the relationship between DesignOps and engineering is less about process and more about education. DPMs enable engineers to understand how design dependencies are scoped and sized, ensuring that the design process—including its artifacts and timelines—is factored into engineering milestones, and operationalizing how engineers interact with and consume design artifacts, such that both the details *and* the intent of the designer are translated into code in a meaningful way for the end user.

The number of engineers required to develop a great product varies tremendously based on the size and maturity of a company. One engineer can create the same experience as a team of twenty; nonetheless, there is a reason that both large engineering teams and the rare "army of one" exist, due to the technical infrastructure and maintenance required to support increasingly complex projects. While we admire the uncommon 1:1 (engineer:designer) ratio, we believe that a healthy, desirable target is 16:1 (engineer:designer), which often represents one or two Scrum teams. When an engineering org starts to head north of 200 engineers and engineering managers, that is a strong signal that a DesignOps practitioner is necessary to be added to the product org.

DESIGNOPS DECODED

BEYOND DESIGN: A CALL FOR OPS INTEGRATION

Kamdyn Moore, former head of R&D Enablement and head of Design Operations at Spotify

In the latter part of my tenure at Spotify, it became clear that Design Operations required a significant overhaul in order to support the broader business needs. As our design teams worked to create increasingly sophisticated experiences, our operational practices needed to evolve to serve more than design— we needed to serve the entire product development organization. By establishing a highly-effective, centralized enablement team that served engineering, product, research, and design, we could provide greater cross-disciplinary synchronicity and rigor in our processes at scale, without neglecting the nuanced requirements of each function.

DesignOps often falls short by narrowly focusing on serving the design discipline alone, maybe with occasional nods to ResearchOps or design system engineering. This siloed approach is where DesignOps fails. If you're entrenched in DesignOps but lack robust relationships with cross-functional counterparts in engineering and product teams, or if you're not fully integrated into strategic business operations, you're inadvertently undermining the success of design across the business.

What makes DesignOps different from design management? DPMs and managers are equally focused on the team, the conditions in which they work, and the end user experience. In our view, the biggest difference—beyond the actual people management aspects—is that design managers are focused outward, on the product, while the DPM is focused inward, on the process. Beyond that, the two roles are very complementary, and we believe that one of the greatest signals of DesignOps success is a DPM's ability to partner with design managers and execute through them, not just individual designers.

Design leadership is more varied, but a similar question exists: What makes a design manager (and design program manager) different from their respective leaders? Here, the primary difference is the proximity to the work each has, with managers typically much closer to the day-to-day work and leadership much closer to the business objectives and end users, as shown in Figure 9.2

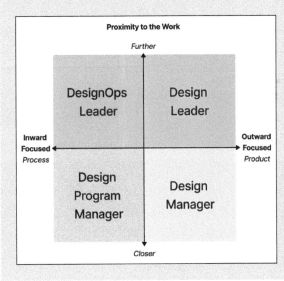

FIGURE 9.2
The Design and DesignOps Management and Leadership, inspired by Patrizia Bertini's *Roles and Remits Matrix*.

Designers

Reader, this section will be quick. The previous chapter is all about how DesignOps is shaped by its partner design org. And to a greater extent, this entire *book* is about how our two functions work together. Suffice it to say, DPMs who find themselves in a design-led product trio are likely to be in an organization where the *desirability* of the product is tantamount, and all decisions are framed through the rubric of increasing usability and creating a loveable experience.

Regarding ratios, we believe that the designer to DPM golden ratio is 16:1. (Chapter 12, "Maintaining Your Rhythm," covers how DesignOps can prioritize and reorient when this ratio becomes untenable.) At this scale, there is likely to be a design leader, and perhaps two or three design managers, equaling a total team size of around 20. If any of these numerical triggers are met on *your* design team, you (or your org) need to prioritize a design program manager—pronto. This ratio is the point at which the "force multiplier" effect of a DPM outmatches the additive effect of a new designer and is the strongest signal that a team is ready to invest in Design Operations. In all likelihood, a designer or manager is already performing DPM functions at this level of maturity, so the investment will be *more* than paid back in the time returned to the existing team!

The Program Managers: TPMs and Scrum Leaders

In many organizations, the engineering org is the largest and most complex discipline among the product trio. (Don't believe us? Just look at those ratios again!) Many companies have long employed specialized program managers to work closely with engineering teams to ensure that their projects are executed effectively and free of technical challenges. Specifically, the roles of technical program manager (TPM) and Scrum leader exist to help plan and execute software projects, making these functions valuable contributors to the development lifecycle (Figure 9.3). Moreover, these functions are familiar partners to DesignOps practitioners, with both roles often having *significant* overlap with the day-to-day responsibilities and skillsets of a DPM.

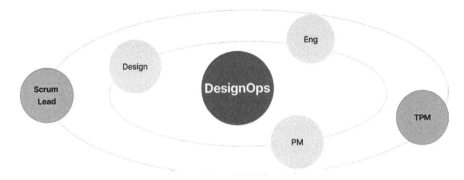

FIGURE 9.3

As product delivery becomes more complex, TPMs and Scrum leaders enter the orbit of DesignOps to ensure program health.

Technical Program Managers (TPMs)

A TPM typically uses technical expertise to help engineers manage complex projects, such as those that span multiple engineering teams or that have an element of technical risk (new tools, short deadlines, scaling up, etc.). Success is usually measured as a function of project goals, which neatly aligns the TPM's day-to-day work with their organization's business priorities. For tech-savvy program managers, being a TPM is an excellent role where immediate impact can be made.

The TPM role doesn't so much contrast with the DPM role as it complements it. The "program manager" parts of their roles make their functions very similar in nature, and depending on the specific requirements, some companies can deploy TPMs or DPMs interchangeably to manage (or even co-manage) a given program. The notable differences in the roles are defined by where the "T" and the "D" take prominence in the software delivery cycle: TPMs may be heavily involved in the technical engineering phases of development and delivery, while DPMs may be more in charge during the discovery and definition phases. (We want to emphasize that engineering and design teams—and TPMs and DPMs, too—are partnered throughout the entire cycle, just at different levels of engagement.)

Another common difference is that TPMs are often tasked with a single program, whereas DPMs may have the bandwidth to manage several. This is due to the lopsided ratios of engineers to designers, and also because design programs tend to be focused on behavioral consistency and pattern reuse across multiple products—programs which, when operationalized, benefit from the economies of scale.

Because the day-to-day responsibilities of TPMs and DPMs are very similar (hello, program management!), it's important for practitioners of each to establish an operating model with one another whenever they work together. A common model envisions the TPMs owning the "vertical" planning rituals and cadences required to deliver a product or feature, while the DPM owns the "horizontal" activities which ensure that designer capacity, design consistency, and overall governance across those products or features are delivered in harmony. In this model, TPMs and DPMs both work cross-functionally; what differs is that TPMs coordinate deeply with specific engineering teams and a handful of PMs and designers, while DPMs have a much lighter role coordinating the engineers but work deeply across the entire departments of product management, content, research, and—of course—design (Figure 9.4).

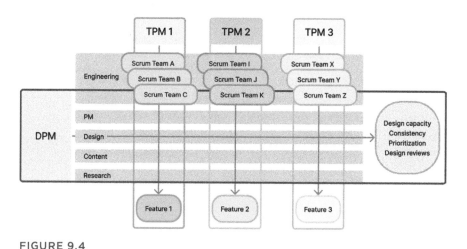

FIGURE 9.4

A common operating model for TPMs and DPMs to work together in complementary ways is to organize vertically and horizontally across the product delivery functions.

TPM roles are typically ratioed to engineering teams, with one TPM supporting one to four teams. This could mean a single TPM works with anywhere from 15 to 60 engineers, with a 40:1 (engineer:TPM) ratio being an approximate average. An 8:1 (TPM:DPM) ratio would be considered extremely healthy in a design-led organization, with 10:1 (TPM:DPM) being a more common average. An increase in TPM roles is a signal of increased investment in engineering, which in turn *should* trigger an increase in design resources. It's also a signal of program complexity and organizational change, all of which can be disruptions to a design team. If your company has eight to ten TPMs on staff, it should seriously consider adding a DesignOps practitioner to its ranks.

Scrum Leaders

All rugby teams follow the Scrum framework, but the same cannot be said for product teams. Those that do typically are managed by someone who functions as a Scrum leader—the person who makes sure that everyone is following the Scrum processes of Sprint planning, daily stand-ups, and reviews. In smaller organizations, this role may fall to a TPM or engineering manager; larger orgs may have dedicated Scrum leaders. Whoever performs this task, the role is critical for removing internal and external roadblocks and ensuring that the development team stays focused on the delivery roadmap.

At a tactical level, Scrum leaders keep product teams—inclusive of all the product trio roles described previously—focused on completing work during a specific "Sprint" cadence. Whether this Sprint is two weeks, fifteen days, one month, or something else, the team's "velocity" during this time-boxed period is what matters most: the amount of work the team completes versus the amount it thinks it can complete at the start of the Sprint. Since Scrum teams often include designers, a DPM's skills of orchestrating work and managing deliverables can sometimes be redundant when placed alongside a Scrum leader.

The best way for DPMs and Scrum leaders to work together is *not* to double up the jobs of Sprint planning and retrospectives, but rather to focus on enabling the Scrum team (and leader) to sequence the Sprint deliverables so that they align to the design team's processes. *Discovery* needs to happen before product managers can commit a roadmap; *definition* needs to happen before engineers can scope their development efforts, and so on. In other words, DesignOps should

WHY WE SAY SCRUM LEADER

In traditional Agile practices, this role is often referred to as the *Scrum master*. But terms like *master* have multiple meanings; in certain uses, these words are historical relics of a past that can be painful and hurtful. As DesignOps practitioners (and as decent human beings), we should be mindful of legacy words that our practice has inherited that no longer belong in a product team's—or anyone's—vocabulary.

defer to Scrum leaders when it comes to running the rituals of a Sprint, and instead be accountable for helping the Scrum team define which design deliverables are needed within each Sprint for the release to be successful.

Given that many roles can be ordained as Scrum leader, we lack any recommendation on ratios between this role and Design Operations. (And for that matter, all the other roles described in this chapter!)

The Operators: ES/HR, Finance, and Recruiting

It (unfortunately) takes more than a Design Operations team to run an effective business. And while the many, many roles required to operate a company may be invisible to the typical DPM, there are a few key functions that tend to partner with DesignOps in significant ways. There are three operator roles: employee success (ES), finance, and recruiting (Figure 9.5). ES is also known as *human resources* (HR).

In a startup business, many of these day-to-day responsibilities might be co-owned or shared by folks who have "Ops" somewhere near their title. As the company matures, and the specialized skills required to do these jobs properly come into focus, these functions get staffed appropriately, and most of these responsibilities shift away from the ad-hoc operators, including DesignOps. But the legacy and dependencies between these groups means there will always be strong DPM partners to be found among these operator roles!

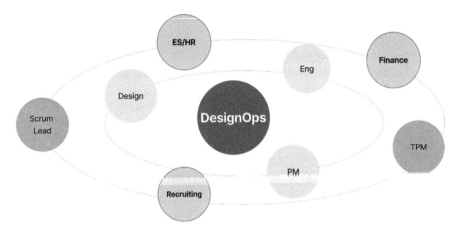

FIGURE 9.5
Relationships with the operator functions ensure that DesignOps, and this orbit of roles, are advocating for the team's needs.

Employee Success (ES)/Human Resources (HR)

DesignOps and ES/HR teams are similar, in that they are both responsible for fostering a positive and productive work environment. The obvious difference is that DPMs do this for their *design teams*, and ES/HR do this for the *entire company*. Critical areas of overlap include onboarding, employee engagement, and establishing career leveling frameworks. While ES/HR practitioners are accountable for these goals at the business level, they often partner with DesignOps to define and deliver the specific elements that make design a unique function in any organization. We see this partnership most often in the realm of career competencies, performance evaluation, and learning and development, where the landscape of design tools and role expectations are constantly evolving and are benefited by a knowledgeable expert who can articulate and codify "what good looks like" in a fair, relevant way.

Finance

Finance may not be a role every DPM works with, but for those who do, they may be your *most* important partner. Through their own seemingly mystical machinations (read: forecasting and spreadsheets), finance managers are responsible for creating annual budgets and controlling teams' spending. DesignOps works with finance to communicate the design team's financial plans and needs, and to prioritize what gets spent and when. This work falls under the "platform" focus outlined in Chapter 2, "Learning the Score," and can include maintaining current software contracts, investing in new design tools, and augmenting design capacity with external agencies or contractors. DesignOps may also manage the design team's internal budget to fund supplemental training, access to design conferences, internal events, and offsites—all of which need to be coordinated with finance to ensure that they can be funded year over year, and for a (hopefully) growing team!

Recruiting

If you like your design team, thank your recruiter. If you *love* your design team, buy your recruiter a coffee. Recruiting is instrumental in building a high-performing and diverse workforce through the acquisition of top talent. Recruiters attract, hire, and help "re-plant" designers internally to ensure your company's growth and success. But given the low ratio of designers relative to other roles, some recruiters may lack the skills and criteria to properly evaluate design candidates and assess their capabilities. DesignOps can partner with recruiting to establish functional competencies, objective standards for screening résumés, and interview questions. Some DPMs also design the interview process itself, ensuring a fair portfolio review experience and diverse interview panel. Recruiting personnel greatly appreciate when DesignOps people partner with them, because DPMs make their jobs better *and* help move the best designers forward in the recruiting process.

The Experience Partners: Research, Content Experience, and Design Systems

Ask a dozen companies which roles comprise their "user experience" team, and you'll get a dozen different responses. The least helpful answer is simply, "The ones who make the UX," which may be a sign that someone at the company doesn't know anything about UX, and that their organization could use some serious operational rigor. (If you hear this reply, pitch the responder on DesignOps, immediately!)

In many businesses, UX often equates specifically and solely to the design role. But there are a number of related experience roles that contribute to user experience; these roles may be organized as part of the design team or adjacent to it and may or may not report into a head of design or chief design officer. We call this family of experience roles the *experience partners*, which include the critical UX roles of research, context experience, and design systems. Whether these partners all sit at the same organizational table or separately, it's critical that DPMs understand how these roles work alongside design to deliver a successful end user experience, and how to partner with these roles regardless of what organizational boundaries might exist (Figure 9.6).

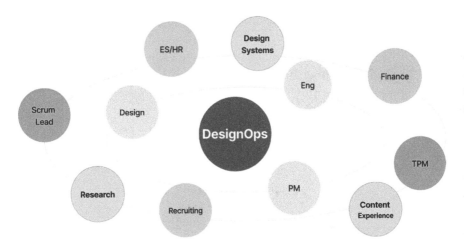

FIGURE 9.6
In some design organizations, these experience partners' functions also fall under the DesignOps' purview.

Research

Research teams help drive product innovation by gathering customer insights, analyzing user data, and reporting out on industry trends. As a partner to design, UX researchers specifically help product teams understand user needs and behaviors by conducting usability studies, interviews, and gathering and synthesizing product feedback. They also conduct strategic research on user preferences, technological advances, and changes in the market.

If your DesignOps team doesn't also include ResearchOps practitioners, a common way for DPMs to partner with research is by facilitating how their insights reach the design team; for example, by coordinating readouts and enablement sessions of research studies co-hosted with the research team. DesignOps may also partner with the research team to organize funding of research tools and vendors or co-create research milestones during release planning. Lastly, if the research team needs to navigate the product or engineering team (say, to request a certain feature get instrumented to capture user behavior in greater detail), they may call upon their DPM partner to help find the right contact.

Content Experience (CX)

Content experience (CX)—also known as *content design, UX writing*, or *content strategy*—is the discipline that shapes the experience users perceive via written content and mixed media in a product, as well as defining the strategy for how and when that content will be delivered. CX both aligns to and shapes the user experience (UX) of digital products, through the skills of information architecture, content personalization, and content design. If a product ever feels like it "speaks" to you or has a recognizable voice and tone, that is content experience in action.

When CX sits *inside* the design org, we often see very little difference in how DesignOps is organized to partner with this role versus the design role. CX and UX may operate using different tools (words and pixels, to put it simply), but their methods and outcome are entirely aligned. If CX sits *outside* the design org, then it's beneficial to everyone—including the end user—when a DPM includes CX practitioners in key design rituals and decision-making moments. In essence, DesignOps has a responsibility to ensure that this partner feels welcome as a critical part of the experience-making family. Accomplishing this means building relationships with the CX org to better understand its players and contributors, and to advocate for CX inclusion in release planning activities organized by product trio leaders.

Design Systems

We briefly covered design systems in the previous chapter. We defined a design system as "the organization and standardization of composable elements and the corresponding guidelines for how these elements should (and should not) be used to create a consistent user experience." Design systems allow product teams to experiment and develop with confidence, knowing that their UI and user journeys adhere to common principles and best practices.

Design system teams run the gamut of organizational maturity. On one end, design system teams might be resourced and run like a business, as (or sometimes even more) critical as profit-making product. On the other end, the design system team might be composed of designers and engineers for whom maintaining the design system is a side project. It's also common to see smaller dedicated design system teams that have a sort of "misfit" relationship with their partners—not quite design, not quite engineering, and certainly not building any end user product. Whether created by part-time enthusiasts or dedicated misfits, by its definition, a design system should touch every part of the user experience, and therefore it is worthy of any DPM's attention. (In fact, in many companies, the design system team is actually a function and responsibility of Design Operations!)

Some critical ways in which DPMs partner with design system creators is through enabling and scaling their communications to stakeholders; creating processes to manage inbound dependencies; operationalizing programs related to design system audits, governance, and accountability; and finally, by partnering as a Scrum leader or program manager for the team on high profile projects and deliverables. In other words, being a design system DPM can (and should) be a full-time job, one that is equally complex and rewarding for even the most seasoned DesignOps practitioner.

The Creatives: Marketing and External Design Agencies

Not all design is product design. Companies of all shapes and sizes will typically employ a variety of designers, from pre-sales solutions designers to end-to-end service designers. But the most common design roles that DesignOps partners with *outside* of product design are the ones we call the *creatives*: internal marketing design teams and external design agencies (Figure 9.7).

Not only do DPMs frequently partner with these functions, but many DesignOps practitioners often come from these backgrounds themselves! For example, 26% of DPMs surveyed in 2023[1] started their career as a marketing project manager, agency producer, or something similar. For this DPM cohort, partnering with the creatives may come naturally; for the remainder, understanding how DesignOps partners with these roles is critical to managing some of the most important UX relationships in your company.

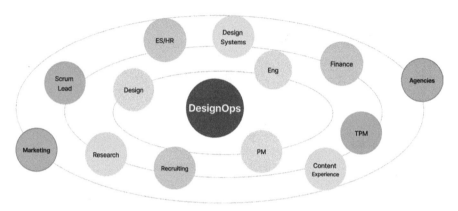

FIGURE 9.7
Creatives contribute to the same product, but at different stages of the customer journey (or "funnel," as they might say).

Marketing

Marketing is the team that promotes a company's products and services. They drive brand awareness, buyer consideration, and customer acquisition. Marketing is all about the "funnel"—engaging potential customers at different stages of their purchase intent. When moving people through the funnel, one of the key drivers of marketing's success is a close partnership between the marketing and product design teams; it is at this crossroads where DesignOps often finds itself working.

Marketing organizations typically employ their own designers who are specialists in graphic design, content design, web design, social media, etc. These designers know how to optimize their work for marketing channels, but this work often needs to draw upon the

---

1   *2023 DesignOps Benchmarking Report* (DesignOps Assembly, 2023), www.designopsassembly.com/2023report

Fast forward to the present, and the design industry looks very different. The mega-growth era has slowed, small design teams have proven they can be exceptionally mature, and this has prompted us to rethink what "mature" truly means for design and DesignOps.

In retrospect, our 2020 framework was more of a *growth* matrix than a holistic measure of maturity. Despite the common assumption that larger organizations are more mature, a study by Nielsen Norman Group revealed what should now be obvious: that company size does not correlate with design maturity.[1] This makes sense when you consider the diverse ranges of maturity among teams of similar size. In today's marketplace, headcount quantity does not necessarily equal design quality: a small, highly skilled and tightly knit team can outshine a larger one—especially if that team is mired in complexity and indecision. For example, the banking industry, known for its large UX teams, often lags when it comes to its design maturity. Larger enterprises have a surprisingly hard time reaching design maturity; smaller companies are twice and three times more likely, respectively, to reach high design maturity compared to large ones.[2]

As the design landscape has shifted and evolved, we've refined our matrix to better reflect this landscape. While size isn't the sole factor that defines maturity, it still shapes the dynamics of a design organization and the DesignOps practice alongside it. We've come to see team growth as just one aspect of development (albeit a core one), and ultimately, it is the holistic development of design teams that most affects how DesignOps works. Our modernized matrix now considers the frameworks of maturity and size (of both design and DesignOps practices) as distinct but complementary components of this development:

- **Maturity:** This component focuses on an organization's continual advancement in user-centered design, encompassing both the desire and capability to deliver great user experiences. This includes the refinement of design and DesignOps skills, capabilities, and quality of outcomes.

---

1 Kate Moran, "The State of UX Maturity: Data from Our Self-Assessment Quiz," Nielsen Norman Group, January 16, 2022, www.nngroup.com/articles/state-ux-maturity-quiz

2 Leah Buley, *The New Design Frontier* (InVision, January 2019).

- **Size:** This component focuses on the scaling and expansion of the design and DesignOps teams, encompassing both team size and the interactions within the team and its surrounding ecosystem.

Maturity and size are related; *both* must be understood to achieve a complete view of a team's development. Routinely examining your design team's maturity and growth isn't just good practice, it's essential for maximizing both impact and organizational health. Aligning DesignOps initiatives with the current state of design team development ensures that DesignOps is not just a responsive partner, but a driving force that elevates the entire design practice. If you fail to align, DesignOps can fall behind your design team's development—or worse, jump ahead of it. Either outcome hinders effective scaling, disrupts career growth, and can result in frustration and burnout.

The Development Matrix, Side 1: Maturity

Defining "maturity" for design and DesignOps in our ever-changing world can feel like cracking a constantly shifting code. Markets evolve, technology advances, skills broaden, and customer expectations are on a constant rise. It's no wonder the topic of maturity matrices pops up constantly on design and DesignOps forums—it's a complex area ripe for ongoing discussion and exploration.

Design has some generally accepted maturity frameworks; DesignOps does not. We believe that aligning these two recognizes the interdependent nature of DesignOps and design. After some tinkering, we've harmonized our new model (Figure 10.2) with some existing design maturity frameworks to better visualize the maturity touchpoints between DesignOps and design.

Decoding this model is pretty straightforward. The Maturity Matrix is divided into three sections: the first is integration—how design is integrated into the business and DesignOps is integrated into design. The second is design maturity. The third section lists the DesignOps drivers governing how Design Operations responds and where it focuses at the four developmental stages of design. In this section, we'll demystify these three factors and then show how each appears at the different stages of design and DesignOps development.

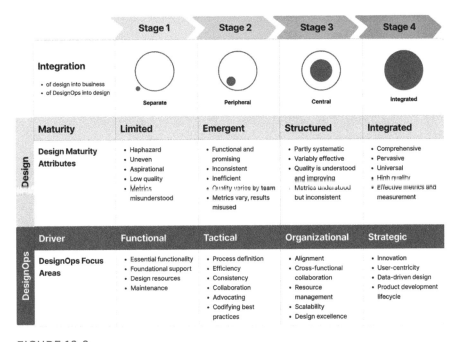

		Stage 1	Stage 2	Stage 3	Stage 4
Integration • of design into business • of DesignOps into design		Separate	Peripheral	Central	Integrated
Design	**Maturity**	**Limited**	**Emergent**	**Structured**	**Integrated**
	Design Maturity Attributes	• Haphazard • Uneven • Aspirational • Low quality • Metrics misunderstood	• Functional and promising • Inconsistent • Inefficient • Quality varies by team • Metrics vary, results misused	• Partly systematic • Variably effective • Quality is understood and improving • Metrics understood but inconsistent	• Comprehensive • Pervasive • Universal • High quality • Effective metrics and measurement
DesignOps	**Driver**	**Functional**	**Tactical**	**Organizational**	**Strategic**
	DesignOps Focus Areas	• Essential functionality • Foundational support • Design resources • Maintenance	• Process definition • Efficiency • Consistency • Collaboration • Advocating • Codifying best practices	• Alignment • Cross-functional collaboration • Resource management • Scalability • Design excellence	• Innovation • User-centricity • Data-driven design • Product development lifecycle

FIGURE 10.2

The Development Matrix, Side 1: Maturity.

Integration

The integration of one group into another involves aligning and merging their operations, systems, priorities, and culture. The extent of integration between a smaller and larger group serves as a significant indicator of the smaller group's maturity (Figure 10.3).

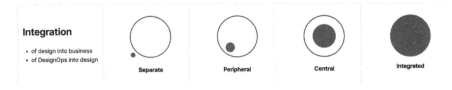

Integration
• of design into business
• of DesignOps into design

Separate   Peripheral   Central   Integrated

FIGURE 10.3

The four stages of integration, which we reviewed in Chapter 8.

Drawing upon Dr. Sabine Junginger's model in Chapter 8, there are four "orientations" that describe progressively stronger design integration: *separate, peripheral, central,* and *integrated.* These orientations reflect the positioning of design within an organization and also offer insight into the level of organizational maturity.

The effectiveness of design relies on its integration with other parts of the business. Design maturity is *way* bigger than design itself—achieving it is not possible without a mature product organization. Attaining the highest levels of maturity extends beyond the capacity of designers alone; it requires commitment from the entire business, embracing and integrating user-centricity at all levels and in all roles.

While Apple is known for its extreme secrecy, it also stands as one of the prime examples of mature product design and development (especially under the leadership of former CDO Jony Ive). The company as a whole embraces user-centered decision-making. Strategic product decisions are *initiated* by the design team, which wields significant decision-making power throughout the entire development process. In fact, reports suggest that design holds such prominence in Apple's product development that the design team sets its own budgets and can ignore manufacturing practicalities.[3]

Apple's product development environment incorporates validation and customer feedback at every stage of the product development process, making it, to the best of our knowledge, a pinnacle of design and product maturity. This meticulous approach ensures that Apple consistently delivers products that not only meet but often exceed customer expectations.[4]

What does Apple's design maturity say about DesignOps? In a sense, it shows that achieving DesignOps maturity is unattainable if the design organization itself lacks maturity and is not integrated into the business. The position and impact of DesignOps is largely shaped by the understanding, support, utilization and advocacy from design leaders and decision-makers. In more mature DesignOps organizations, there is a deeper integration into the design organizations.

---

3   "Apple's Product Development Process—Inside the World's Greatest Design Organization." Interaction Design Foundation—IxDF, December 15, 2023,. www.interaction-design.org/literature/article/apple-s-product-development-process-inside-the-world-s-greatest-design-organization

4   John Carter, "New Product Development Process at Apple (4 Steps)," TCGen, April 16, 2021, www.tcgen.com/product-development/product-development-process-apple/

Design Maturity

The next developmental factor to consider is design maturity. We've shared that there are a handful of popular maturity frameworks; we've synthesized them as follows (Figure 10.4).

Maturity	Limited	Emergent	Structured	Integrated
Design **Design Maturity Attributes**	• Haphazard • Uneven • Aspirational • Low quality • Metrics misunderstood	• Functional and promising • Inconsistent • Inefficient • Quality varies by team • Metrics vary, results misused	• Partly systematic • Variably effective • Quality is understood and improving • Metrics understood but inconsistent	• Comprehensive • Pervasive • Universal • High quality • Effective metrics and measurement

FIGURE 10.4

The four stages of design maturity: limited, emergent, structured, and integrated.

"Maturity," as defined by the Nielsen Norman Group's (NN/g) *The 6 Levels of UX Maturity* framework, reflects an organization's desire and ability to successfully deliver user-centered design. We focus on the four key stages that represent a realistic and achievable progression: *limited, emergent, structured,* and *integrated*. (We exclude the initial *absent* stage, as it predates the need for DesignOps, and the final *user-driven* stage, which is highly aspirational, with only 0.04% reaching it.) Each stage within the framework is characterized by specific maturity attributes: descriptors that indicate a company's evolving capabilities, understanding, and implementation of user experience best practices.

DesignOps Drivers

Finally, here are the DesignOps drivers, which reflect how Design Operations is shaped by design's maturity and integration (Figure 10.5).

Driver	Functional	Tactical	Organizational	Strategic
DesignOps **DesignOps Focus Areas**	• Essential functionality • Foundational support • Design resources • Maintenance	• Process definition • Efficiency • Consistency • Collaboration • Advocating • Codifying best practices	• Alignment • Cross-functional collaboration • Resource management • Scalability • Design excellence	• Innovation • User-centricity • Data-driven design • Product development lifecycle

FIGURE 10.5

The four stages of what drives DesignOps: functional, tactical, organizational, and strategic work.

"Drivers" describes how the priorities that drive DesignOps evolve from supporting functional needs, through tactical and organizational focuses, to finally becoming a strategic partner. These drivers adapt to the evolving needs of design teams and ultimately drive their success. Alongside these drivers, the underlying focus areas illustrate what DesignOps does at each stage of maturity. It's important to remember that the design landscape varies across organizations—factors like size, structure, and design maturity directly influence the pace and path of the DesignOps maturity journey. Ultimately, these factors determine both what DesignOps focuses on and the level of impact it can achieve.

Developing Through the Stages of Maturity

The factors of integration, design maturity, and DesignOps drivers each align to one of four developmental stages. These stages can be considered as snapshots in time, providing DesignOps practitioners with the tools to identify and address the distinct needs of their design teams. In this section, we'll review the unique design and DesignOps nuances of each stage.

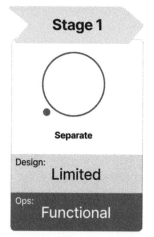

Stage 1: Separate, Limited, and Functional

A survey of over 5,000 UX professionals revealed that 17% of design organizations were categorized in the limited stage of design maturity.[5] This stage signifies the *very* early phases of design development, where the concept itself is largely unknown and its value remains unappreciated. Organizations at this stage might acknowledge the existence of UX, but they lack a fundamental understanding of its benefits and impact.

Limited budget and lack of formal recognition hinder design efforts in this stage, which leads to scattered, inconsistent efforts, resulting in shallow design capabilities and an uneven user experience across the organization. Passionate

---

5   Moran, "The State of UX Maturity."

advocates may emerge, utilizing whatever resources they can find, but quality is low, and their efforts are often hampered by insufficient tools and experience.

At this stage, design is *separate* from the core business and product development functions. Designers, if present at all, might work as isolated contractors or solo employees. This siloed approach creates a disconnect, preventing them from collaborating effectively and contributing to the bigger picture.

The DesignOps side is even less developed. With no formal design or DesignOps practice, there are no full-time DPMs. The operational responsibilities fall on the shoulders of a scattered ensemble: designers, leaders, even program managers in other organizations. These individuals, essentially "accidental DesignOps practitioners," adopt the necessary mindsets (as discussed in Chapter 4, "It's All About Practice") out of necessity, often lacking the corresponding skill sets and experience.

They approach DesignOps as a functional driver, handling operational tasks on an "as-needed" basis—simply enough to keep the design engine running. Growth and improvement are not top priorities here. (Think duct tape repairs, not sleek upgrades.) To make it work, the few designers who exist become resourceful "MacGyvers," crafting operational solutions with whatever limited resources they can find. Because operations is not the core of their work, they are usually reacting to timely needs vs. proactively planning ahead.

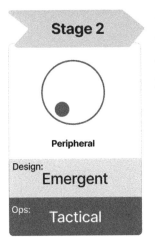

Stage 2

Peripheral

Design:
Emergent

Ops:
Tactical

Stage 2: Peripheral, Emergent, and Tactical

At least 50% of all design organizations[6] find themselves in this second stage. While more individuals may hold design roles, the overall organization falls short in terms of both quantity and skill level. Designers are often stretched thin—their skill sets sometimes incomplete. While design efforts exist across certain teams, they tend to be limited in scope, inconsistent, and lacking strategic direction.

---

6   Moran, "The State of UX Maturity."

Securing budget and headcount remains a challenge, and there is still a lack of centralized design resources and processes.

The good news is that even these nascent design teams are starting to show their value, with more stakeholders recognizing the benefits of their work. Research and design methods are gaining traction, and overall design quality is improving. While individual champions within the organization advocate for design, it hasn't yet become a strategic priority. Successes are largely driven by individual managers, leading to inconsistent impact and limited reach.

In an emergent organization, design often plays a peripheral role: on the fringes of the broader product organization, contributing to specific products, but not deeply integrated into the larger organization. Some companies have a centralized UX team, while others embed designers directly in their product teams. This can lead to a frustrating hodgepodge of design approaches, with everyone using different tools and methods—which, in turn, creates an opportunity for DesignOps. Here, DPMs exist at the periphery of the developing design team, serving as a tactical driver focused on defining how the design organization operates. DPMs contribute to specific programs and products, but their integration into the design organization is minimal. Close to 50% of DesignOps teams are in this ramping up stage of DesignOps maturity.[7]

In emergent design teams, DPMs often find themselves in a reactive mode, tackling immediate and short-term challenges and removing roadblocks as they arise. They are focused on defining processes and implementing systems that enhance consistency, efficiency, and collaboration. By establishing cadences and rituals where there were none, a sense of stability begins to emerge. And, since a broader understanding of design's value is still not widespread, DPMs also prioritize advocating for design and securing budget and resources.

---

7   *2023 DesignOps Benchmarking Report* (DesignOps Assembly, 2023), www.designopsassembly.com/2023report

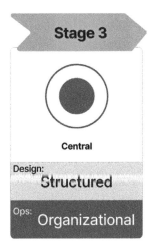

Stage 3

Central

Design:
Structured

Ops:
Organizational

Stage 3: Central, Structured, and Organizational

In this stage, design teams have established their foundation and emerged as a full-fledged design practice; 28% of surveyed orgs are here.[8] Design is widely valued and understood, and research and user-centered principles are respected and actively participated in by partners outside design. Leadership is supportive, integrating design into broader strategies. While some areas of the business might still exhibit resistance, the overall company culture recognizes the value of design, providing budgets and resources to run their teams effectively.

Increased support translates to greater investment in design resources and tools for teams. This influx of resources often empowers teams at this stage to start to tackle an important initiative: building a design system. A design system acts as a centralized library of reusable design components and guidelines, ensuring consistency, efficiency, and brand integrity across the expanding product landscape. At this stage, there also becomes a more pressing need to hire consistently and assess performance fairly across design, which prompts the creation of the design competencies framework.

In a structured practice, design is often *central* to the organization, playing a core role in the product development process. Engineers, product managers, and other stakeholders understand the value of user insights and readily collaborate with designers to translate them into impactful solutions. However, the priorities are mainly informed by product and business needs rather than user needs.

---

8   Moran, "The State of UX Maturity."

This stage of maturity represents nearly 25% of all DesignOps teams.[9] DesignOps sits at the heart of the design organization, positioned centrally and playing a pivotal role by acting as a bridge between designers and other functions. DPMs act as catalysts for organizational alignment, cross-functional collaboration, resource management, and design excellence. DesignOps propels the organization forward by codifying best practices and creating scalable programs that support the growing design practice and elevate the quality of design work across the company.

DPMs can be more proactive. While operational issues still arise, the team is prepared to handle them. When it comes to culture, DesignOps focuses on preserving a close-knit connection, connecting dots across the organization, and maintaining the fabric of the community. For most organizations that have structured design organizations, this stage is where they land and stay—it becomes their maturity ceiling.

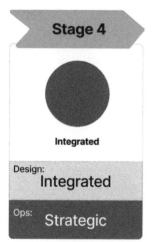

Stage 4

Integrated

Design: **Integrated**

Ops: **Strategic**

Stage 4: Integrated and Strategic

Design teams that reach this stage are among the 4% of organizations to have achieved this gold standard.[10] Here, design becomes a driving force behind decision-making, from product development to marketing. The vision of design and the user are well understood company-wide. Design teams operate with efficiency, effectiveness, and deliver very high-quality work. Sometimes, these integrated organizations even contribute to the broader field of design, setting new benchmarks and developing innovations that resonate across the industry.

Integrated teams no longer need to expend as much energy advocating for budget, resources, and headcount. They are well funded with support and respect from leadership. Things like design systems, processes, rhythms, career pathing, tooling, and training are comprehensive and high quality, largely due to the dedicated investment in DesignOps by this stage.

---

9 *2023 DesignOps Benchmarking Report.*

10 Moran, "The State of UX Maturity."

DESIGN IMPACT VS MATURITY: THE CHICKEN OR THE EGG?

A thought-provoking LinkedIn post by design leader Bob Baxley ignited a hot discussion with the statement: "The ONLY measure of design maturity is outcomes. All the rest is process, and process is meaningless without outcomes." Yes, this is the same Bob Baxley whom we quoted in Chapter 2, "Learning the Score," about the importance of process. While Baxley admits his intention to spark discussion, his claim prompted this question for me:

Is design maturity the *cause* of impactful design or the *result* of it?

On one hand, mature design teams, equipped with strong capabilities (skills and processes), are more likely to deliver impactful solutions. Processes, like Agile methodologies, have proven to increase product quality, faster time-to-market, and higher customer satisfaction—all critical factors for long-term success. However, some practitioners, echoing Baxley, argue that maturity is defined by impact alone. This perspective suggests that the means matter less than the ends.

But here's the thing: the impact we create on stakeholders and the broader ecosystem absolutely matters on the journey from A to Z. While I agree with Baxley that aiming for positive outcomes is ultimately the goal, I define "outcomes" more broadly than just immediate product or business results. In DesignOps, we value team health and well-being, continuous learning, and fostering strong connections, all contributing to long-term excellence. Maturity isn't just about sporadic "wins," but about consistently delivering positive results over time.

Nearly 20% of Design Operations organizations operate at this level.[11] This suggests that these design mature companies recognize the value of DesignOps and have made significant investments in building out their DesignOps capabilities. With DesignOps fully integrated into the design organization, DesignOps becomes a strategic driver, executing on priorities like design innovation, user-centricity, and data-driven design methodologies. At this stage, DesignOps can be much more strategic and forward looking, developing longer term DesignOps roadmaps in support of the design org's vision and driving product development lifecycle transformations.

---

11 *2023 DesignOps Benchmarking Report*.

The Development Matrix, Side 2: Size

Design organizations grow, shrink, and change shapes constantly. Through these ups and downs, DesignOps needs to be adaptable and responsive. And while it's important to stay attentive to these changes in org size, the *real* opportunity for DesignOps practitioners comes by understanding which stage of growth the design team is in (Figure 10.6). Each of these stages corresponds to a set of similar growing (or shrinking) pains—recognizing these helps our discipline respond proactively to the challenges that designers face. Similarly, these stages underscore some fundamental dynamics of the design and DesignOps practices, influencing the behaviors, interactions, and communications within a team. In this section, we'll explore the development dynamics at each stage of growth.

		Small	Mid-size	Large	Enterprise
Design	**Size**	1–15	16–45	46–150	151+
	Design Dynamics	• Strong family feeling • Easy communications • Quick decisions • Mostly clear priorities • Designers wear multiple hats	• More processes and comms • Mostly made of generalists • More complex priorities • Clearer organizational lines	• Weakening of strong family feeling • More org shifts • Harder to find answers and make decisions • More meetings and formal processes	• Mature product • More specialists and new capabilities • Team and leadership turnover • Organizational complexities • Hard to remain connected
DesignOps	**Size**	0–0.5	1–3	4–9	10+
	DesignOps Dynamics	• DesignOps is likely done part time by a designer • "Accidental DPM" focused on ensuring designers have what they need to do their work	• A budding team • Focused on putting processes into place and establishing best practices across the team	• Dedicated DPMs aligned to product areas • Focused on solving team specific challenges and creating repeatable processes that scale	• Larger DesignOps org is scaling in new ways • Focused on creating stability, culture, and optimizing across and down to stay connected

FIGURE 10.6

The Development Matrix, Side 2: Size.

Small Team Stage and Dynamics

Small design teams, usually fewer than 15 people, are the prototypical "tiny but mighty" pioneers, paving the way for great design at their business. These groups are often newly formed, growing, and sometimes under stress. At this stage, designers and their partners

Small

Design: **1-15**

Design Ops: **0-0.5**

often grapple with operational, personal, and growth hurdles. However, the smaller size means that communication is uncomplicated, and decisions are made quickly. In compact design groups, everyone covers a broad range of responsibilities; they are scrappy, close-knit, and agile.

At this stage, DesignOps doesn't really exist as a team or group. Although DesignOps work exists, there are no full time DPMs: 22.5% of practitioners reported that they cover DesignOps out of necessity, but don't formally have the role.[12] These "accidental DPMs" are designers and design managers by trade. In organizations of this size, the primary focus of DesignOps work is to establish an environment where designers are well-equipped to execute their tasks effectively. Designers—doing the work of DesignOps—need to be a champion for their Ops needs while simultaneously carrying out their own design work.

Mid-Size Team Stage and Dynamics

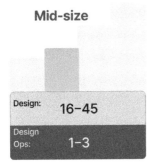

Mid-size

Design: **16-45**

Design Ops: **1-3**

Mid-size design teams typically range from about 16–32 designers. At this stage, there is a mix of self-organization and leadership. Design swim lanes emerge at the upper end of this size range; as the team grows, repeatable processes and clear communication become key. Teams at this stage may consist of design generalists who wear many hats, an advantage carried forward from the small group stage that allows individuals to tackle diverse tasks and take on varying responsibilities.

As design teams grow beyond 15 members, keeping everyone coordinated and focused can be chaotic; design leaders frequently find themselves drowning in operational and coordination tasks. We believe this stage is the ideal tipping point to add a dedicated DesignOps role—someone who can take on the role of conductor, bring structure to the team, set up adequate operations, manage processes, and free the design team to focus on design.

---

12 *2023 DesignOps Benchmarking Report.*

At this stage, DesignOps teams are a squad of one to three DPMs, with 30% being a "team" of one.[13] These teams adopt a flexible approach, splitting up prioritized tasks without relying on a lot of formal structure. Similar to design at this stage, DesignOps teams are often staffed with generalists; their primary focus is fulfilling the design leader's most pressing needs for the organization and supporting the broader design team. At the upper bounds of this stage, DesignOps is aligned to a strategic program or product to help with complex and high-priority delivery.

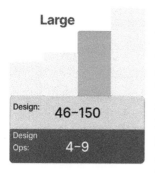

Large

Design: **46–150**

Design Ops: **4–9**

Large Team Size and Dynamics

Large design teams employ from 46 to 150 designers. At this size, new obstacles arise to challenge what was once a small, nimble team. The complexities of operating a design department demand a more structured approach to role hierarchy, leadership, and organizational layers. Some designers thrive with more structure and clarity; processes and playbooks mean (ideally) less ambiguity, and a larger team provides more opportunities to learn and grow. On the other hand, some designers bristle at bureaucratic slowness; for them, increased approvals, meetings, and milestones make decision-making too slow.

Designers at this stage have moved beyond generalist roles and specialize in particular types of design (interaction design, visual design, service design, etc.). As the team grows, and as the practice of design becomes more established, designer competencies and career paths must be developed to create a clear path for growth. And as designers start to diverge in skills and levels (and possibly regions), maintaining a sense of camaraderie and connection requires intentional effort and dedicated nurturing.

At this stage, DesignOps has expanded to around four to nine DPMs. This stage marks a well-established operations practice, with DesignOps coverage throughout the design department. DPMs start to specialize, too; individuals who once partnered with the *entire* design org may now be supporting individual *product* teams, or hired to own a specific workstream that delivers for the entire department globally, such as designer onboarding or training. DPMs deeply embedded with

---

13 *2023 DesignOps Benchmarking Report.*

their product design teams in turn focus on delivery-focused challenges and manage the business aspects of individual products.

Enterprise

Design: **151+**

Design Ops: **10+**

Enterprise Team Size and Dynamics

When a large team surpasses 150 designers, it reaches the enterprise stage. At this size, designers reap the benefits of a well-established structure, abundant resources, clarity in roles, and robust support. Collaboration is easier with partners who deeply understand the value that designers bring. Professional development allows designers more ways to improve their skills and explore diverse roles within the organization. Smaller teams emerge within the larger structure, rekindling a close-knit atmosphere at the team level. Sounds great!

Obviously, organizations of this size bring their own challenges. Complex organizational structures and numerous spans and layers slow down decision-making. Frequent leadership changes, turnover, and reorganizations can disrupt teams and priorities. Resource allocation also becomes a balancing act, ensuring that each member utilizes their skills effectively and avoids under- or overwork.

At this stage, DesignOps plays a vital role. There should be ten or more DPMs to comprehensively cover all DesignOps functions, with the actual number determined by the relative ratios of the roles with whom DesignOps practitioners partner most often (see Chapter 9). About 9% of organizations have DesignOps practices of this size or greater.[14]

Managing large design teams requires a synchronized effort across all groups. Consistency is paramount, and DesignOps facilitates this by sharing and organizing information, tools, and resources. This goal is paired with optimizing workflows that aim to enhance consistency, productivity, and overall design excellence. Building and nurturing a vibrant design community within a large and increasingly dispersed organization is a top priority for DPMs at this stage; so, too, is solidifying partnerships with cross-functional counterparts. The focus on collective growth becomes a vital challenge as DesignOps itself scales and adapts.

---

14 2023 *DesignOps Benchmarking Report.*

Coda: The Design and DesignOps Development Matrix

This chapter explores the intricate relationship between design and DesignOps development. We demystified the individual components of our Maturity Matrix and Size Matrix, which unite together into the comprehensive Design & DesignOps Development Matrix (Figure 10.7a and 10.7b).

Locate your teams' positions within each matrix and identify your design and DesignOps development stages. Are you a Stage 2 team supporting a Stage 3 department? Are your dynamics in harmony or disarray?

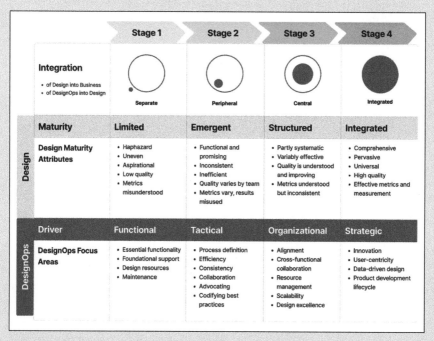

	Stage 1	Stage 2	Stage 3	Stage 4
Integration • of Design into Business • of DesignOps into Design	Separate	Peripheral	Central	Integrated
Maturity	**Limited**	**Emergent**	**Structured**	**Integrated**
Design Maturity Attributes	• Haphazard • Uneven • Aspirational • Low quality • Metrics misunderstood	• Functional and promising • Inconsistent • Inefficient • Quality varies by team • Metrics vary, results misused	• Partly systematic • Variably effective • Quality is understood and improving • Metrics understood but inconsistent	• Comprehensive • Pervasive • Universal • High quality • Effective metrics and measurement
Driver	**Functional**	**Tactical**	**Organizational**	**Strategic**
DesignOps Focus Areas	• Essential functionality • Foundational support • Design resources • Maintenance	• Process definition • Efficiency • Consistency • Collaboration • Advocating • Codifying best practices	• Alignment • Cross-functional collaboration • Resource management • Scalability • Design excellence	• Innovation • User-centricity • Data-driven design • Product development lifecycle

FIGURE 10.7a

The Design & DesignOps Development Matrix showing the Maturity models.

Many combinations are possible but know that maturity mismatches are one of the *most* disruptive forces to any DesignOps practice (discussed in Chapter 13, "The Wrong Notes").

Ultimately, development through these stages isn't always linear or synchronized. What works for one design organization might not be suitable for another. As you navigate the evolving landscape of organizational growth and maturity, remember that flexibility and adaptability are your superpowers on your DesignOps journey.

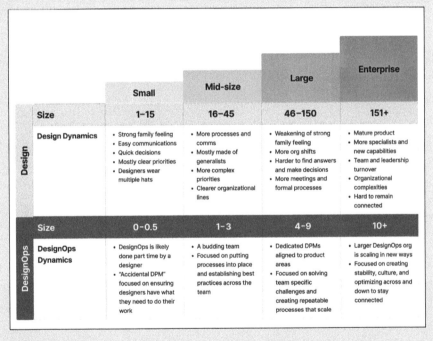

		Small	Mid-size	Large	Enterprise
Design	**Size**	1–15	16–45	46–150	151+
	Design Dynamics	• Strong family feeling • Easy communications • Quick decisions • Mostly clear priorities • Designers wear multiple hats	• More processes and comms • Mostly made of generalists • More complex priorities • Clearer organizational lines	• Weakening of strong family feeling • More org shifts • Harder to find answers and make decisions • More meetings and formal processes	• Mature product • More specialists and new capabilities • Team and leadership turnover • Organizational complexities • Hard to remain connected
DesignOps	**Size**	0–0.5	1–3	4–9	10+
	DesignOps Dynamics	• DesignOps is likely done part time by a designer • "Accidental DPM" focused on ensuring designers have what they need to do their work	• A budding team • Focused on putting processes into place and establishing best practices across the team	• Dedicated DPMs aligned to product areas • Focused on solving team specific challenges and creating repeatable processes that scale	• Larger DesignOps org is scaling in new ways • Focused on creating stability, culture, and optimizing across and down to stay connected

FIGURE 10.7b

The Design & DesignOps Development Matrix showing the Size models.

CHAPTER 11

Ready to Take Up the Baton
Designing Your DesignOps Org

In the world of Design Operations, context is everything. As a discipline that exists to lift, accelerate, and streamline a sibling organization (the design org), each DesignOps team is—by the very nature of its practice—shaped by the unique business factors and boundaries present in any given company. We've written about how Design Operations is shaped by the four most common design org models, and how our discipline often leads (and follows) different levels of design org development. We also showed how the size and influence of design-adjacent roles shape the way a DesignOps team is organized and run.

But Design Operations teams are not just lumps of clay to be molded by external forces. Those outside factors may shape the approximate borders in which DesignOps operates, but the DesignOps team defines the rest. And regardless of whether that's a team of one, a few, or many, once the organizational context of Design Operations is understood, the time is right to start shaping the DesignOps practice from the inside, and get to work.

Defining and giving shape to your Design Operations practice is a critical milestone in its maturity. DesignOps teams of all sizes and tenures might exist within an organization without any clear sense of purpose. Because they can be influenced by other teams and roles, DesignOps teams can come to be defined by what those groups *don't do* and *need*, versus what DPMs *can do* and *provide*. Taking the bold step of declaring and clarifying what your DesignOps team is, and its role within your particular organization, signals to your designers and stakeholders that your practice is ready to take up the baton and lead.

There are many components required to build a DesignOps team (budget, leadership, software, etc.), but we maintain that just a few are necessary to define it. These are a mission statement, an operating model, and a clear set of workstreams. These elements should be informed by the organizational context in which your DesignOps team exists, but not constrained by it. Moreover, these defining elements are crucial for teams of *any* size—even the scrappy teams comprised of one or two DPMs—because they also define the ways in which your practice can and should grow in the future. (More on the principles and pitfalls of growing a DesignOps team in Chapters 12, "Maintaining Your Rhythm" and 13, "The Wrong Notes.")

Ultimately, the outcome of this exercise should be a scalable, durable charter that articulates how your Design Operations team is shaped to support the activities it *should* do to provide the maximum value to the design org and its partners, and to support the organizational and career growth of the DesignOps team and its practitioners.

Establishing Your Mission Statement

Your DesignOps mission statement is an articulation of what your team does and seeks to achieve in the present. It's the sentence or two you'd use to describe DesignOps to somebody in your organization, who, when stuck in an elevator with you, asks, "So, what exactly is it that you do?" But a mission statement is more than an elevator pitch; it's a brief and purposeful declaration that defines a team's actions and identity as it stands today. Laura Gatewood, lead design program manager at Salesforce and former program manager at Children's Hospital Los Angeles, sums up this connection between purpose and a mission statement:

> Mission statements are the heartbeat of a team, department, org, company—they not only convey the what but even more importantly the why—they state the raison d'être. This echoes the now-famous story of John F. Kennedy's visit to NASA, where a janitor, when asked about his job, proudly responded, "I help put a man on the moon," highlighting a shared dedication to a larger mission.

The mission statement's emphasis on being declarative and active is critical to its utility. To unpack this concept, it helps to look at some examples. We presented the following DesignOps mission statement at a conference in 2022:

> DesignOps accelerates confidence and clarity for our design community and their development partners.

At the time of that conference, this mission statement declared everything that was important to our DesignOps team: confidence, clarity, community, and partnership. We had organized our operating model around these four pillars, hired DPMs skilled in communications and bridge-building, and more. This statement also included the verb that best summarized the action we were seeking to take with our design org that year: "accelerate." The design org was growing exponentially relative to DesignOps, and our mission was to accelerate the adoption and implementation of new onboarding processes, software tools, and global ways of working. If anyone asked what our DesignOps team did, we could respond with this mission statement and use it to provoke a deeper conversation about our specific workstreams and methods.

Here are a few other DesignOps mission statements that we particularly like, which also illustrate the importance of being declarative and strong on action:

Miro: DesignOps improves the circumstances in which good design can happen.[1]

Airbnb: DesignOps provides agility to the whole product organization through centralized tools, systems, and services that enhance speed and quality of execution.[2]

Capital One: DesignOps creates the conditions for success, surfaces design's business and experience value, and strengthens well managed practices.[3]

These DesignOps mission statements have several elements in common. First, they're brief and direct. Second, they have strong methods that signal what's most important to each team: "good design," "centralized tools," "well managed practices," etc. Third, each statement contains strong verbs that summarize the actions the DesignOps team is rallying behind: "improve," "provide agility," "create the conditions," etc.

These mission statements make their point simply and clearly; in addition, they capture what the DesignOps teams are seeking to achieve *at that moment*. This is because a good mission statement is all about the present, and should be grounded in the goals and objectives most critical to success *today*. Anyone reading or hearing these mission statements should immediately understand the action and methods the DesignOps team is going to accomplish within the next twelve or so months. And as business objectives change, so should

---

1   Peter Boersma, DesignOps Manager at Miro (2021–2022), posted on DesignOps Assembly Slack workspace, 2022.

2   Adrian Cleave, "How We Manage Effective Design at Scale Airbnb," https://airbnb.design/designops-airbnb/

3   Tim Gilligan, "The Power of Crafing a Design Ops Mission" (presentation, DesignOps Assembly Event, 2020).

the DesignOps mission statement. Ours, as an example, has evolved its focus over time from "acceleration" to "enablement" and more recently "performance," and it continues to change each year.

Mission Versus Vision

A *mission statement's* near-term view is in contrast to a *vision statement*, which gets to look into the future and describe a team's long-range direction and aspirations many years out. Vision statements are important, too, but we recommend DesignOps teams establish a mission statement first. This is because, for the purpose of defining your practice to the design org and its partners, your team needs a statement that declares the practical, tactical, and immediate actions and methods it owns as a product partner. And for newly formed DesignOps teams, the mission statement establishes what the team does to the DPMs actually on the team—it is this kind of clarity that your Design Operations practice should be seeking early on.

Declaring Your Mission

Even a DesignOps team of one or two needs to start with a mission statement. For the solo practitioner, the value lies in defining oneself to the design org, before the design org defines them. For small and scrappy teams, a mission statement can align the practice to a common purpose. Teams of two or more can start this process by sharing a mutual set of methods—keywords, mostly—that capture the team's primary areas of focus through the lens of the design org's primary obstacles. Following this, establishing what action the team needs to take keeps everyone moving in the same direction and ensures that they "spend their calories" in ways that are complementary and not wasteful. A DesignOps team's action might map to the design org's maturity level, with verbs like "establish" and "simplify" being prerequisites to "accelerate" and "scale."

As the final step in this process, mash the methods and actions together with a focus on the present, and ultimately a succinct, durable declaration of the DesignOps team's mission will emerge. (Generative AI can help here, too!) This mission statement establishes the domains the DesignOps team is responsible for, and may create some very high-level ways to divide and delegate work. And critically, the mission statement sets boundaries for what the DesignOps team is *not* going to do!

Defining Your Operating Model

With a mission statement in place, it can be tempting to think you're ready to lace up your shoes and start sprinting. But this is like deciding the rules of a race and expecting runners to compete with no starting line or lanes. Moving too fast to "operationalize the mission" creates the risk that DPMs collide into one another and crash into each other's programs. Each DPM needs to know which lane is (and isn't) theirs, and the best way to bring clarity to this goal is to define your DesignOps team's *operating model*.

An operating model articulates how your DesignOps team is organized to deliver its mission. It gives structure to how DPMs work together in ways that are complementary and harmonious. Operating models also provide a rough framework for how your DesignOps team might grow in the future, when you're at the inflection point of expanding from a "small and mighty" team to a proper DesignOps org.

In theory, there could be dozens of successful DesignOps operating models in practice today; in reality, there's a relatively small handful that most teams follow. Whether this is a sign of some "best practices" in the Design Operations space, or simply the result of teams learning from one another, the following common models work for the vast majority of design practices; they are the following:

- **The Agency Model:** DesignOps is a central service unit, with roles focused on specialized areas.

- **The Embedded Model:** DesignOps is distributed across individual design teams to provide dedicated support.

- **The Hybrid Model:** DesignOps is a blend of the two models above, typically organized into horizontal and vertical practices.

The Agency Operating Model

The agency operating model is not just for DesignOps at design agencies. In fact, it's one of the most common models used in companies of all sizes and domains. The "agency" name stems from the way this model organizes the DesignOps and design teams, with an implicit agency relationship between the two. Here, Design Operations is the agency, staffed with project and program specialists whose expertise augments and supports the ever-changing needs of the design team "client."

In this operating model, the DesignOps team is its own entity (Figure 11.1), and its practitioners have specific, unique focus areas like communications, program management, workflows, and tooling. These skills are deployed to design teams with the greatest needs at any given time, with levels of support changing frequently.

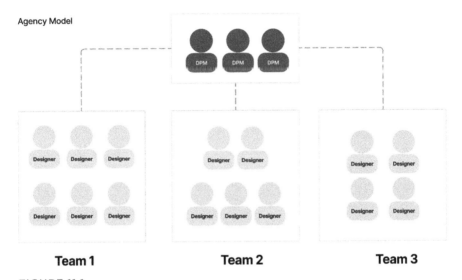

FIGURE 11.1
In the agency model, the DesignOps practice supports multiple design teams.

The advantage of the agency operating model is its specificity—in these teams, DesignOps is shaped specifically by the needs of the design team and its designers, with DPMs hired to be subject matter experts (and sometimes firefighters) for design leaders who lack an operational background or need certain burdens shifted to a specialist. Another advantage: prioritizing a DPM's work is somewhat easier, because the DesignOps team's primary focus is (by definition) the top goals and priorities of the business.

But this model can also challenge the DesignOps team's identity and cohesion. Specialists might tend to self-silo or operate without interaction with other Design Operations practitioners, potentially muddying the *team's* role and mission within the design org. Another potential obstacle of this model is funding DPM headcount for a team that stands apart from the more direct revenue-generating parts of a product. (More on these growing pains in Chapter 13.)

The Embedded Operating Model

Another framework to help define your DesignOps swim lanes is the embedded operating model. In this model, design program managers are distributed throughout individual design teams, partnering directly with those teams' leaders and stakeholders. This embedded relationship brings the DPM closer to the short-term delivery challenges and long-term operational vision of each team, positioning each DPM as a "mini COO" (chief operating officer) of their team (Figure 11.2). Here, each DesignOps role is differently shaped due to the unique operational needs of each design team; however, we find that in the embedded operating model, there are common areas of focus, including workflow optimization, managing cross-functional relationships, team health, release planning, and "running the business" of the design team.

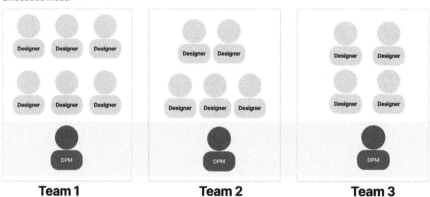

FIGURE 11.2

In the embedded model, dedicated DPMs are assigned to teams that need them.

The embedded model is common because it's an organic approach to solving for operational excellence. In many instances, an operationally-minded designer takes on the DPM role full-time for their team. Another way this model emerges is when teams hire someone who's worked with Design Operations in the past, and that person advocates for the value of adding a DPM to the roster. These two scenarios both involve *growth* teams, which is why the embedded model is common when the design org is scaling fast: everyone adds DesignOps to their teams—however and whenever the opportunity presents itself!

The advantage of this model is that each DPM's skill set specifically suits each design team's greatest needs. And because teams typically have *lots* of unmet operational needs, embedded DPMs tend to be more generalist in nature, bringing broad program management experience and a problem-solving mindset to the role. Embedded DPMs also are expected to build deeper cross-functional partnerships than those in the agency model, especially with their stakeholders in product, engineering, and the other roles described in Chapter 9, "Your Performance Partners." Finally, some DPMs just prefer this model, feeling closer to the creators and decision-makers of the product.

The downside to the embedded operating model is that it doesn't incentivize strategic and business-wide DesignOps initiatives—those that should be standardized for all designers, everywhere. Activities like onboarding and software licensing tend to get distributed among DPMs, meaning the practice lacks the economies of scale available to a centralized team.

The Hybrid Operating Model

Larger DesignOps teams or more mature design orgs may use a hybrid operating model. This model blends the best of the centralized specialists and embedded generalists into one practice, organized along two dimensions (Figure 11.3). These two axes have many different names, which we usually call the *horizontal* and *vertical disciplines* of Design Operations. The horizontal dimension typically focuses on operations for the entire design org; names for this lane might be *Central Ops*, *Practice Ops*, or *People Ops*. The vertical dimension is shaped according to what the design teams collectively do; names for this lane might be *Product Ops*, *Delivery Ops*, or *Design Team Ops*.

We currently practice a hybrid operating model. We call our two dimensions *Central DesignOps* and *Product DesignOps*, summarized as follows:

> Central DesignOps optimizes for the whole design org. It goes wide and focuses on scale. Product DesignOps optimizes for a product design team. It goes deep and focuses on delivery.

DPMs in the Central Ops (horizontal) lane focus on anything that impacts all designers equally, such as onboarding, tooling, and community events. This half of the practice delivers programs at scale to a global design org, with the purpose of scaling best practices and building a singular design culture. Befitting its agency model roots, Central Ops is organized to grow via specialized DPMs that meet the design org's evolving needs. Experts in event management, learning and development (L&D), and other specializations find a welcome home in this space!

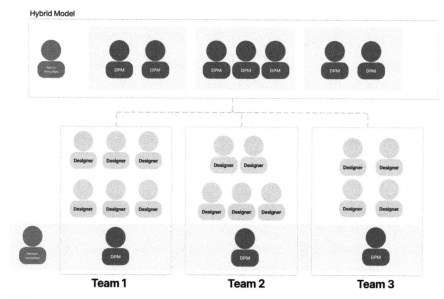

Team 1   **Team 2**   **Team 3**

FIGURE 11.3

In the Hybrid model, one team of DPM delivers centralized programs, while other DPMs are aligned to their delivery teams.

DPMs in the Product Ops (vertical) lane focus on the specific needs of design teams and their partners. Often having roots embedded *within* these teams, practitioners here are fluent in capacity planning, vision workshops, delivery milestones, and more. They prioritize the integration of design processes and practices into product development, and partner closely with cross-functional stakeholders to ensure seamless design execution throughout the product life cycle.

A designer working with a hybrid DesignOps team will regularly partner with DPMs from both sides, even though the operating model itself might be totally opaque. ("Wait, aren't you all just the DesignOps team?") The advantages of a hybrid operating model are most pronounced not for designers, but for the DesignOps team itself. Consider this operating model from a DPM's perspective: the horizontal and vertical dimensions create space to both own and delegate specific functions. A DPM can be confident that work *outside* their lane (say global onboarding, or the design partnerships of a specific product) is being taken care of. Program managers in this kind of team are not duplicating work, being stretched thin, or swinging wildly between competing priorities. Instead, the operating model allows DPMs to be responsible to the design org in a sustainable way.

The hybrid model is not perfect, nor suitable for all design orgs. For one, it assumes a moderate to high design org maturity—one that necessitates hiring multiple DPMs into a relatively complex structure. This model also creates healthy tension within the DesignOps team. What product team's best practices get elevated up? Which org-wide workflows get passed down? Moreover, hybrid Design Operations teams need established leaders to navigate potential roadblocks and to have a strategy for growing a practice that is both centralized and distributed. (Signals of brewing tension are discussed in Chapter 13.)

TWO SIDES OF THE DESIGNOPS COIN

Rachel and I don't call our operating model *hybrid*, even though that's how it works. We've sometimes called our way of working the "two sides of the DesignOps coin," which kind of makes sense (maybe?) for DesignOps practitioners, but doesn't really work as an explanation of our partners. Sure, it connotes one thing—the coin!—with two sides, but our partners benefit when we're clearer.

Central DesignOps and *Product DesignOps* are the terms that most clearly express our model. Yeah, they're wordy, and a firewall between centralized and embedded DesignOps functions is kind of implied, but it's a good way to start the conversation. We follow up by explaining that there's one public channel for our team, one shared calendar, one way to put something on our radar, etc. The truth is, we tweak our own operating model often enough that it's not necessary that partners understand the specifics of how we work together, so long as they understand that we are ONE team, mutually responsible for managing the operations of our design org.

Maybe we should just mint DesignOps coins and hand them out?

There are more, uncommon operating models that design orgs might employ, and no model is the "right" one for DesignOps teams to follow. Nor is there any expectation that your model will stay the same year over year. In fact, learning to recognize when your operating model is no longer serving your team's mission is a critical skill for established DesignOps practices (one which we'll talk about in Chapter 12). But this is predicated on the basis that your team has an operating model in the first place! The right model for any team should establish boundaries that enable two or more DPMs to operate *without* getting in each other's way. It should organize the practice to successfully deliver on the DesignOps mission statement and create a framework for future DPM growth. Ultimately, the goal is for every DPM (and the designers they support) to clearly understand how the DesignOps team is set up to contribute to the success of the design org.

Organizing Your Workstreams

With its mission statement declared and operating model defined, the DesignOps team's structure starts to take shape. This structure might resemble two halves of a whole, three co-equal branches of government, a construction crew of trade specialists, etc. Whatever metaphor your team lands on, the next action to take is to organize the workstreams each group is responsible for.

In our DesignOps vernacular, a *workstream* is a set of similar programs, functions, and deliverables that collectively achieve a common outcome. More simply, a workstream is a bunch of DesignOps work that logically belongs together. Your team's focus areas might be somewhat intuited via your mission statement or operating model, but the step of articulating your workstreams in clear, unambiguous terms is required to connect the DesignOps team's structure to tactical, tangible work that anyone—inside and outside the design org—can easily understand and appreciate.

To give an example of what organizing your workstreams looks like in practice, consider a team using our Central DesignOps and Product DesignOps operating model, with our mission statement declaring *"DesignOps accelerates confidence and clarity for our design community and their development partners."* The exercise for this team is to use the affinity mapping process to ideate and map out all the possible programs and deliverables that might contribute to this goal. After dozens of stickies, this process might yield something like Figure 11.4.

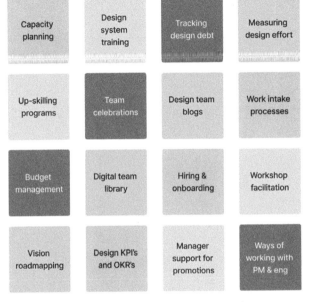

FIGURE 11.4
The ideas derived from your mission statement should also be aligned to your team's Jobs to be Done described in Chapter 15, "Measure by Measure."

Next, sort these functions and outcomes according to your operating model structure. For agency and hybrid models (which are defined by specialties and dimensions, respectively), this is relatively straightforward. For embedded operating models (which tend to be flatter and decentralized), this exercise can be more complicated. Here, the activity could be more about sorting by which programs should be standardized vs. bespoke; for embedded DesignOps teams that map to different design functions—say, design systems, product, and creative—the sorting can be done at this elevation. For the Central and Product DesignOps example cited previously, the outcome of this exercise might look something like Figure 11.5.

If some programs seem like they should be co-owned, that's totally fine. Operating models are not intended to create firewalls between DesignOps team members. They exist to describe how the DesignOps team is organized to deliver its mission—and sometimes that organization implies partnership!

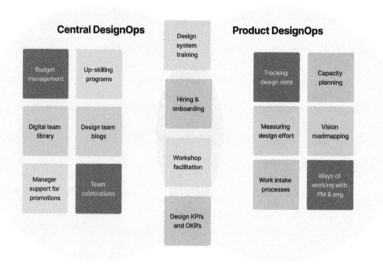

FIGURE 11.5
Aligning workstreams with your operating model doesn't mean you can or will do it all now. But it helps to map out who owns what.

Finally, you can cluster the programs and outcomes into logical families, labeling each when the identity of the cluster reveals itself. (And, of course, refine and edit along the way.) These clusters are the DesignOps team's workstreams, logically sorted by its operating model. The outcome of this exercise will naturally be different for every team, but here is how the workstreams look for our current Central and Product DesignOps operating models (see Tables 11.1 and 11.2).

TABLE 11.1 CENTRAL DESIGNOPS WORKSTREAMS

Community & Events	Learning & Growth	Scale & Enablement
• Internal org-wide events • Industry events • Design culture and community building • Team celebrations • Team health programs • DEIB Programs • Giving back programs • External design presence (blog, recruiting, social)	• Hiring & onboarding programs • Skill building & development programs • Trainings & speakers • Career paths & competencies • Talent cycle support • Tool transitions • Manager support	• Org communications • Facilities • Tools & systems management • Org dashboards • Policies & governance • Budget management • Playbooks & toolkits • Internal knowledge hub and management • Operational partnerships (HR, recruiting, etc.)

TABLE 11.2 PRODUCT DESIGNOPS WORKSTREAMS

Productivity & Delivery	Project & Program Management	Design Partnership
• Tracking design work and key metrics across teams • Process & workflow optimization • Managing design project life cycles • Curating digital spaces and work processes • "How we work" guidelines and operating models	• Strategic program management • Resourcing & capacity planning • Design team vision and culture • Tracking milestones and team health • Team communications • Prioritization and accountability	• Cross functional collaboration with eng, PM, and TPM • Design Single Source of Truth overviews • Vendor POC • Offsites • Design leader proxy

As an example of how this might look with a different DesignOps team and operating model, here's a workstream view by Adam Fry-Pierce and Diane Gregorio from their article "5 Keys to Scaling DesignOps"[4] (Figure 11.6).

---

4   Adam Fry-Pierce and Diane Gregorio, "5 Keys to Scaling DesignOps," *Medium* (blog), February 3, 2022, https://medium.com/docusign-design/5-keys-to-scaling-designops-b938e1bc4499

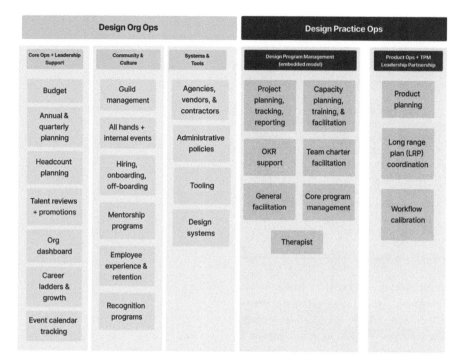

Design Org Ops			Design Practice Ops	
Core Ops + Leadership Support	**Community & Culture**	**Systems & Tools**	**Design Program Management (embedded model)**	**Product Ops + TPM Leadership Partnership**
Budget	Guild management	Agencies, vendors, & contractors	Project planning, tracking, reporting / Capacity planning, training, & facilitation	Product planning
Annual & quarterly planning	All hands + internal events	Administrative policies	OKR support / Team charter facilitation	Long range plan (LRP) coordination
Headcount planning	Hiring, onboarding, off-boarding	Tooling	General facilitation / Core program management	Workflow calibration
Talent reviews + promotions	Mentorship programs	Design systems	Therapist	
Org dashboard	Employee experience & retention			
Career ladders & growth	Recognition programs			
Event calendar tracking				

FIGURE 11.6

The DesignOps Business Menu by Adam Fry-Pierce and Diane Gregorio takes similar ingredients found in Tables 11.1 and 11.2, but puts them together into their own unique "dishes."

When fully built out and organized, DesignOps' workstreams tend to look like tall, skinny columns, often referred to as *pillars*. As in, "the three pillars of Central DesignOps are Community & Culture, Learning & Growth, and Scale & Enablement." The term *pillars* is common when describing your workstreams among the DesignOps community, but we recommend using *workstreams* when communicating your operating model to internal stakeholders, as it implies an important component that your designers, developers, and partners care about deeply: the work itself.

PILLARS! PILLARS, EVERYWHERE!

Wouldn't it be beautiful if you've built these workstream "pillars," and they all neatly support your operating model like columns supporting a roof? Ah, the symmetry! The organization! The ancient Greeks would love it.

Congratulations if your DesignOps operating model ends up looking like the Parthenon. Because in my experience, defining workstreams looks more like playing blocks with my kids. Pillars everywhere, some knocked over, some holding nothing up, some bunched together supporting the tiniest fragment of a balcony. It's an architect's nightmare.

If you've got some DesignOps pillars and can't figure out where they should go, what can you do about it?

- **Go back to the drawing board.** Set aside your current workstream definitions and try again. Re-cluster your programs and functions in a different way. You may find that regrouping the deliverables creates a new pillar (or two) that makes more sense for your operating model.

- **Let some workstreams be co-owned.** Maybe it just makes sense for some groups of programs to be a part of everyone's role. I see this a lot with anything involving communications or onboarding, which tend to have overlaps with multiple people or groups.

- **Turn that pillar into a foundation.** Maybe the problematic workstream isn't really program or deliverable-based. Perhaps you've created a pillar that actually describes fundamental competencies of being a DPM. In this case, that's no pillar—it's a foundation. Remove it, flatten it, and add it to your DesignOps career competencies, like we talked about in Chapter 4, "It's All About Practice."

- **Change your operating model.** I think this can be a bit "tail wagging the dog," but if the outcome of your workstream exercise is a bunch of beautiful pillars that simply don't support your operating model, maybe it's time to rethink or evolve the model itself?

I love building with blocks, so if you find yourself with too many pillars, or oddly shaped pillars, have fun with it. You ultimately want to build something that stands up on its own, and doesn't just look good on paper, so a little playful experimentation is definitely the right call.

Coda: Taking Shape

For individual DPMs and small teams ready to invest in the long-term success of their practice, the exercises described in this chapter demonstrate to the design org (and its stakeholders) that the DesignOps team is ready to lead. Give shape to the practice by first establishing the DesignOps team's mission statement, which articulates its purpose for its partners and yourselves. Define the operating model, to create boundaries for growth and the effective operation of multiple DPMs. Finally, organize the workstreams, which give shape to the pillars into which all DesignOps work happens. In doing so, the DesignOps team not only solidifies its role as a strategic enabler, but also establishes a foundation that aligns its efforts with the goals of the design organization—paving the way for innovation, efficiency, and continued operational excellence.

CHAPTER 12

Maintaining Your Rhythm
Evolving DesignOps from One to Many

There are many ways that Design Operations can be introduced into an organization. The designer who finds they are the "accidental DPM" might decide—or be asked—to formalize this role and take it on full time. Program managers from other parts of the business (especially the creative and technical sides) might slide over to the design org and own critical operational needs. A new design leader, having worked with Design Operations in the past, might look around their team and prioritize a DPM partner as their next hire. Perhaps a CEO reads this book and decides to fund an entire DesignOps practice from scratch!

In whatever way the seeds of DesignOps are planted, there are specific steps (described in the previous chapter) that need to happen first: establish a mission statement, define an operating model, and organize the workstreams. But once DesignOps has germinated in an organization, what ensures that it takes root? Inspiration is easy, but nurturing and sustaining a DesignOps practice for years to come takes *perspiration*—and a lot of it.

We have shown how Design Operations adds lasting value to any business, accreting long-term benefits of productivity, clarity, and values-driven leadership to design teams and their stakeholders. Unfortunately, these outcomes only come about when the DesignOps discipline is permanently established in an organization. If Design Operations is only employed as a temporary solution to a specific problem, the business will never reap these benefits. Therefore, no matter *how* the practice is introduced, it's important for its practitioners to know how to *keep it going*, find opportunities to grow, and expand DesignOps' influence—and indirectly, its team size—so that its partners and stakeholders get the greatest return on their investment.

The Three Phases of DesignOps Evolution

Growing a DesignOps team should always be a means to an end. Simply increasing the team's size is never the objective, and it's a terrible measure of success. It's also true that not all DesignOps growth is disruptive. For example, adding a DPM to an existing team of four or five may simply add much needed operational capacity, but won't fundamentally change how the DesignOps team functions.

Yet there are *some* stages of growth that fundamentally change how Design Operations is run. When a DesignOps team reaches one of these phases, an additional DPM doesn't just "add capacity"—it profoundly changes the team's mission, relationships, and services it provides to the design org. So, to maintain the long-term success of the practice, it's important to recognize what triggers these evolutionary phases and to know what to do when these critical moments rise.

The most trusted and durable signal that a DesignOps team is ready to evolve is when its stakeholder design org reaches a new developmental stage. In Chapter 10, "From Soloist to Symphony," we defined development as a function of maturity and size, with the stages of growth (size) described as small, mid-size, large, and enterprise. Design teams grow faster than DesignOps, i.e., designers will reach the large team stage while DesignOps may still be in the mid-size stage. Although our Design and DesignOps Development Matrix provides some head-count numbers for these stages, for the purposes of identifying when it's time to evolve Design Operations, it's more important to be attuned to the *inflection points* in maturity and size—not simply the number of designers and DPMs. These inflection points represent the key evolutionary phases of DesignOps (Figure 12.1), which are triggered at these three moments of design growth.

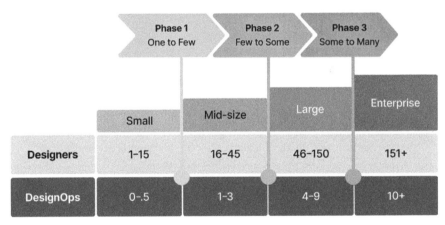

FIGURE 12.1
The three phases of DesignOps evolution.

Each of these three phases share common characteristics and actions that a DesignOps team needs to take to evolve from one level to the next. We define these evolutionary phases as:

- **Phase 1: One to Few**—The point at which the DesignOps "Army of One" becomes a proper team of two or more DPMs, co-owning and prioritizing projects together. Here, clearly organized workstreams are critical. (21%[1] of DesignOps practices are at this "soloist" inflection point!)

- **Phase 2: Few to Some**—The point at which the DesignOps team matures, with multiple DPMs operating in harmony alongside a possible people manager or player-coach. Here, a well-defined operating model is paramount to success.

- **Phase 3: Some to Many**—The point at which the DesignOps team is at the enterprise stage, requiring DPM managers to delegate and up-level work, and a DesignOps leader to ensure that the org's mission statement is aligned to the company's business objectives.

Taking Action to Evolve

When a Design Operations practice enters one of these evolutionary phases, it's time to take action. This chapter will delve into the basic DesignOps principles that need to be reevaluated at each phase; however, the most *important* action to take is to revisit the foundational elements discussed in 11, "Ready to Take Up the Baton." These are the team's mission statement, operating model, and workstreams, and it's imperative to validate that each one is still relevant. If, in the face of a fundamental change to the DesignOps team, any (or all) of these no longer serve the needs of the DPMs or design org, the very first step should be revisiting these core elements and realigning them to meet everyone's new level of maturity.

Resetting its purpose and ways of working can technically be the *only* step an evolving DesignOps practice needs to take. But, time permitting, there are additional questions to ask and actions to take that the team should consider, in order to effectively operate at its new level of maturity. These all involve reevaluating some of the

---

1 *2023 DesignOps Benchmarking Report* (DesignOps Assembly, 2023), www.designopsassembly.com/2023report

basic elements of Design Operations and understanding how they change when the practice grows and evolves. These elements are:

1. Which fundamentals the team prioritizes
2. With whom the team sets expectations and boundaries
3. How the team assesses the state of operations
4. How the team measures its success

1. Prioritizing the Fundamentals

In Chapter 2, "Learning the Score," we outlined the three tenets of DesignOps; these are where Design Operations focuses, how it acts, and what it delivers (Figure 12.2). Recall that each of these tenets is further broken down into a few sets of fundamental principles, as follows.

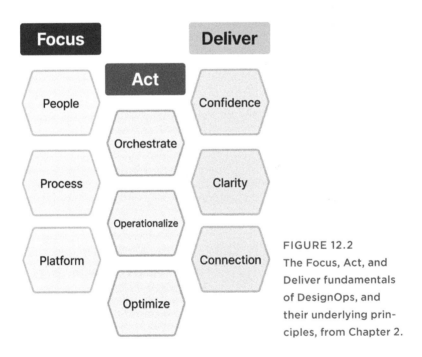

FIGURE 12.2
The Focus, Act, and Deliver fundamentals of DesignOps, and their underlying principles, from Chapter 2.

Can a team of DPMs effectively implement all these aspects of DesignOps simultaneously? Theoretically, yes; in practice, no. These fundamental principles are not equally relevant at all levels of maturity; as a DesignOps team evolves, it must know which principles take priority at each phase. We believe that at each of the three evolutionary phases, the following fundamentals are the ones that most need to be addressed to lay a solid foundation for future growth, as shown in Figure 12.3.

	Phase 1 One to Few	Phase 2 Few to Some	Phase 3 Some to Many
Focus	People	Process	Platform
Act	Orchestrate	Operationalize	Optimize
Deliver	Confidence	Clarity	Connection

FIGURE 12.3
Prioritizing the fundamental principles by phase.

- **Phase 1: One to Few**—At this phase, DesignOps needs to prioritize its *people*, providing what they need for success. This might include the right workspace, equipment, and essential design tools and skill sets. In addition, it should focus on *orchestration*: aligning teams, reducing roadblocks, and designing a way forward to get work done. Lastly, DesignOps should deliver *confidence*: ensuring that designers feel empowered to tackle the right tasks, at the right time, with the right tools.

- **Phase 2: Few to Some**—At this phase, DesignOps should prioritize its *processes*: establishing standards and guidelines and creating consistent workflows. It needs to design efficient systems that allow work to be streamlined. DesignOps should also focus on *operationalizing*: simplifying and codifying processes to make them easier to repeat. Finally, it should deliver *clarity*: articulating what "good design" looks like, defining clear roles and responsibilities, and measuring how design work aligns to long-term business goals.

ALWAYS BE PRIORITIZING

When I first joined Salesforce, I quickly learned that one of the constants of its culture was "order matters." I mean anything that ended up resembling a list, no matter its purpose, elicited comments confirming "this is in priority order, right?" At first it felt like an extra unnecessary step, but over time it became second nature, something I now truly stand by.

It makes sense because each year Salesforce goes through its planning process where everyone creates a V2MOM (our version of Vision and Goals). This document, which cascades from the very top all the way down, outlines your vision, values, methods, obstacles, and measures for the year ahead, and you guessed it, order very much matters. Methods are prioritized, and measures within methods are also ordered. Taking this simple step to signal priorities, not only in the big yearly planning motions, but also in our everyday communications and planning makes a difference. It means that everyone is on the same page about what matters most from the start, and it's built into the way we work.

- **Phase 3: Some to Many**—At this phase, DesignOps must prioritize its *platform*: strategic planning, managing the "business of design," future investments, and implementing processes that help the design org scale. Further, it should focus on *optimizing*: continuously improving by analyzing past iterations, trying different solutions, and refining all components of the platform to achieve excellence. And lastly, it should deliver *connection*: fostering rich connections and partnerships, formal communication channels and rituals among teams and stakeholders, and elevating the design org's work to its industry peers.

2. Resetting Stakeholder Expectations and Boundaries

One of the riskier outcomes of the DesignOps practice evolving is that its stakeholders stay oblivious to any changes in how Design Operations is organized and run. On the lesser end of the spectrum, this obliviousness might just look like miscommunication, possibly resulting in longer delivery times; for example, a design leader continuing to ask a specific DPM for support, rather than using a new intake process. But at its worst, DesignOps practitioners risk getting stuck in an "expectations gap" between how they worked in the past, and how they *need* to operate moving forward. Design stakeholders might expect DPMs to execute at past and present levels of scale, pigeon-hole DPMs into limited lanes of responsibilities, or believe they can simultaneously deliver team-specific solutions *and* org-wide consistency at the same time.

Some of these evolutionary pain points are discussed in Chapter 13, "The Wrong Notes," but for the self-aware DesignOps practice that recognizes it's at an inflection point, there *is* an important action to take to reduce these risks: *reset your stakeholder's expectations and boundaries*—publicly and intentionally. Here are some tactical recommendations for DesignOps practitioners who are ready to reset and move forward with their evolution:

- **Phase 1: One to Few**—At this phase, DesignOps practitioners are working alongside one or more design teams and operate primarily at the project level. The most common stakeholders are design ICs; with them, expectations must be set that a growing DesignOps practice is not going to be a "fixer" for all team woes. DPMs should clearly communicate that they are collaborative partners with the team, and not a role to which operational tasks are off-loaded. DesignOps practitioners need to articulate their workstream boundaries to ensure that their stakeholders understand what work is in and out of bounds. Lastly, DPMs should set expectations about which design teams they do and do not partner with, as DesignOps is probably at an inflection point when not all teams have nor should expect DPM support.

- **Phase 2: Few to Some**—At this phase, the DesignOps team is partnered with a large design team and operates at the program level. Stakeholders at this phase are design leaders; with them, expectations must be set about how the DesignOps team has reorganized to support all teams and how this changes the ways design ICs and leaders engage with DPMs. There will likely be a formal "front door" to the DesignOps team—direct requests will no longer scale. Critically, DesignOps practitioners will need to establish that they are responsible for designing workflow processes and frameworks, and, in return, will expect that design teams will adopt, use, and provide feedback on these new ways of working.

- **Phase 3: Some to Many**—At this phase, the DesignOps team finds itself working inside a mature, enterprise-sized design org. Evolving to meet the needs of this moment requires resetting expectations not only with design teams, but their cross-functional and business partners, too. These partners might be holding on to an outdated understanding that DesignOps is simply a service or perk to the design org, focused on a narrow set of workstreams. To disabuse this notion, it is important to establish how its practitioners are expected to show up externally to the performance partners described in Chapter 9, "Your Performance Partners." For example, DesignOps should set the expectation that DPMs will proxy for design leaders in cross-functional events, that they co-own program management alongside TPMs, and are strategic planners to product leaders and GMs who need to understand the capacity and capability of their design org.

DESIGNOPS DECODED

EVOLVING THROUGH THE PHASES

How would you describe some of the stakeholder challenges you face when growing a DesignOps practice?

Kristine Berry,
IBM Z DesignOps program director

The first challenge is just getting cross-functional leaders to grow! Some might think of DesignOps as the design leader's responsibility and not a separate dedicated practice. That's the first hurdle—getting the ears of those leaders and helping them understand the value in DesignOps. You're not only getting design on board with this practice, but also other parts of the business, too. And when DesignOps grows, you also have to help the people who have worked with you before. "Now this person will do the product stuff, and that person will do the program stuff." Or maybe it's split by research and tooling, or whatever. Scaling the team, everything gets a little more complicated, so you have to make sure that you're communicating well.

3. Reassessing the State of Operations

The operational side of design needs to get done, whether or not there's a dedicated person or team to do the work. We call the assessment of operational work that is (and is not) getting done the *state of operations*, and it's important to reevaluate this state whenever Design Operations enters a new evolutionary phase. Practitioners and teams that don't reassess the state of operations risk carrying forward their existing workstreams as-is, missing the opportunity to evolve them in the context of a maturing practice. Further, this action is important to uncover operational needs that exist but are not owned or are only being partially met within the current DesignOps operating model.

Here are a few tips and questions to consider when reassessing the design practice's state of operations:

- **Phase 1: One to Few**—At this phase, the most important question to ask is, "What DesignOps work already exists and is being owned by a designer or leader?" This inflection point marks a moment when DPM supply is unlikely to meet operational demand; therefore, rather than chase new workstreams—adding even more DesignOps work to the backlog—it's more important to first fulfill the basic promise of Design Operations and take over existing operational work from your design makers and doers.

DesignOps Decoded

Evolving Through the Phases

What did the state of operations look like as you were evolving your DesignOps practice from one DPM to a few?

Patrizia Bertini,
DesignOps strategist and leader

When you go into startups, it's important that you start thinking about Design Operations when the business is growing and scaling. One day there is one designer that is doing everything, and the next day, it's 20 designers from 20 different companies doing the same thing in 25 different ways. Everyone has their own way. So, what happens is, you have the most fantastic people, but they just speak different design languages. They use the same tools in very different ways. They don't have naming conventions; they don't have the same culture. They work with PMs differently, etc. So, it becomes critical in startups to have visibility as a DesignOps leader.

- **Phase 2: Few to Some**—At this phase, the right question to ask is, "What DesignOps needs exist, but are not being addressed?" At this evolutionary phase, it's OK for the DesignOps team to acknowledge that the full breadth and depth of operational work might exceed its capacity. What matters most is identifying the complete state of operations and focusing on the highest priority work. (To this end, the "Start, Stop, Keep Doing" framework is a great exercise to run.) Recall that this phase focuses on creating processes and operationalizing the design org—two principles that, when tackled head on, should create sustainable efficiencies that allow DesignOps practitioners to incrementally take on more "below the line" Ops needs in the future.

- **Phase 3: Some to Many**—At this phase, DesignOps must ask itself, "What can we do new or differently to deliver design excellence across different functions and business units?" This is the phase at which the state of operations must actually *expand*, reaching beyond the design org to include the needs of its cross-functional and business partners. Often, these "design + X" workstreams are net-new, requiring DesignOps practitioners to not only identify them, but also articulate why they matter, how they will be run, and who is accountable for their success. Examples might include new delivery methods that better integrate design with its endpoint engineering or marketing partners, and elevating design thinking into strategic planning and product roadmapping.

4. Rethinking How Success Is Measured

It's probably obvious at this point that success is going to look different as a DesignOps team evolves from one phase to the next. Completing a project versus orchestrating a program, as an example, will both earn a DPM a gold star, but require very different measures to know if the jobs have been completely successful. Similarly, design leaders and executive stakeholders will want DesignOps to define success criteria before green-lighting a new workstream. It's bad business to invest in a new initiative, like upgraded design software or a revamped recruiting process, without knowing if DesignOps can measure whether the effort has made things better or worse.

Knowing how to measure DesignOps success is a complicated topic, which is reviewed in Chapter 15, "Measure by Measure." But recognizing that success won't always be measured the same way—especially as a DesignOps practice matures—is an important acknowledgment to make, especially when that practice is evolving. When DPMs are at one of these inflection points, here are some important points to consider as the team transitions into its next stage:

- **Phase 1: One to Few**—At this phase, DPMs are typically aligned to teams, prioritizing people and projects, and focused on keeping them orchestrated in harmony. Success here is measured at the individual (person or project) level, meaning it is atomic, enumerated, and countable. How many designers completed their training? How did the audience members rate that last presentation? How many design system components have been implemented compared to plan? Did the project complete on time? (Yes, measures at this phase can be binary, too.) These are somewhat basic success measures, but that does not make them any less powerful. Enumerable metrics are a simple yet meaningful way to measure DesignOps success and create the foundation for how DPMs measure their effort even as their practice evolves.

DesignOps Decoded

Evolving Through the Phases

You've been at different places that cover the full spectrum of DesignOps maturity. What are some of the things you've observed about how you measure success?

Brennan Hartich, director, Design & Research Operations at LinkedIn

At the most simple and easy level, it's basically product delivery. Like, getting an actual designed product out the door. I don't have to convince people of that, they just see a DPM on the team, and they see the output increasing, and you can measure that through project plans or Agile methodologies, those kinds of things.

At more mature levels, I measure success as design org health. We've never figured out how to measure this directly, but for us it's a mix of biannual surveys and pulse surveys on team health. We also run our own surveys after programs and events to gather what people are looking for.

- **Phase 2: Few to Some**—At this phase, the DesignOps team is likely aligned to a large design team, prioritizing process and programs, and focused on operationalizing these elements so they can scale effectively. Success here is measured at a multi-dimensional level, requiring multiple inputs and data points. A program to, say, change the design pipeline to accommodate building with a new visual language, will have multiple moving parts—each with its own unique success metrics. DesignOps must evolve to match this complexity. Success is not just measured in discrete sums or percentages, but rather as functions of multiple values, sometimes measured at different times, and occasionally with no "apples-to-apples" comparisons between them. Because of this, DPMs need to up-level how they communicate design success to their stakeholders, so that the complexity of the metrics doesn't obscure a great win. Dashboards are a common tool at this phase, as are simple (but slightly subjective) "Red, Yellow, Green" overviews of program health.

- **Phase 3: Some to Many**—At this phase, the DesignOps team might be more aligned to the product or business, prioritizing how the practice benefits those inside and outside design, and focused on optimizing its contributions. Success at this level is often defined top-down, as key performance indicators (KPIs) or business goals. In this context, design metrics are just one of many factors to overall success. At this stage of maturity, Design Operations is responsible for identifying which design metrics are relevant to the business's KPIs, and how to connect the dots between them. Sometimes this requires implementing new ways to measure design success (i.e., by instrumenting in-app telemetry, or soliciting user feedback) that see DPMs working cross-functionally and externally, two actions befitting this phase of DesignOps evolution.

The More Things Change...

In the world of overused expressions, "The only constant is change" is one that's stubbornly familiar to DesignOps practitioners. Our discipline can feel like it's constantly stuck in the second gear of change management, and that no two days will ever feel the same. (More on this topic in Chapter 14, "Tuning Your Instrument.") Thankfully, there's another well-worn saying that is equally true of DesignOps: "The more things change, the more they stay the same."

Just because your practice evolves, not everything needs to change. After our cumulative decades of experience, we've seen that some parts of the job tend to stay relatively stable throughout the different phases of DesignOps evolution. No matter your practice's level of maturity of size, you can count on the following jobs to be a constant, dependable part of your DesignOps suite of services:

- **Design work tracking:** The demand for managing work intake, prioritization, and commitment.

- **Design crits and reviews:** Coordinating people and artifacts at the right time to receive feedback.

- **Aggregating knowledge:** Maintaining a searchable library of best practices, templates, research insights, trainings, etc.

- **Team recognition:** The corporate and personal ways to celebrate and acknowledge team milestones (hello, birthdays, team anniversaries, and spot bonuses!).

- **Communications:** Newsletters, pass-downs, org change announcements, and more.

- **Integrating systems and connecting dots:** Managing complexity through design planning and tooling.

Regarding integrating systems and connecting dots, this DesignOps job is so remarkably stable, and such a consistent part of our discipline, that innovations have started to emerge that support this domain specifically. In particular, the rise of platforms that provide a durable infrastructure for connecting design and business processes

DESIGNOPS DECODED

EVOLVING THROUGH THE PHASES

What's one thing that stands out to you about how the fundamentals of DesignOps change when the practice evolves?

Alana Washington,
head of design, Platform at Rippling

I think there's a proactivity pivot that happens when the team is ready for the next level. DPMs aren't being shown what to do, they're asking for feedback on a plan. (I'd say that's true for designers, too.) This shows they're able to take on greater and greater complexity. When that proactivity muscle gets stronger, DesignOps can say "We think that's the right decision," or "Based on my past experience and based on these inputs, this is what I expect to see change or happen." This shows they are deeply thinking about a problem and a solution, which is something I look for when I think about the team's maturity.

not just through templates and artifacts, but also through data. Jon Fukuda, partner and design principal at Limina, is on the forefront of exploring "integrating design processes as a service." He states:

> Research and designers need the proper integrated infrastructure to plan and validate their work. They have tools and protocols, but the processes and workflows between these are not integrated, leaving out an auditable history of effort, duration, artifacts, outcomes, and impact. There's an entire ecosystem of tools today to support engineers in their development cycle, but the infrastructure to support end-to-end discovery, design, and deployment of great design is still fragmented and lacking.

We'll share some of these "design process as service" examples in our toolkit at the end of this book.

Coda: You Say You Want an Evolution

DesignOps growth does not always trigger DesignOps evolution. Adding DPMs or managers to a Design Operations team usually happens without any major disruption to how the team operates. It's when this growth coincides with an inflection point (or mismatch) in the development levels of the design and DesignOps practices that "how the team operates" is something that will need to fundamentally change. By recognizing and embracing these evolutionary moments, and being mindful of the actions to take when they happen, DesignOps will be prepared to morph alongside their design org and sustain its lasting value.

And what happens if the DesignOps practice overlooks that it's in this moment, and fails to evolve or take action? Well, we discuss some of those obstacles and pitfalls in the next chapter.

CHAPTER 13

The Wrong Notes
Managing Risk, Obstacles, and Challenges

The hard work of establishing and expanding a DesignOps practice is a study of contrasts. It requires equal parts art and science, soft and hard skills, and personal and group effort. That building a functional Design Operations team requires so much balance should come as no surprise to its practitioners, who themselves have followed a career path for which "the balancing act" is a skill valued above nearly all others. As the practice grows, this constant vigilance of weighing and balancing contrasting forces to keep the team aligned to its mission is what ultimately makes the best Design Operations teams successful.

But the path to success is never a straight line. In the previous chapters, we covered the steps and actions you might take to establish and then evolve your DesignOps team. And while these are the right steps for aspiring (and veteran) DPM leaders to move their practice forward, what wasn't described are all the obstacles that might force these leaders to take a step back, too. And knowing how to stumble backward is just as important a skill to master as leaping forward. Remember: with Design Operations, it's always a balancing act!

Most of the obstacles a DesignOps team faces will be unique to the context of their organization. However, we maintain that some obstacles and pitfalls are rather common, particularly those that challenge a DesignOps team's long-term growth and stability. The most frequent roadblock is a basic misunderstanding of DesignOps by design teams and their partners—even in practices where DesignOps may be at the mid-size or large stage. We get it! The discipline is new and is shaped so specifically from company to company that no two DesignOps practices will look the same. When the novelty of Design Operations wears off, so, too, can design org support; Alison Rand, author and design leader, puts it this way:

> People seem very sold on Design Operations, and then you get there and realize you're a team of one or maybe two, and there's no clear support or scope around what your work is supposed to be. So, you build and build and build, even though there's no clear definition from the company. So, I think that often because design leaders don't understand DesignOps, they give you carte blanche to help figure it out—and then you do, and there's a misalignment in their expectations and needs.

Having navigated this and similar challenges many times throughout the years, we've learned to tune in to the specific signals that often predict obstacles ahead. And we've seen that the most challenging obstacles to DesignOps stability—from both internal and external forces—are actually quite similar for most practices, regardless of their operating model or the shape of their design organization.

Accepting that your DesignOps team will face obstacles is easy; anticipating where these obstacles will come from is tricky, but only if you don't know where to look. Organizational pitfalls can come from anywhere, but the two signals to be most attuned to come from the internal misalignment of your design and DesignOps teams' respective maturity levels and the external cyclical rhythms that govern your company's business. These two forces couldn't be more different: in fact, they're almost polar opposites! But they are also a balanced pair of obstacles, likely to challenge your DesignOps team's forward progress, and just as equally likely to be overcome—if you know what to look for.

Maturity Level Misalignment

Growing pains are not always subtle. Sometimes they are written out like the proverbial writing on the wall, or, in the case of Design Operations, documented in lengthy email chains, ever-growing backlogs, and frustrated one-on-one conversations. It's plain to see the obstacles of a DesignOps team that is vastly under-resourced relative to its design org and to take corrective action (hiring, reprioritization, de-scoping, etc.). What's less obvious—and potentially more challenging—is when the development path of both the design and DesignOps teams deviates only slightly, creating a long-term misalignment in the maturity levels of both. Rather than presenting itself as an acute growing pain, this misalignment grows steadily and unnoticed, experienced more like a slow rise in temperature that never seems to reach a boil—until it does.

Recognizing this moment before it happens can remove a huge number of obstacles from your DesignOps team's path. These inflection points when the design and DesignOps teams' maturity get out of sync signal that growth (or contraction) in either discipline is disrupting the DesignOps team's mission and operating model, and something needs to change. The clues that your org is at this inflection point are DPMs feeling stretched and DesignOps partners feeling unclear about what the DPMs are doing. We described this condition at the 2020 Rosenfeld DesignOps Summit, when we said:

> Our DPMs felt stretched, had too many competing priorities, and were covering an overly broad set of responsibilities. And our partners, inside and outside design, were asking for more clarity, a stronger POV on tools and process, and more Ops time dedicated to helping design teams do great work.

Sound familiar? If a maturity level misalignment isn't this clear from a high-level perspective, then be attuned to the bottoms-up pain points described by your team's DPMs and partners, like those in Figure 13.1.

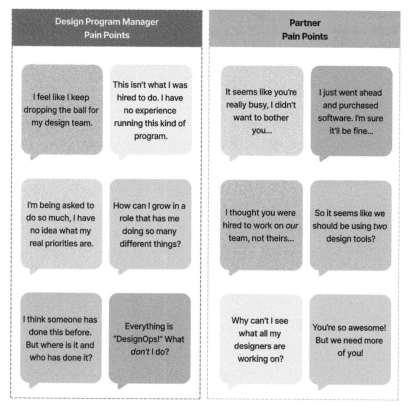

FIGURE 13.1

When maturity levels are misaligned, both DPMs and their partners feel the pain.

Misaligned levels of org maturity threaten to stretch your DPMs too thinly and muddy your team's mission in the eyes of its partners. They can cause DesignOps' solutions to fall out of sync with design org problems, as experienced when DPMs think they need to be solving the needs of a mid-sized design team, when what they actually need to be solving are the needs of a large design org (see Chapter 10, "From Soloist to Symphony"); in effect, solving the wrong problems entirely.

But the real threat to Design Operations is that these challenges appear slowly and subtly, prompting complacency or band-aid solutions that don't do anything significant to address the obstacle. So, if you happen to miss the signals, then it's important to have on your radar some of the most common problems that manifest as a result of a maturity level misalignment. And because it's easier to recognize symptoms than to diagnose an illness, knowing which problems to look for can help you recognize organizational misalignment, in order to take appropriate action. The following are some common problems to be attuned to (with solutions appearing later in this chapter):

The Pendulum Problem

The *Pendulum Problem* is when do-it-all DPMs have priorities that swing wildly, from helping the entire org to helping a single project. Each of these takes 100% of their time, and swinging in either direction can lead some partners to assume their needs are not a priority. Examples of this include DPMs needing to focus on an org- or business-wide priority at the expense of design team programs and product release planning, and then, suddenly swinging back to specific product design work, at the expense of necessary org-wide functions, like onboarding and software management.

The Mind the Gap Problem

With the *Mind the Gap Problem*, quality gaps and blind spots emerge because DesignOps is trying to operate horizontally and vertically at the same time, and at multiple levels of scale. DPMs have difficulty constantly recalibrating to these different detail levels, resulting in work where the fidelity is too high (or too low) than needed, creating quality gaps all around. An example of this might look like a DPM inappropriately using scrappy, small-team methods to solve complex org-wide problems, or a DPM over-engineering a process needed by a close-knit group of designers and making everything more complicated.

The Lone Wolf Problem

The *Lone Wolf Problem* arises when DPMs take on such widely vary-ing responsibilities that they don't feel aligned with each other or with the DesignOps team. Each DPM can end up owning a niche that nobody else needs to occupy, creating artificial silos and eroding a family feeling on the DesignOps team. Examples of this should be obvious, but they include DPMs who always need to start new proj-ects from scratch, don't have the ability to bootstrap or jumpstart new programs based off prior work, and don't see any obvious model for load-balancing work across DPMs (who might have wildly different skill sets and capacity).

The Career Step Stool Problem

When faced with the *Career Step Stool Problem*, the DPM career lad-der resembles more of a step stool. In other words, DPMs get high enough to look around the DesignOps landscape, only to discover there's no next step to take. Lacking clear ways to develop and specialize, DPMs can get discouraged and look elsewhere. Examples of this are also obvious: lack of promotions, lack of job security, attri-tion, and high DesignOps turn-over.

Recognize the Signals, or Feel the Problems

The problems described in this chapter range in severity, but at least they are *obvious*. A DesignOps team is likely to feel the pain of attri-tion or isolation, for instance, and take corrective steps when needed. Our hypothesis is that being attuned to and recognizing the signals of misaligned maturity levels will help your Design Operations team take action *before* problems emerge. And the best way to do this is to bake into your practice a regular assessment (and reassessment) of your org's design and DesignOps maturity, using the criteria from our Development Matrix in Chapter 10. Whether the signals you tune in to are team size, ratios, the level of integration of design into the broader org, or something else, we recommend that DPMs check their maturity alignment at least once per year and commit to taking action if the two disciplines show signs of scaling apart from each other.

Cyclical Rhythms of Business

If misaligned maturity models are the internal source of many DesignOps problems, the *cyclical rhythms* that govern your company's business are its biggest external antagonists. For Design Operations, these forces are usually predictable: release planning, promotion cycles, annual roadmap reviews, and so on. These recurring cycles may cause minor headaches and occasional DesignOps fire drills but are usually of the sort that can be scoped in advance (if not outright planned for). But zoom out further, and this level of predictability becomes impossible. Every business and industry has cyclical rhythms shaped by macro-economic and worldwide forces, and unless your design team is in the business of making crystal balls, there is no way to know when external events will force your org into a boom or a bust.

While impossible to predict, the up-and-down impacts of a cyclical downturn do follow familiar patterns, permitting some degree of contingency planning by DesignOps teams. Your team may not know when these obstacles will stand in their way, but they can certainly be prepared for these moments when they arrive. And, done right, these preparations mean Design Operations can not only support their partners in the design org, but the DPMs on the DesignOps team, too. The following are some recurring rhythms of business, driven by macro forces, that DesignOps teams should be prepared for:

Reorganizations

Reorganizations are, understandably, disruptive and hard for the people being moved around. DesignOps teams tend to be small, and therefore DesignOps practitioners are unlikely to face a situation in which their own team is being reshuffled entirely. More common is a reorganization to (or within) the design org itself, and it is within this situation that DPMs experience the most acute impacts.

There are countless reasons why a design team might reorganize— some of which are positive. For example, a design team might need to reorganize due to a merger or acquisition; design as a business function operates best without silos and firewalls, and two design teams will inevitably be reorganized into one at some point. Design orgs might also reorganize due to organic growth; in this situation, a reorg serves as a positive change moment to rebalance and realign teams and skills.

On the neutral to negative side of the equation, design teams might reorganize due to a change in business priority. Entire design teams may suddenly need to be reassigned and re-skilled to support a critical change in the commercial zeitgeist. (Any DPM who's partnered with a generative AI design team in recent years is probably familiar with this experience!) Another common reorg trigger is when design leaders move up or out of the organization, or switch to an individual contributor track. In these situations, a reorg is necessary to maintain continuity of management and to ensure that designers have the proper reporting structure to grow and do their jobs effectively.

Regardless of the catalyst, a design team reorganization creates a massive amount of work for DesignOps. Org charts need to be revised, meeting cadences need to be revisited, distribution lists need to be updated, software licenses need to be reevaluated, design processes need to be resolved, team members need to be onboarded, announcements need to be made, and so on. For DPMs, the notion of taking a design team that has perhaps reached its "performing" peak and forcing it into a "storming" period is anathema to the basic principles of efficiency and productivity. Nevertheless, reorganizations can and will happen. They are part of the cyclical rhythms of any business. Therefore, it's important for the DesignOps team to prepare for the inevitable by making sure some of their key practices are durable and resilient in the face of a reorg. While not an exhaustive list, some of our top recommendations to bake reorg resiliency into one's practice include the following:

- **Centralize and simplify your organizational artifacts.** One org chart is easier to update than two (or twenty). A simple team visualization is easier to revise than one with bespoke images, colors, and complicated layouts. A single design tracker in a table or database is easier to make current than multiple trackers maintained in text-heavy documents. And centralizing *all* of these artifacts in a single depot (and perhaps controlling access via an editor-restricted portal or wiki page) will give DPMs the confidence that when changes need to be made, there will not be any rogue artifacts in the wild to complicate and confuse designers.

- **Validate your manager and IC competencies and levels annually.** In the more positive reorganization case, design teams get bigger through merger or organic growth. But with this change comes the need to have a trusted set of competencies and levels by which designers (and their managers) are measured. This is *especially* true with reorgs triggered by acquisitions, where titles and levels may

FORMING, STORMING, NORMING, AND PERFORMING

When I consider team growth (or any team change for that matter), one of my favorite frameworks to keep in mind—and to keep me sane—is the "Forming, Storming, Norming, and Performing" model. It basically describes the different phases any new team can expect to encounter. And if you're in a growing DesignOps team, or in any organization that constantly restructures, these four phases are good to remember:

- **Forming:** The team has come together!
- **Storming:** Uh, oh. Roles are unclear, swim lanes are poorly defined, we're duplicating work, etc. The team is producing less than the sum of its parts. Quick—invest in an operating model!
- **Norming:** Ah, we've paid that "growth tax." The team is coming together, and we're producing like normal.
- **Performing:** Now we're excelling! This is why we grew or restructured our team in the first place—we're producing more than each of us would individually.

Whenever I find myself with a re-org'd team that doesn't seem to be firing on all cylinders, I just remind myself of where we are in this framework, which builds confidence that we'll get to where we need to be...eventually.

not align between the two teams. The DesignOps team should make it an annual practice to validate the competencies, skills, and levels they maintain with their design team, so that these definitions are accurate and ready whenever change happens.

- **Establish or adopt a change management process.** We talk about DesignOps' role in change management and some change management processes in Chapter 14, "Tuning Your Instruments." There are *many* different frameworks a team could adopt, but the key thing is that a DesignOps team should prepare by having a change management process of *any* kind ready to deploy in case a reorganization happens. Basic criteria could include a criteria for which stakeholders should be notified, examples of previous communications, a playbook for which areas of operations need to be reviewed, and more. If a DesignOps team has improvised its way through a reorg once, it's a good practice to retro that experience and codify best practices into a change management rulebook for next time!

Reductions in Force

More isn't necessarily better; less isn't necessarily worse. But when it comes to reducing a design team's workforce, dealing with the pain (and occasional heartbreak) of operating with less is extraordinarily hard for Design Operations. Setting aside the painful fact that reductions in force can impact designers *and* DPMs alike (in 2023, 24% of DesignOps teams experienced a reduction in force, and 34% had a hiring freeze[1]), the challenging job of figuring out "What comes next?" often falls to DesignOps and their leadership partners—a difficult task that always comes at a difficult time.

A reduction in force *is* a reorganization—it will trigger all the work described previously, ameliorated by the preparations described earlier, too. But a reduction in force is so much more: it's a layoff (to be blunt), meaning that team sizes in design and DesignOps are going to significantly change. Subject matter and domain experts might inexplicably be let go. The design team's capacity will go down, alongside its ability to allocate time and personnel to vision work, research, and usability testing. Moreover, a reduction in force threatens the morale and well-being of employees "affected" but not "impacted" by the layoff, who have to manage increased workloads, overcome sudden knowledge gaps, and strike a balance between being productive and burning out.

It's a little cynical, or even callous, for DesignOps to have a layoff playbook. So, don't. For a practice built on relationships and trust, an off-the-shelf "layoff guide" risks reducing humans to cogs in a machine, which is definitely *not* the goal of Design Operations. Rather, managing a design team through a layoff requires DPMs to draw on their team values (see Chapter 7, "Playing Your Part") to stay anchored to their mission and vision. More crucially, it underscores how important some DesignOps practices are to the daily operations of the design org—practices DPMs should implement, *regardless* of whether the current business cycle is trending up or spinning down. Some of these practices include:

- **Aggregate institutional knowledge.** In established design orgs with little attrition, the default mode of storing institutional knowledge often relies on the least durable medium

---

1 *2023 DesignOps Benchmarking Report* (DesignOps Assembly, 2023), www.designopsassembly.com/2023report

of all—human brains. No wiki, hub, or vault can replace the simplicity of a tap on the shoulder, or a DM asking "Do we have any research on this?" The advantages of speed and simplicity in this model break down completely, though, if the subject matter expert exits unexpectedly. A good practice—and one that safeguards against the risks of reductions in force—is to enforce the documentation and aggregation of all artifacts created by the design org, into a system that is searchable and scalable.

- **Establish file-sharing protocols.** Design work might begin on a whiteboard or sketchpad, but often ends up in a digital file. Whether your design org uses Figma, Illustrator, Penpot, or any other number of design tools, how those outputs are shared and organized is crucial to your org's long-term health. A view-only file shared with specific stakeholders can be effectively locked up if the author is no longer with the company. Conversely, a DesignOps-curated library of all artifacts, made possible by a protocol of sharing all files to a team or shared folder, can ensure that critical design files are never inaccessible.

- **Maintain accurate allocation and resourcing docs.** DesignOps often produces work-tracking documents that show how designers are allocated across programs and workstreams, and how those portfolios are (and are not) resourced. These docs are crucial in good times and bad: accurate work-tracking is necessary to ensure that top design priorities are being met and design work-life balance is healthy. But it's also necessary when design capacity is reduced, so that business leaders can see at a glance which programs are suddenly at risk.

These best practices are recommended for all DesignOps teams, regardless of external factors. That they also help prepare design orgs for cyclical downturns and layoffs is simply added value. Beyond these practical measures, though, is the human aspect of personnel loss, and in this, DesignOps practitioners also have an important part to play. The skills of communication, event planning, and fostering a psychologically safe environment are critical for navigating reductions in force and can help design orgs "move forward" and not just "move on."

Recessions and Global Calamities

Companies will reorganize their workforce, and they will periodically expand and reduce it; these events are part of the peaks and valleys of all business cycles. But there is another cycle that governs all businesses—one that affects every company, and yet is entirely out of their control. This cycle is governed by macro-economic and global forces, which manifests itself as boom times (when everything goes great, but nobody seems to notice), and as recessions or downturns (when suddenly, everybody seems to be affected!).

The good news for DesignOps practitioners is that these macro-economic cycles are definitely outside of their sphere of influence. There is nothing a DPM can do to control a global recession, political unrest, or natural disaster. These events will unfairly impact companies, causing them to reduce their staff, or—worse—disappear completely. In these situations, everyone is affected, even if they are not all "impacted," leaving those that remain in a fragile state.

In these situations, Design Operations can have an outsized role to play. Supporting affected design orgs in difficult times requires drawing on all the empathetic skills DesignOps practitioners have to offer—skills which should be directed toward achieving three discrete and important goals: team well-being, continuity of service, and leadership support.

- **Team well-being:** DesignOps can implement initiatives that support mental health, work-life balance, and remote work. Far from being "perks," these programs are vital necessities to ensure that designers can work safely and securely during uncertain times. When individuals are focused on taking care of themselves and their own psychological safety, it's hard to also do the same for their teams. Here, DesignOps (in partnership with HR and internal resource teams) can take the lead to promote well-being initiatives, build events that foster safe spaces and community, and deploy communication skills to spread messages that bring confidence and clarity to those working during uncertain times.

- **Continuity of service:** When the outside world feels unpredictable and scary, many people seek solace in work. The structure and regularity of a workday can bring peace in an otherwise chaotic world. This is why, during times of global uncertainty, it is important for DesignOps practitioners to prioritize continuity of service for their design orgs—being mindful, of course, of the team's well-being first and foremost. Maintaining a reasonable cadence of scheduled events and communications (even if the agenda and content change) can go a long way toward creating a sense of security.
- **Leadership support:** In challenging times, leaders can lose their way, too. DesignOps' proximity to leadership can be deployed here to increase their confidence that they are doing the right things and in a timely matter. Helping design leaders reorient to the practice's values (see Chapter 7) can go a long way when the going gets rough.

Put Your Own Mask on First

Although not part of the job description, DesignOps practitioners are often the "first responders" throughout the crises described in this chapter, keeping a steady pulse on the design org's well-being. Our discipline serves as therapists, mediators, teachers, and firefighters; in these roles, it can be emotionally taxing and easy to forget to take care of yourself. Furthermore, DesignOps managers have the responsibility of supporting their own team's well-being, making it even harder (and sometimes lonelier) to navigate these challenges. In these times, it really is important to "put your own mask on first," to ground yourself in your values, to lean on others, and to prioritize your own well-being.

Coda: You're Ready for This

DesignOps practitioners are super, but they're not superheroes. In the face of outsized obstacles—either internal or external—there's only so much a DPM can be expected to do. But this implies that there *are* expectations: design orgs rely on their Design Operations partners to help them navigate uncertain situations, and to maintain that tricky balance of managing team well-being and team commitments. Tuning in to the signals, problems, and realities of these obstacles can help DesignOps practitioners prepare for these challenges and face them head-on. They can build processes that are sensible and durable for design orgs at *any* point in their business cycle—processes that (fortunately) *also* happen to provide contingencies and continuity when that cycle trends downward.

And in the event that some inside or outside force truly does disrupt the DesignOps team, reorganizing or reducing it in unexpected ways, the best remediation is to replay the steps outlined in Chapter 11, "Ready to Take Up the Baton": reset your team's mission statement, operating model, and workstreams. In short, recalibrate your Design Operations charter to meet the needs of the design org as it exists *today* and in the foreseeable future. This exercise will ensure the long-term health of your DesignOps team, allowing it to adapt to the evolving maturity levels of its adjacent design org and the cyclical business forces in which it operates.

Tuning Your Instruments
DesignOps Tools

A musician tunes their instrument to adjust and calibrate its pitch, ensuring that anything they play is—well, "pitch-perfect." Similarly, DesignOps tests and refines its *own* tools, which are unique—relative to other operations practices—in that they are the same tools *designers* use to create digital products and services.

At the top of the DesignOps toolkit are the methods of *design strategy* and *change management*. These design "instruments" are powerful tools in the hands of a DesignOps practitioner, deployed in a similar manner, and differing only in the outputs the discipline creates (processes, organizational design, and the like). Patrizia Bertini, DesignOps Leader for 8x8, sums up this core tenet of why DesignOps must master these design methods:

> I'm quite vocal about the need to combine design, systems thinking, and change management. Because without those three elements, you have project management, program management, and design, and you lose the power.

We assert that of all the design skills a DPM must hone and keep constantly in tune, design strategy and change management are the most important to the DesignOps practice. In this chapter, we will cover how these methods have been historically defined for designers, and then share how we've integrated these tools in the service of DesignOps.

What Is Design Strategy?

Design strategy is where creativity and business needs intersect. It's a method that uses design thinking to achieve specific goals and make a real-world impact. It posits that the best, most innovative products exist at the intersection of desirability, viability, and feasibility (Figure 14.1), with design operating at the seams and overlaps to align business objectives and user needs.

IDEO championed design thinking methodologies in the 1980s–1990s, influencing a trend toward user-centered design as a means to create desirable products. During the late 1990s and early 2000s, this practice was applied to digital products as well. Today, design strategy has evolved into a core business discipline, leveraging human-centered design to create valuable products and address broader societal challenges.

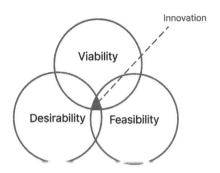

Desirability (human-centric):
Addressing a customer's need or fulfilling a specific job to be done.
Do people want and need the product?

Viability (business):
Having long-term sustainability and value.
Is it financially viable?

Feasibility (technical):
Ensuring that the concept can be realized, delivered, and maintained
Is it even possible to create?

FIGURE 14.1
In IDEO's framework, design focuses on desirability, engineering on feasibility, and the business on viability. However, it's important for all groups to understand each of these spheres.

What Is Change Management?

Change management is the art and science of guiding individuals and organizations through transitions to achieve desired outcomes. The practice dates to the pre-1990s, when social science pioneers like Kurt Lewin and Arnold Van Gennep laid the groundwork by studying human behavior and reactions to change. Simultaneously, management thinkers Mary Parker Follett and Douglas McGregor explored communication, collaboration, and power dynamics in change initiatives, emphasizing the human aspect of change.

The 1990s marked the rise of the "change guru" with consultants like John Kotter and Daryl Conner popularizing change management frameworks. From 2000 on, research and data analysis took center stage, leading to the development of more nuanced and context-specific approaches, notably Prosci's ADKAR model (discussed later in this chapter) that focuses on individual needs for adopting and adapting to change.

Integrating Design Strategy for DesignOps

When DesignOps integrates the design strategy toolkit into its practice, it does so to craft the processes and experiences designers have when creating products. The primary tool in this strategy is *design thinking*, which is a step-by-step process to designing great experiences.

There are many design thinking frameworks, but the most popular one (for designers) is the Double Diamond method. The Double Diamond is a model popularized by the Design Council in the UK in 2005. It consists of four stages: discover, define, develop, and deliver. The model is called the *Double Diamond* because it forms two diamond shapes, representing the two divergent (Discover, Develop) and convergent (Define, Deliver) processes of an iterative design process (Figure 14.2).

FIGURE 14.2
The Design Council's Double Diamond fosters user-centered thinking and exploration, but it can lack clarity in guiding the translation of insights into practical solutions or actions.

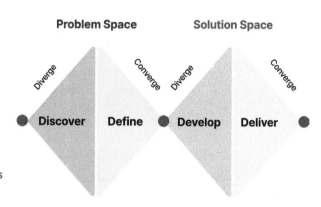

Recently, applying this framework to modern design challenges has sparked concerns that the Double Diamond may be limited. This has given rise to the Triple Diamond, an evolution that adds a third space to address the Double Diamond's perceived gap between solution and execution. There is less consensus on how to visualize and name these spaces. However, because we've adapted this Triple Diamond framework into our own DesignOps practice, we've created a version that is uniquely suited to Design Operations, seen here in Figure 14.3,

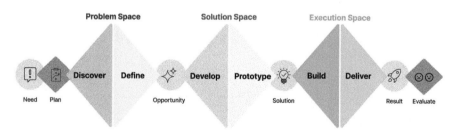

FIGURE 14.3
Triple Diamond for DesignOps includes Delivery and a feedback loop for improvement.

Our adaptation of the Triple Diamond framework incorporates the execution space, and it includes planning and evaluation as "touchpoints" in the design thinking journey. DesignOps can leverage this framework to gain a deeper understanding of design org challenges and to ensure that it is delivering the right things, at the right time, to the right people. This process involves empathizing with designers and other stakeholders, pinpointing key issues, ideating potential solutions, and prototyping strategies for implementation.

Let's take a look at each step of the adapted Triple Diamond framework, with an explanation of how the tool is applied to a specific DesignOps example: establishing an onboarding experience for the design organization.

The First Touchpoint: Planning

Once a need has been identified (in our example, improved onboarding), you begin by planning how you will proceed. This touchpoint reminds us of the adage "plans are useless, but planning is indispensable," because the planning process not only guides *how* you might continue, but *if* you should even proceed in the first place! In other words, should this need even be a DesignOps priority?

Assuming it is, DesignOps should plan how the project will be set up, what deliverables will be needed, agree upon the outcome, and create a single source of truth for program documentation. Here is an out-of-the-box planning toolkit (Table 14.1) adapted for our design strategy process; items with a ★ can be referenced in the toolkit at the end of this book.

TABLE 14.1 PLANNING TOOLKIT

Project Setup	Example Deliverables:
• Project Tools	• Program Plan ★
• Project Team	• Communications Plan ★
• Define Project Purpose	Example Tools:
• Project Stakeholders	• RACI Stakeholder Map ★
• Program Values	• Roadmap ★
• Audience/Customer	• Project Tool (Asana, etc.)
• Timeline and Milestones	Outcome:
• Project Comms Plan	Identified Need & Program Goal
• Task Tracker	Question to Answer:
• List of Resources	*Why and how are we doing this?*

Step 1: Discover

In our example, an onboarding gap was identified and prioritized, and a plan was created. Next, DesignOps initiated a comprehensive discovery phase. Actions included conducting user interviews with new hires and managers, exploring the onboarding problem through a mind map, analyzing existing onboarding processes, and assessing the specific needs and pain points within the UX team.

Through these activities, we discovered that the onboarding process lacked cohesion, leaving each manager to handle it independently. The decentralized approach led to varied experiences for new hires, who faced challenges understanding team processes, and had difficulty acquiring essential tools. Inexperienced managers, lacking past knowledge and tools, struggled to provide adequate support, resulting in new team members having to navigate these aspects independently. We discovered that onboarding involved seeking information from peers, managers, or outdated repositories, diverting time and focus from their core design responsibilities. Our discovery process highlighted the need for a more streamlined and supportive onboarding process, insights we gained by deploying some of the tools from our Discovery phase toolkit, shown in Table 14.2.

TABLE 14.2 DISCOVERY PHASE TOOLKIT

Explore the Problem Space:	**Example Milestones:**
• Understand user needs, landscape, context	• Stakeholder Kick-off Meeting
• Review existing information	• Interviews or Focus Groups
• Research how others have solved similar problems	• Discovery Share-out
Gap Analysis & Research:	**Example Tools:**
• Identify gaps in understanding	• Mind Maps ★
• Research (e.g., surveys, interviews, listening sessions)	• User Research (interviews, surveys, etc.)
Example Deliverables:	• Brainstorming
• Research Plan	• Card Sorting
• RACI Stakeholder Map ★	• Jobs to Be Done
	Question to Answer:
	What do we need to learn?

Step 2: Define

Define

Armed with our discovery data, DesignOps was able to synthesize the information into two overlapping user journeys: one for the manager experience and one for the new employee. This helped us see the gaps, pain points, and breakdowns in the process, as well as where there were opportunities to bring joy and bright spots into the onboarding experience.

These clarifying actions are a hallmark of the Definition phase, when information converges to form a data-backed perspective of what the *real* opportunity is. In our example, DesignOps actually defined two problems (the new hire and manager experience), and then used this knowledge to describe the objectives and scope of the new onboarding program. Our DesignOps spin on converging and defining the opportunities drew from our Definition phase toolkit (Table 14.3).

TABLE 14.3 DEFINITION PHASE TOOLKIT

Synthesis & Sense-Making	Example Milestones:
• Refine assumptions based on the learnings	Share-out of synthesized discovery findings and program updates
• Affinity Mapping	Example Deliverables:
• Synthesize into themes, clear findings, and recommendations.	• Research Findings
Example Tools:	• Recommendations
	• Updated Plan
• Affinity Mapping ★	Outcome:
• Personas	Opportunity Defined
• Journey Map ★	Question to Answer:
• Experience Map ★	*What did we learn and what problem(s) are we trying to solve?*

Step 3: Develop

As teams start to develop solutions, design strategy suggests that processes and tools should allow for divergence and exploration. In our onboarding example, the Development phase involved a comprehensive rebuilding of existing onboarding resources. We also explored onboarding ideas like making Slack more prominent, adding visual onboarding language to our materials, and updating our document's voice and tone. The team not only developed tailored content and generated new onboarding materials, but also overhauled the program framework based on insights garnered in earlier stages. We also collaborated with subject matter experts and content creators, guaranteeing the program's alignment with specific UX requirements. All in all, we used every tool from our Development phase toolkit (Table 14.4).

Develop

TABLE 14.4 DEVELOPMENT PHASE TOOLKIT

Design & Develop:	Example Milestones:
• Explore solutions and evaluate options	Share-out of your narrowed options and recommended solution
• Ideate solution options	**Example Tools:**
• Evaluate your ideas and narrow to your recommended approach	How Might We? (HMW)
• Follow up research	**Question to Answer:**
Example Deliverables:	*What could we do to solve this problem?*
All pilot materials and platforms	

Step 4: Prototype

With our onboarding ideas fully developed, it was time to converge on the best ones and prototype a path to success. This phase is crucial to test how solutions operate under real conditions, with real customers. Challenges of scale can be uncovered, and hidden dependencies brought to light.

Prototype

In our onboarding example, DesignOps planned a small-scale pilot to experiment and gather feedback before full implementation. This revealed two areas that needed further exploration: how new employees would *receive* onboarding information (all at once, or gradually over time), and the *sequencing* of onboarding topics as preferred by managers. For the pilot, an A/B test was designed to compare the effectiveness of providing information in a single batch versus a gradual trickle. In addition to a feedback survey, our teams utilized link tracking to gauge the engagement levels for each type. Additionally, a card sorting exercise was introduced to understand managers' preferences for what topics new hires should prioritize, and how to structure this information. This iterative approach allowed DesignOps to fine-tune the onboarding program based on insights gathered from the pilot, and it drew from some of tools in our Prototyping phase toolkit (Table 14.5).

TABLE 14.5 PROTOTYPING PHASE TOOLKIT

Prototype & Test: • Choose a solution to test • Create a prototype, a version that you can share with a small pilot group • Test/Analyze—get feedback on your solution • Iterate—update based on feedback • Update Program Plan	Example Milestones: Pilot Launch Example Deliverables: • Prototype Detail • Pilot Plan Example Tools: • Prototype Tools • Sketching
Outcome: Solution Defined	Question to Answer: *How would a specific solution work?*

Step 5: Build

After successful prototyping, it's time to advance to the Building phase. In our onboarding scenario, DesignOps scaled up the program by incorporating the Prototype phase feedback. Training materials were finalized, resources were readied to onboard an unexpectedly large group of new hires, and support was given to their hiring managers.

Beyond finalizing all materials and communications, DesignOps collaborated with a vendor to create a new onboarding welcome kit for all new hires, meticulously ensuring brand alignment for a positive first impression. Moreover, we strategically mapped out all interactions, roles, and ownership areas using a service blueprint (Figure 14.4 on page 228), actions drawn from our DesignOps Build phase toolkit (Table 14.6).

TABLE 14.6   BUILD PHASE TOOLKIT

Design & Build:	Example Milestones:
• Define a solution based on your pilot • Define a version that can scale beyond your pilot group • Create all parts of solution for launch • Refine Rollout Plan • Update Program Plan	Finalizing all elements of program **Example Deliverables:** • Solution Detail • Participant Guide • Launch & Rollout Plan **Example Tools:** Service Blueprint ★ **Question to Answer:** *What is needed for a successful rollout?*

Step 6: Deliver

Deliver

The onboarding program was officially delivered to the design team. DesignOps ensured a smooth execution by providing necessary training, resources, and support. Clear communication channels were established to address questions and implementation challenges. DesignOps followed its rollout plan and used a change management framework to help managers transition away from established (and outdated) onboarding processes to our new and improved way. Some of these actions were inspired by our Delivery phase toolkit (Table 14.7).

TABLE 14.7   DELIVERY PHASE TOOLKIT

Rollout & Execute	Example Deliverables:
• Follow your rollout plan • Announce the program • Communicate along the way • High-quality implementation **Example Milestones:** • Launch • Mid-point Check	Program Rollout **Example Tools:** ADKAR Framework **Outcome:** Final Result **Question to Answer:** *How can I deliver this?*

The Final Touchpoint: Evaluation

Job done? Not exactly. Our DesignOps Triple Diamond framework includes an evaluation touchpoint at the end of the process. Closing out our onboarding example, our DesignOps team made sure to evaluate the new program's effectiveness. They collected participant feedback, analyzed key performance indicators, and assessed the program's alignment with its defined objectives. DesignOps conducted a retrospective to gain comprehensive insights into the program's performance and identify areas for improvement. They synthesized program data, considering factors such as open rates, question patterns, and survey results.

Using these insights, DesignOps created a roadmap for future updates to evolve the program further. Additionally, they took the opportunity to narrate the program's story, articulating its impact, and incorporating visual elements like photos and feedback from stakeholders. This holistic summary ensured that design leaders thoroughly understood the program's performance, and it is one of the tools we recommend in our evaluation toolkit (Table 14.8).

TABLE 14.8   EVALUATION TOOLKIT

Evaluate & Follow-Up	Example Milestones:
• Send Surveys • Retrospective • Analyze Outcomes • Synthesize the Program Data • Outline Recommendations for Future Iterations • Post Delivery Follow-up • Project Summary	Retrospective **Example Deliverables:** • Program Summary • Maintenance Plan • Roadmap for Program Evolution ★ **Example Tools:** • Surveys • Data Tracking **Question to Answer:** *How did it go and what did we learn?*

The previous example of how we adapted design thinking methods and the Triple Diamond framework to overhaul our onboarding program (Figure 14.4) is a perfect encapsulation of this book's core theme: that DesignOps *is* design. The behaviors, actions, and skills our discipline deploys each day are rooted in proven design frameworks, and the more these two practices are integrated, the better our combined creations will be.

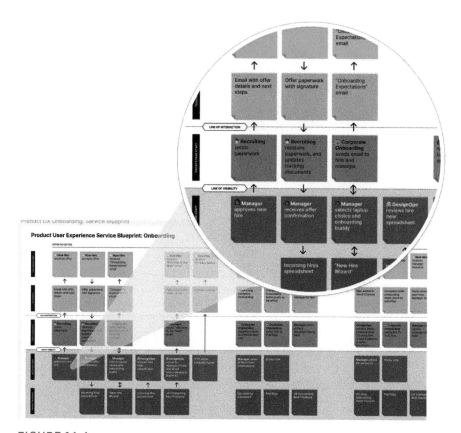

FIGURE 14.4

This onboarding service blueprint by Laine Riley Prokay, Principal DPM at Salesforce, was used to ensure a smooth delivery of the program and helped identify opportunities to improve the experience.

Integrating Change Management for DesignOps

The second important design tool in the DesignOps toolkit is change management. Change, especially in the fast-paced world of technology and design, is inevitable. It can also be stressful and disruptive: 73% of employees experience moderate to high stress when change occurs, impacting performance and potentially leading to job departures.[1] The reason can be associated with a phenomenon known as *uncertainty bias*, which influences how individuals handle change.

---

1   Gartner, 2019, www.gartner.com/en/corporate-communications/insights/
    change-communication

When faced with significant changes, the brain tends to perceive them as negative by default, which can increase feelings of anxiety and stress. Also, when individuals are uncertain about how a change will affect them personally, they are more likely to perceive it as stressful, especially if they strongly identify with their personal roles and responsibilities within the organization.[2]

DesignOps helps individuals and design teams navigate change confidently. This support and partnership is so crucial to the role that we believe there is effectively no Design Operations *without* change management—change is embedded in just about all aspects of this discipline.

As a strategy, change management prioritizes people as its primary focus, emphasizing the importance of empathetic guidance, and bringing equal attention to the technical aspects of change (the "what") and the often-overlooked *human* elements (the "how and "why"). Recognizing that 70% of transformation efforts fail because they neglect the impacts of change on people,[3] it's important that DesignOps understands and dedicates energy to responsible change management practices.

Change can vary in size and scope, but here are five things to keep in mind for the responsible management of change:

- **People-first:** Prioritize the well-being and psychological safety of the people impacted by change.
- **Intentionality:** Ditch the improvisation. Be structured and guide people through change with clarity and purpose.
- **Values-driven:** Champion organizational values and use these as your compass to navigate change management.
- **Inclusivity:** Partner and collaborate with diverse perspectives to drive change that benefits everyone.
- **Sustainability:** Consider the long-term impact and footprint of change management for all of your stakeholders.

---

2 B. Wisse and E. Sleebos, "When Change Causes Stress: Effects of Self-construal and Change Consequences." *Journal of Business and Psychology* 31, no. 2 (2016): 249–264.

3 Michael Beer and Nitin Nohria, "Cracking the Code of Change," *Harvard Business Review*, May–June 2000, https://hbr.org/2000/05/cracking-the-code-of-change

The DesignOps practice is rooted in responsible change management, equipped to skillfully guide teams through many forms of change. These forms exist as "layers of change," with different layers being closer (and further) from the sphere of control a DesignOps practice can reasonably expect to have. Our Layers of Change framework (Figure 14.5) define this spectrum, visualizing how change impacting an individual and team is closest to our sphere of control, with organizational and macro-environmental level changes further out. This framework helps DesignOps practitioners identify which layer of change they are dealing with and understand how much control they have over the outcomes.

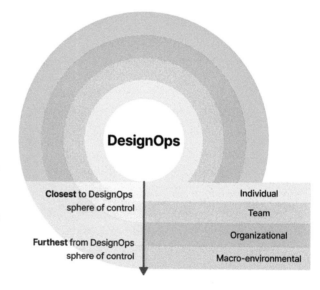

FIGURE 14.5
The Layers of Change framework illustrates that change occurs across multiple facets of our lives, within different spheres of control.

Individual Change

This layer of change focuses on *individual transitions*, both personal and professional, and is closest to what DesignOps practitioners can control. Here, DesignOps offers one-on-one support to design leaders, aids in onboarding new team members, and serves as an organizational guide. DesignOps can also help navigate life transitions like parenthood and medical leave, providing valuable resources like extended-leave planning templates and re-entry onboarding checklists. By providing this holistic support, DesignOps empowers individuals to manage change with confidence and clarity.

Team Change

When design teams grapple with new tools, priorities, workflows, and rhythms of work, DesignOps steps in as the central guide. It facilitates smooth transitions by providing training and guidance, helps teams adapt to shifting priorities while maintaining alignment, fosters new ways of engaging and collaborating effectively, and even introduces new team forums or rituals to strengthen connection and understanding. Essentially, DesignOps empowers the design team to navigate change *collectively*, building a more resilient and cohesive organization.

Organizational Change

DesignOps plays a critical role in supporting organizational transformations by helping teams adapt to leadership transitions, restructurings, strategic shifts, and workforce reductions. It can facilitate communication, clarify expectations, map new team structures, define roles, manage knowledge transfer, guide resource allocation, and support team morale during challenging times. Even though DesignOps may have reduced control or influence during such changes, it is still instrumental for establishing continuity and stability.

Macro-Environmental Change

Beyond organizational shifts, DesignOps helps teams navigate broader societal and environmental changes, like economic fluctuations, political unrest, or pandemics. While it (obviously) can't control these macro-environmental forces, it can empower design teams with the tools and resources to manage change effectively, by creating well-being initiatives, maintaining clear communication, and advocating for inclusive team practices. By acknowledging and adjusting to external factors, DesignOps fosters resilience, mental health, and even the ability to contribute positive change in wider contexts.

Change Management Models for DesignOps

Similar to the diverse array of models found for design thinking (double diamonds, triple diamonds, and the like), change management *also* has many methodologies. One popular framework is the Prosci method, championed by Jeff Hiatt. After studying how hundreds of organizations navigated change, Hiatt developed the Prosci method to help teams clearly and practically approach change. This method provides two distinct models, suited to how close or far the change exists from the DesignOps sphere of control. The first model focuses on helping organizations adapt, while the second empowers individuals to embrace change with confidence.

The Prosci Model for Organizational Change

The Prosci method proposes a three-phase process (Figure 14.6) for managing change at the organizational level. It provides a structured framework for planning, implementing, and sustaining change initiatives. Each phase is broken down into three stages, and each stage includes important activities to support the success of change initiatives.

These phases are:

1. **Prepare your approach.** In the first phase, you focus on defining goals, identifying affected groups, specifying adoption strategies, and planning the necessary steps for project success.

2. **Manage your change.** The second phase focuses on bringing the change to life by developing plans, actions, and tracking progress. This phase also encourages adaptation based on continuous learning.

3. **Sustain your outcomes.** In the third phase, you focus on establishing an approach to ensure the adoption of change and implement actions to sustain the achieved changes over time.

FIGURE 14.6

Where design strategy frameworks sometimes lack operational guidance, the Prosci 3-Phase Process for organizational change steps in to offer clear action steps.

The ADKAR Model for Individual Change

While the Prosci 3-Phase Process provides a clear roadmap for navigating *organizational* change, it is too high-level to guide *individual* transformations. This is where the Prosci method's ADKAR Model comes in. ADKAR is a guide for individual journeys through change, designed to fit inside the "manage your change" phase (described earlier). It ensures that each person not only has the support and understanding they need to move forward, but also the desire and vision to explore new horizons with confidence. This model for individual change is reminiscent of Antoine de Saint-Exupéry's advice:

> If you want to build a ship, don't drum up the [people] to gather wood, divide the work, and give orders. Instead, teach them to yearn for the vast and endless sea.

Each letter of the ADKAR acronym (Figure 14.7) represents a crucial step in this personal journey:

FIGURE 14.7
The ADKAR framework is an excellent blend of user centricity and operational rigor.

- **Awareness:** Start by getting clear on why this change is happening. What problem is it trying to solve, and what are the anticipated benefits? Knowing the "big picture" helps people understand how the individual change impacting them personally fits into the overall vision. Here, compelling narratives, visuals, and FAQs can spark individual understanding and buy-in.

- **Desire:** Don't just inform, inspire! Help people see how the change aligns with their personal goals and aspirations. Does it offer new skills, career growth, or contribute to a bigger purpose? Tailor messaging to different groups, highlighting individual benefits so that people can see what's in it for them and embrace the change with enthusiasm.

- **Knowledge:** Empower people with the skills, tools, information, and resources they need to navigate the change. Develop comprehensive training programs, clear documentation, and accessible support channels. Remember, knowledge builds confidence and reduces anxiety.

- **Ability:** Help people move from theory to action. Provide ample opportunities for people to practice and learn by doing. Design workshops, training sessions, and office hours to ensure that everyone feels comfortable and competent using the new approach.

I vividly remember attending a conference years ago. As the speaker dove into change management, I felt a wave of realization—not a comfortable one. Like a lightbulb flickering on, I saw how I'd been neglecting a crucial aspect of my role: the "human" side of change.

As a seasoned design program manager, user needs and empathy were second nature. Yet, embarrassingly, I admitted to myself that I was "winging" the people side of change within my own team. The "what" part of the change equation came naturally. I think in systems, so I can make project plans in my sleep, and breaking down big programs into manageable chunks is clear to me. But guiding them through the emotional rollercoaster of new processes and tools? That, I hadn't honed in on a structured approach.

The model I learned that day, and is now my North Star, was the ADKAR model, a beacon of clarity developed by Jeff Hiatt. This model is based on the analysis of hundreds of successful and unsuccessful organizational changes over many years. It outlines five outcomes an individual needs to achieve for a change to be successful.

Now, these five steps form the backbone of many of the DesignOps programs we design. Every new process requiring behavior change gets planned with each ADKAR principle in mind. I have found this process to be cyclical since most of our DesignOps programs are ongoing and require regular iterative refreshes.

This journey, from that conference realization to the ADKAR framework, has fundamentally shaped my approach to DesignOps. It's a constant reminder that even the most well-designed systems need compassionate human guidance to truly succeed.

- **Reinforcement:** Sustain the momentum over time. Recognize and celebrate efforts, progress, and successes along the way. Offer ongoing support, address challenges collaboratively, and create a culture of continuous learning. Remember, positive reinforcement keeps motivation high.

ADKAR reminds DesignOps practitioners that they're not just implementing a change—they're guiding people through a journey. By using ADKAR as your roadmap, you can equip your team with the understanding, motivation, and skills needed to embrace change, and ultimately drive success.

Design Strategy and Change Management Together

We've explored design strategy and change management as discrete toolkits within DesignOps, but they are also complementary. And like peanut butter and jelly, these frameworks are even better when paired together.

Design strategy excels at human-centered problem solving, revealing deep user needs and discovering innovative solutions. Putting those solutions into action is where change management shines. It seamlessly bridges the gap between creative ideation and real-world implementation, ensuring smooth adoption and lasting impact. Working hand-in-hand, these methodologies create a holistic problem-solving approach: design strategy ensures that solutions resonate with people, while change management equips those people to embrace these new solutions. Ultimately, this collaboration fosters lasting positive change for both users and organizations.

Merging the Triple Diamond framework and the Prosci 3-Phase Process (Figure 14.8) reveals a natural alignment between their respective phases.

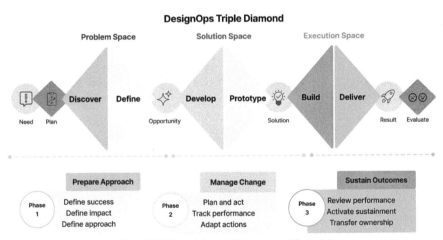

FIGURE 14.8

Combining design strategy and change management practices is a powerful approach for addressing DesignOps problems, leveraging the strengths of both design and operations.

Returning to our onboarding program example, it became evident that DesignOps had to manage dual tracks: to both *design* a new solution and to *transition* individuals from an outdated approach to a new one. The demand for design strategy and change management was right in front of us, underscoring their importance in the Design Operations toolkit. And seeing this has driven *our* practice of deploying these powerful tools from the beginning for all major DesignOps programs.

Coda: Staying in Tune

Implementing these processes and frameworks into your daily DesignOps work may seem (initially) to be unrealistic or daunting. However, these tools give DesignOps *superpowers*, not constraints. They're meant to guide and empower you, not dictate a rigid process. If strictly following every step proves too complicated, don't do it. Instead, understand the "why" behind each tool; then adapt and apply them flexibly to your programs and ever-evolving organizational landscape. *Embrace* these methods—experiment, play, and discover what works best for you. In doing so, you'll equip yourself to meet challenges head-on and to transform them into opportunities for growth and improvement within your dynamic design environments.

Measure by Measure
Measuring What Matters

M usic moves forward in measures. They're the basic unit of time that unify a song's beat, rhythm, and melody into a segment that musicians use to decode how a piece should be played.

DesignOps also relies on measures—but for our discipline, the word connotes something entirely different. *Measures*, as a noun, are quite literally anything that can be measured and compared: attendee count, survey ratings, time-on-task, Net Promoter Score, and the like. DesignOps practitioners also use *measure* as a verb, literally meaning to measure or count quantifiable values like those described above. But the way in which Design Operations most often talks about measures and measuring is in the context of "measuring DesignOps value"—capturing and quantifying the (seemingly elusive) evidence of how DesignOps programs and practitioners are contributing to and improving design health and delivery.

Measuring DesignOps value is surprisingly complicated. Many practitioners would agree with the sentiment that measuring their impact feels aspirational at best and theoretical at worst. Anecdotal evidence and praise from partners ("I don't know what we'd do without you!") is nice but doesn't add up to proof that DesignOps is a worthy return on investment. We feel this way, too, and believe there are a few reasons that measuring DesignOps value can seem so tricky.

First, ours is a relatively new discipline supporting a relatively misunderstood practice; in other words, business leaders lack a shared understanding of design's values, let alone DesignOps'. In Chapter 10, "From Soloist to Symphony," we shared how only 20% of design organizations demonstrate mature measurement practices, meaning a full 80% of design orgs lack effective or consistent ways to measure the impact of their contributions. Second, one of the basic principles of DesignOps is something that makes this discipline nearly impossible to standardize: our practitioners are malleable, molded by the needs of their particular business and design teams. No two DPMs look exactly alike—even when they work on the same team! DesignOps is a flexible and adaptable practice, meaning its goals and outcomes are more fluid than stable, and more challenging to measure consistently.

Team sizes and ratios further compound this challenge. DesignOps teams are often small and stretched thin. Just doing the work is hard enough; finding time to establish a comprehensive measurement system can feel out of reach and may even get in the way of delivering actual value. Larger, established DesignOps teams face similar hurdles. For them, operating models and workstreams create differentiation between DesignOps roles, which challenges their ability to measure and summarize how the organization is doing as a whole.

Measuring Value Means Defining Value

Here's the good news: even with those challenges, 52% of DesignOps practitioners report that their work has clearly defined objectives and outcomes, and 41% report that they have measures to assess DesignOps impact.[1] That feels like a pretty good start!

Given that design exhibits a wide range of maturity in measurement practices, we don't suggest that all DesignOps practitioners go out and set up a robust measurement system right away. Being data-driven is good, and being data-influenced is better; but recognizing that there are many ways to show value beyond purely quantitative methods—i.e., *just doing good work*—is best of all. While measures certainly have their place, the most compelling proof of DesignOps' value lies in the quality of the work itself. As design leader and author Sara Wachter-Boettcher eloquently puts it:

> Endlessly justifying yourself rarely changes others' opinions. It just positions design [and DesignOps] as something that's up for debate. It also does nothing to create that elusive "impact." Because the more time we spend explaining why design matters, the less time we have to improve the actual product.[2]

Focusing on the work itself, being consistently present in its impacts, and loudly championing those achievements, are powerful means for DesignOps to showcase its value. In the end, leaders are more likely to invest in what they can witness directly rather than what requires extensive justification. By showcasing exceptional work, DesignOps can authentically demonstrate its significance.

---

1   *2023 DesignOps Benchmarking Report* (DesignOps Assembly, 2023), www.designopsassembly.com/2023report

2   Sara Wachter-Boettcher, "Hey Designers, They're Gaslighting You," *Medium* (blog), October 25, 2023, https://medium.com/nice-work-from-active-voice/hey-designers-theyre-gaslighting-you-e02e5a4d9cff

Design leader Jared Spool says this on the importance of making the invisible, well—visible:

> Visibility is the most vital thing for UX leaders to be focusing on. You can't expect executives and stakeholders to invest in and prioritize your team's efforts without making your UX work visible at every level of an organization. This is a strategic imperative.

It's also important to see that value is bigger than a quantifiable measure; it is the worth, significance, and importance that something holds for individuals and organizations. Value exceeds the narrow confines of financial or functional usefulness—it's the very thing that makes us human, like our experiences, aspirations, and even our identity. In her essay, "The Value of Design Is Holding You Back," Jen Briselli challenges readers to think differently about value. Instead of focusing on the value of design, she suggests focusing on *designing value*.[3] Designing value is the process of intentionally creating, improving, or optimizing value for stakeholders through thoughtful and strategic design practices. This perspective moves the conversation away from purely transactional considerations and toward the transformative potential of design and DesignOps.

The way people perceive and define value is often influenced by powerful corporate systems. We, as authors, want to challenge these ingrained definitions of value to foster a more comprehensive and human-centered approach, considering not just shareholders but *stakeholders* and their broader ecosystem. And to achieve this goal, we need to rethink the traditional ways in which value is defined and how it's measured.

New Approaches to Measuring DesignOps Value

To be clear, DesignOps must maintain basic measures of its impact; don't toss out those easily-accessible numbers, percentages, and spreadsheets just yet. But we maintain that there are more radical approaches to defining DesignOps measures—methods that break from the traditions and norms described previously and make it easier to center success on the concept of "designing value."

---

3   Jen Briselli, "The Value of Design Is Holding You Back," *Design Museum Magazine*, Issue 021, 2021.

In this chapter, we'll share two of these methods: the Jobs to Be Done framework and the DesignOps HEROES framework. These unconventional approaches can be used to uncover and define value measures that more accurately capture the impact that DesignOps and design have on a business and its stakeholders. And because using either (or both) of these methods will generate a huge new set of measures to consider, we also share some tested rubrics that your DesignOps practice can use to prioritize and implement these new measures. Through this strategy of using new frameworks to define your outcomes, and new tools to prioritize and bring them to life, we hope that teams will feel more connected to the work they do and be better able to understand how that work is connected to the value they create.

The Jobs to Be Done Framework

The Jobs to Be Done (JTBD) framework is a theory from marketing and business development. In short, the concept states that customers buy products—or hire services—to get a specific job done. Sounds obvious, right? But the beauty of this framework is its focus on understanding these jobs, and the job performers' motivations and needs while doing the underlying tasks, to effectively reverse-engineer a better product or service. The concept is sometimes best understood via this quote: "People don't want to buy a quarter-inch drill. They want a quarter-inch hole."

Simply put: don't start with the solution in mind—start with the customer's need. The JTBD framework can be used just as effectively in DesignOps to better understand the motivations and needs of design orgs. In our slightly modified version of this framework, DesignOps itself is the product, and designers are the customer. In this relationship, the JTBD question becomes: "How well does DesignOps know its customers' jobs to be done? Given the chance to rehire (or "buy") DesignOps again to help them accomplish their jobs, would our customers choose us again?"

Getting to the heart of that question requires researching DesignOps' "customers" through the lens of the JTBD framework. The answers can lead DesignOps to new insights about how to meet the needs of its customers, define its measures, and prioritize and improve its work. Figure 15.1 shows how to do it.

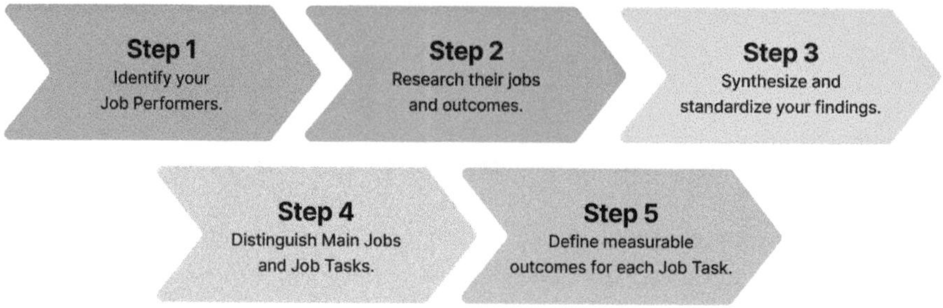

Step 1
Identify your
Job Performers.

Step 2
Research their jobs
and outcomes.

Step 3
Synthesize and
standardize your findings.

Step 4
Distinguish Main Jobs
and Job Tasks.

Step 5
Define measurable
outcomes for each Job Task.

FIGURE 15.1

The five steps of the JTBD framework. This marketing and business development methodology can be applied to DesignOps.

Step 1: Identify Your Job Performers

Your DesignOps customers aren't a monolith. Numerous types of designer have hired DesignOps to help them accomplish their everyday tasks. The first step of the JTBD framework is to identify these *job performers*: the groups of roles, personas, and individuals that can be categorized together based on similar jobs and outcomes. Workshops and affinity mapping are great ways to accomplish this step. Your outcome should be a well-defined set of job performer categories to share with your stakeholders, such that everyone you work with can unambiguously point to a group and say, "Yes, that's me!"

When we ran this exercise on our stakeholders, we identified the following six categories of job performer:

- Design Individual Contributors
- Design Managers
- Design Executive Leadership
- Design Development Partners
- Design Business Partners
- Designer Ecosystem

Step 2: Research Their Jobs and Outcomes

Next, research what *jobs* your job performers do regularly and what *outcomes* they are seeking. You may use surveys, interviews, and your own prior knowledge. For each job performer category, seek to understand the following:

- **The When:** The circumstances that triggered their jobs
- **The What:** The social and emotional motivations surrounding their jobs
- **The Why:** The outcomes to be achieved by doing their jobs

Remember not to insert your own current DesignOps jobs into the conversation. For example, you wouldn't ask about the processes or programs your DesignOps team already creates—those are the solutions to what you think your customers need. Instead, have a conversation about your customers' work in a world in which they (hypothetically) haven't hired you.

Step 3: Synthesize and Standardize Your Findings

Make sense of your research by simplifying and standardizing the responses; this will help you classify and find patterns among your job performers. In the JTBD framework, a common standardization method is to use the "Verb + Object (+ Clarifier)" format. Use this technique to define the job the performer wants to do, not the process they are currently doing.

Some examples of how jobs and outcomes might be restated using this V+O (+C) format:

- Connect with designers from other product areas.
- Measure your team's progress.
- Discover existing templates, assets, and components.
- Validate your designs with end users.
- Educate your product stakeholders on your UX processes.

Step 4: Distinguish Main Jobs and Job Tasks

With these standardized job statements in place, the next step is to distinguish between *main jobs* and the underlying *job tasks*. Main jobs are what your customers actually want to get done; job tasks are the incremental steps. It's important to distinguish between the two, because you don't want to risk optimizing your DesignOps team to deliver on tasks and accidentally miss critical customer jobs. In other words, if customers say they want to "boil water," and also say they want to "prepare a hot beverage to drink," it's your responsibility to know which is the main job, and which is the underlying task.

Here's a small sample of what this step looked like for our design manager customer. Using the V+O (+C) format, some of their main jobs might be:

- Deliver design strategies.
- Enable individual growth.
- Foster team connections.
- Access organizational knowledge.
- Amplify the team's voice.
- Access qualified staffing pipelines.

And the underlying job tasks (using the same format) for that first main job are:

Deliver design strategies to:

- Educate your stakeholders on your design processes.
- Staff design priorities according to business needs.
- Establish collaboration frameworks for designers and developers.

Step 5: Define Measurable Outcomes for Each Job Task

This is the step that brings the JTBD framework back to measuring DesignOps value: *defining measurable outcomes* for each job task. This is the level of granularity at which the work your DesignOps team does can be connected to the observable, measurable changes in the outcomes your customers value most. Accomplishing this step requires you to define outcomes of each job task in measurable language; we choose the "Direction + Object + Outcome" format to define our outcomes:

- **Direction:** The change the object takes when the outcome is successful.
- **Object:** The object you can observe and measure.
- **Outcome:** The thing changed by the job task.

Putting it all together—the main job, the job task, and the measurable outcome—creates a concise, simple articulation of what your customers want to do, and how to know that your DesignOps solutions are helping them do those jobs better. Here are two examples of what the JTBD framework produced for our Design IC job performer—notably aligning to the DesignOps outcomes of clarity, confidence, and connection from Chapter 2, "Learning the Score."

TABLE 15.1 DESIGN IC MAIN JOB #1 WITH TASK AND OUTCOMES

Main Job #1: "Build my skills and experience" to confidently develop within and for our product ecosystem			
"I want to…" (Job tasks)	"…so that I can" (Measurable outcomes)		
V+O (+C) format	Direction	Object	Outcome
Sharpen my competency with our design tools	speed up	delivery of	quality artifacts I need to successfully and efficiently collaborate with my stakeholders.
Discover existing templates, assets, and components	speed up	delivery of	pattern and behavior explorations I need to rapidly experiment with solutions.
Master my understanding of our design system and patterns	maximize	confidence in	how my solutions are compatible with our existing implementations and expectations for usability.
Become a certified designer	maximize	confidence in	how my deliverables are consistent with the values and principles of my design org.
Discover existing product journeys and feature click-throughs	increase	clarity of	our products' existing (and intended) user experience flows.
Learn about internal tooling and support groups	increase	connection with	the teams that can help me get more efficient working at my company.

TABLE 15.2 DESIGN IC MAIN JOB #2 WITH TASK AND OUTCOMES

Main Job #2: "Deliver product value and impact" to my users, customers, stakeholders, and our designer ecosystem			
"I want to…" (Job tasks)	**"…so that I can"** (Measurable outcomes)		
V+O (+C) format	**Direction**	**Object**	**Outcome**
Navigate the roles of our (and our functional partners') organization	increase	connection with	the right people or roles with whom I need to partner.
Work within familiar, trusted collaboration frameworks	increase	confidence in	the digital artifacts I create to share, review, and hand off to my development team(s).
Validate my designs with end users	increase	confidence in	the efficacy and relevance of my solution to what our users are trying to achieve with our products.
Partner with other service teams (Design Systems, Content, A11Y)	increase	confidence in	how my designs align to the right patterns these groups depend on to get their jobs done.
Democratize access to our shared planning and prioritization artifacts	increase	clarity of	how my designs' estimates, commitments, and deliverables are shared with my partners.
Understand the needs of the customer and their pain points	increase	advocacy for	product outcomes that make our customers' lives easier.

Why Use the JTBD Framework?

Compared to the HEROES framework (discussed in the next section), the JTBD framework is recommended when the design org is relatively mature and can confidently state what its jobs and outcomes are. There is an assumption, too, that the DesignOps team is capable of measuring the necessary objects—time, confidence, delivery, clarity, etc.—to show that its processes and programs have moved the outcome in the right direction.

FUTURE-PROOFING OUR PRACTICE

Allison Rand, strategic design and operations lead

Blending qualitative and quantitative data ensures that the disciplines of design and DesignOps remain relevant and evolve. This integration improves the practice and empowers designers. It involves taking the core element of design—behavior as a medium—and combining it with complex data to improve the practice and achieve tangible business outcomes.

A unique opportunity exists to expand our capabilities, mainly through Design Intelligence. This frontier allows for the fusion of strategic foresight, ethical considerations, and artificial intelligence capabilities. The challenges (and opportunities) are in realizing the full potential of this convergence to future-proof our practices and to delve into its wide-ranging implications.

Design Operations can be incredibly influential in creating not just design change but human change. The next phase for DesignOps is about taking everything we know about craft excellence and design work acceleration and evolving it to become less siloed and more impactful across the organization. Talking about planned obsolescence is controversial but likely inevitable, so we should get ahead of it. Remember what Eric Shinseki said: "If you don't like change, you're going to like irrelevance even less."

Although rooted in marketing, using the JTBD framework on the design org enables DesignOps to move upstream and think holistically about how its customers are working every day, and embrace their jobs and outcomes as its own. This shift in mindset can enable DesignOps to:

- **Advance DesignOps relationship with its customers.** How well do customers see themselves in DesignOps' goals and roadmap? Are its deliverables and solutions things they would "hire" DesignOps to do? The JTBD framework asks customers the right questions to prioritize DesignOps work according to *their* needs.

- **Measure DesignOps value and impact.** Inherent to JTBD is defining outcomes in measurable language: What's the object you'll measure? What direction do you want it to move in? Measuring your outcomes is a clear and direct way to demonstrate how DesignOps adds value and impact.

- **Uncover new DesignOps opportunities.** What opportunities exist that DesignOps hasn't discovered or prioritized? Is there something innovative and high-value to say *yes* to? (And, at the same time, say *no* to things that aren't providing a similar impact?)

The DesignOps HEROES Framework

The aptly-named DesignOps HEROES framework (Figure 15.2) is our tool to help DesignOps teams navigate the complicated task of

H	E	R
Health	**Effectiveness**	**Readiness**
How healthy is the design org, and how happy and fulfilled are the teams?	*How effective and efficient are teams at delivering their work?*	*How prepared are teams with the skills and knowledge to excel in their roles?*
• Employee satisfaction scores • Job satisfaction index • Job security confidence score • Leadership confidence score • Turnover rate • Attrition rate • Regrettable attrition rate • Retention rate • Engagement rate • Morale score • Participation rates • Burnout score • Number of designers with mentors, or sponsors • Promotion rate • Utilization of education reimbursement • Diversity of hiring pipeline • Diversity of leadership • Diversity of workforce • Work-life-balance scores • Recognition & reward scores • Workplace environment scores • Value alignment scores	• Process adoption rate • Template utilization rate • Tool utilization rate • Design system adoption rate • Team charter count • Design sprint count • Velocity • Task completion rate • Deadline achievement rate • On-time delivery rate • On-time release milestone rate • Make vs. meet time • Hand-off cycle time • Design debt • Design quality score • Definition of ready compliance rate • Definition of done compliance rate • Design consistency score • Talent utilization • Goal completion rate • Stakeholder satisfaction scores	• Training completion rates • Training effectiveness scores • Skills assessment scores • Tool utilization • Playbooks and guide utilization • Communication open rates • Internal event engagement rate • Tool utilization • Participation in development opportunities • Participation in mentorship programs • Participation in leadership programs • Skills assessment scores • Adherence to UX best practices • User research participation rate • Design system adherence rate • Self-service improvement (i.e., reduction in questions to DesignOps)

FIGURE 15.2a

The DesignOps HEROES framework by Rachel Posman.

measuring its impact when the design org is less mature or needs some help defining its own success measures and outcomes. Less of a step-by-step process and more of a menu and questionnaire, the HEROES framework accelerates DesignOps' ability to define a set of outcomes and measures that matter to their design org and start executing on these.

In the next few pages, you'll learn some desired outcomes your DesignOps team can measure and deliver for each of the six HEROES categories.

O	E	S
Outcomes	**Ecosystem**	**Sentiment**
To what extent do the products and services prove useful, valuable, and impactful?	*How do the products/services we design and the DesignOps choices we make influence the broader ecosystem's impact?*	*What is the perception and understanding of design outside of your design org?*
• Customer-satisfaction score (CSAT) • Net promoter score (NPS) • System usability scale (SUS) • Ease of use rating • Confidence rating • Task completion rate • Time on task • Success rate • Frequency of use rate • Error rate • User engagement rate • User conversion rate • User retention rate • Design-quality scores • Feature adoption scores • Product accessibility scores • Competitive and industry benchmark scores • Perceived value • Patent count	• Sustainability policy adherence • Swag sustainability score • Event sustainability score • Volunteering hours • Teaching and giving back hours • Diversity of guest speakers • Diversity of hiring pipeline • Diversity of recruiting channels • Diversity and responsibility of vendors • Bias in job descriptions • WCAG compliance level • Product accessibility score • Inclusive design score • Ethical design score • User trust score • Privacy standard compliance (GDPR, CCPA) • Privacy impact assessments (PIA) • AI fairness impact assessment • Fair or anti patterns	• Number of non-design internal advocates • Design budget allocation total • Number of positive design mentions internally • Number of external champions supporting design initiatives • Cross-organizational meeting participation rate • Number of design leadership roles • Number of non-design recognition and awards • Number of design blogs and articles published • Designer participation rate at customer events • Event speaking engagement rate • Participation in design training sessions (e.g., design thinking) for non-designers • Non-designer participation rate in design programs

FIGURE 15.2b
The DesignOps HEROES framework.

Health

This category considers design org health. Measures like employee satisfaction, attrition, and morale are all objects that can be directly measured to answer the questions: *How healthy is the design org? And how happy and fulfilled are the design teams?* Some measurable outcomes and impact delivered in this category include:

- **Improved designer well-being and morale:** DesignOps fosters a supportive environment with clear roles, responsibilities, and communication channels, leading to reduced stress and increased job satisfaction.

- **Enhanced team collaboration and trust:** DesignOps encourages open communication and collaboration, creating a sense of belonging and fostering a healthy team dynamic.

Effectiveness

This category considers design org effectiveness. Measures like delivery times, task completion, and capacity are all objects that can be directly measured to answer the question: *How effective and efficient are teams at delivering their work?* Some measurable outcomes and impact delivered in this category include:

- **Increased design efficiency and productivity:** DesignOps streamlines workflows, eliminates bottlenecks, and optimizes processes, leading to faster design cycles and higher output.

- **Reduced rework and errors:** DesignOps establishes clear guidelines, playbooks, standards, and tools, minimizing the potential for rework and time spent outside of design work.

Readiness

This category considers design org readiness. Measures like tool usage, training completion, and participation rates are all objects that can be directly measured to answer the question: *How prepared are teams with the skills and knowledge to excel in their roles?* Some measurable outcomes and impact delivered in this category include:

- **Upskilled and empowered design teams:** DesignOps facilitates continuous learning and development opportunities, ensuring that designers possess the necessary skills and knowledge to excel in their roles.

- **Future-proofed design capabilities:** DesignOps helps teams adapt to evolving technologies and industry shifts, keeping them well-prepared for future challenges and opportunities.

Outcomes

This category considers the outcomes created by the design organization. While DesignOps' influence on these measures is less direct, they still reflect the impact DesignOps has on enhancing the quality of design deliverables, particularly for product-oriented DesignOps teams striving to improve the overall standard of design work. Measures like satisfaction ratings, competitive benchmarks, and time-on-task are all objects that can be directly measured to answer the question: *To what extent do the products and services prove useful, valuable, and impactful?* Some measurable outcomes and impact delivered in this category include:

- **Delivering user-centered and impactful products and services:** DesignOps promotes and facilitates user research and feedback loops, resulting in designs that are not only usable but also valuable and impactful for users.
- **Measurable and demonstrable ROI (return on investment):** DesignOps facilitates the tracking and measurement of design impact, enabling teams to showcase the tangible value they bring to the organization.

Ecosystem

This category considers stakeholders and the broader ecosystem in which the design org exists. Measures like environmental impact, volunteering time, and diversity can all be directly measured to answer the question: *How do the products/services you design and the DesignOps choices you make influence the broader ecosystem's impact?* Some measurable outcomes and impact delivered in this category include:

- **Positive societal and environmental impact:** DesignOps encourages thoughtful consideration of the broader ecosystem with vendors, speakers, partnerships, and design processes, leading to operational decisions that are mindful of their social and environmental impact.
- **Responsible and ethical design practices:** DesignOps promotes ethical and responsible design practices and operations, ensuring that designs are inclusive, accessible, trustworthy, and responsible (think gen AI and data privacy).

Sentiment

This category considers the sentiment of design (as a discipline and as a team) outside the design org. Measures like UX budget allocation, number of design leadership roles, and number of participants in design training programs are all objects that can be directly measured to answer the question: *What is the perception and understanding of design outside of your design org?* Some measurable outcomes and impact delivered in this category include:

- **Empowering cross-functional collaboration and increasing design literacy:** DesignOps fosters a shared language and breaks down departmental silos. This allows teams across the organization to work together more effectively, with a deeper understanding of design's strategic role in achieving common goals.

- **Design evangelism and storytelling:** DesignOps facilitates internal and external methods for highlighting design's impact on user experience and business results. They celebrate and recognize design's successes and empower designers, fostering informal and formal knowledge sharing opportunities.

Why Use the HEROES Framework?

Compared to the JTBD framework, the HEROES framework is recommended when DesignOps needs to jump-start its ability to measure its contributions to a design org's success. This framework visibly and confidently connects DesignOps' outcomes with the design org's. The exercises and questions can be considered with or without the participation of design, although we certainly recommend the former. While the HEROES framework provides off-the-shelf measures and some associated example outcomes, remember that each category should reflect measures specific to *your* unique organizational context.

Prioritizing and Refining Measures

We recommend the JTBD and HEROES frameworks as a means of discovering and defining measures that more accurately capture the impact that design and DesignOps have on a business. The exercises can be inspirational; they can also generate a lot of measures—some of which are not necessary, feasible, or even advisable to pursue.

While it can be tempting to say *yes* to anything that even remotely sniffs of impact and value, be mindful of William Bruce Cameron's advice from *Informal Sociology: A Casual Introduction to Sociological Thinking*:[4] "Not everything that can be counted counts, and not everything that counts can be counted." Not all measures matter, and not everything that matters can be measured. Pretending otherwise is just an exercise in boiling the ocean.

Unsurprisingly, prioritization is a critical skill to help you move forward with your measures. But what happens if your JTBD or HEROES framework exercises yield dozens upon dozens of measures to consider? Prioritizing a list of one hundred measures is arduous, but also pointless—organizations and executives alike can only comprehend so many data points. As Harry Max explains in his book, *Managing Priorities*,[5] prioritization is "a defense against the infinite distractions that keep individuals, teams, and organizations from operating at peak potential."

To get beyond the distraction of "measuring all the things" to "measuring the things that matter," there are several factors you can consider to help guide your prioritization process. Some of these are *organizational factors*, both internal and external to DesignOps; some of these are *outcome-driven factors*, where prioritization is driven by the outcome being achieved. The former will help you narrow your measures to a set that is manageable and relevant to your DesignOps team; the latter will help you refine (and redefine) the remaining set in ways that are meaningful and sustainable long-term. By weighing your measures against the factors that matter most to your design org, you can confidently prioritize the most important work.

Organizational Factors

Examining the internal and external organizational factors that govern your DesignOps team is an important rubric through which you can prioritize. This exercise will help you narrow down and focus on the measures that matter. Internally, we believe the most relevant factors are those discussed in Chapter 11, "Ready to Take Up

---

4   William Bruce Cameron, *Informal Sociology: A Casual Introduction to Sociological Thinking* (New York: Random House, 1963).

5   Harry Max, *Managing Priorities: How to Create Better Plans and Make Smarter Decisions* (New York: Two Waves, 2024).

the Baton": the DesignOps building blocks of a mission statement, an operating model, and clear workstreams. These elements not only guide the structure of your DesignOps team but can also heavily influence which measures you should prioritize.

- **The mission statement factor:** A well-crafted mission statement acts as your North Star, guiding how you prioritize the right DesignOps measures. For example, if your DesignOps mission is "championing design value," relevant measures could include increased mentions in cross-company communications and events and measuring the effectiveness of design-thinking programs.

- **The operating model factor:** Your operating model may help you prioritize using your model's top "customers." An embedded DPM's customers are the design team itself; measures to prioritize might include reducing design-dev handoff friction or improving designer utilization. A centralized DesignOps group's customers encompass the entire design organization and key partners; prioritized measures here might include improving designer tooling fluency and increasing rates of design system adoption.

- **The workstreams factor:** Workstreams clarify the specific work you're responsible for; consequently, they can help you scope your most relevant measures. A workstream that is laser-focused on design health might prioritize employee satisfaction measures, while a productivity workstream might prioritize measuring design effectiveness through measures like new process adoption impact.

Sometimes the most important organizational factors impacting what you prioritize are external to DesignOps. We believe the cyclical rhythms of business discussed in Chapter 13, "The Wrong Notes," should top your prioritization list.

- **The expansion factor:** During boom times, companies focus on fostering a positive culture and employee well-being. Retention, satisfaction, collaboration, and innovation become key measures. DesignOps should change its priorities to assure it is contributing to this strategy.

- **The contraction factor:** During economic downturns, companies prioritize efficiency, aiming to do more with less. Measures like productivity, velocity, and delivery speed take center stage as streamlining operations becomes crucial.

Whether in a boom or bust, neglecting employee well-being can have long-term consequences. As Adam Fry-Pierce suggests, "If you don't regularly pay the culture tax, you will feel it later." A balanced approach that prioritizes both efficiency *and* people is essential for sustainable success. Neglecting these measures, especially in challenging times, can have short-term and long-term consequences.

Outcome-Driven Factors

Another important rubric to help you prioritize, and ultimately build *sustainable measures*, is to define them through the *outcomes* those measures drive. Jared Spool, a prominent expert in usability and design, argues that traditional UX measures often fail to capture the true value of UX work. These "traditional UX measures"—velocity, delivery time, etc.—can obscure a design team's achievements, in the sense that you can't see the forest when you're only looking at the trees. Jared proposes a shift toward three outcome-driven factors that prioritize and measure sustained improvement over time: success, progress, and problem-value measures. Applied to DesignOps these are:

- **DesignOps success factors:** These measures quantify the positive outcomes and achievements resulting from DesignOps improvements. For example, imagine DesignOps launches a new learning series. A traditional measure might be *event attendance;* an improved outcome-driven measure would be an *increase in event engagement.* While event attendance is a conventional indicator of engagement, event engagement increase focuses on a broader spectrum, including time spent, participation, survey results, and other qualitative aspects.

- **DesignOps progress factors:** These measures track the efficiency and effectiveness of current DesignOps procedures and help identify areas for improvement. For example, consider DesignOps rolling out a new plug-in to reduce repetitive tasks. A traditional measure might be *task completion time;* a better outcome-driven measure would be *time-to-task completion.* The difference is that task completion only measures the time to finish a task, while time-to-task completion emphasizes the progress made in reducing the time it takes to complete tasks.

- **DesignOps problem-value factors:** These measures quantify the costs associated with poor experiences and operational gaps. For example, imagine DesignOps is developing a new design tool adoption initiative. A traditional measure might be the *number of inactive licenses*; an improved outcome-driven measure would be *reduction in cost of inactive licenses*. The difference is that this measure calculates the improvement achieved by decreasing the number of inactive licenses, including the expense of purchasing the license, potential maintenance fees, and the opportunity cost of not utilizing the tool for its intended purpose.

Narrowing your measures through the lens of your organizational factors will help you focus on what matters; refining them through the rubric of outcomes will make them durable and lasting. Through it all, this prioritization and definition process will lead you to discover how the activities that your DesignOps team undertakes, and the outputs they produce, can ultimately be related to achieving measurable outcomes that have broad and long-lasting impact on the design org (Figure 15.3).

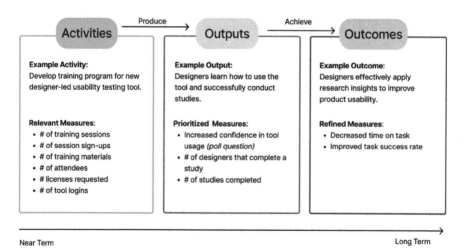

FIGURE 15.3

Building outcome-driven measures starts with your basic activities, which produce outputs, which achieve outcomes.

By adopting outcome-driven measures in DesignOps, you can establish a clearer connection between your efforts and the design organization's desired outcomes. This increased visibility strengthens the impact and value proposition of DesignOps within the organization.

Getting Scrappy With It

Michelle Chu, program, product and operations management

You might need to roll up your sleeves and just start counting *something*. Perhaps you heard a complaint about "too many projects" not being shipped on time. See if you can provide a count and do a percentage of how many projects this actually applies to. Or maybe comments were made about poor communication. Can you count the feedback rounds based on multiple Slack comments? Decide what you can measure and try to measure it. If you have Jira tickets or something you can query, even better: pull counts and see what you find. I actually love this part: it gives me the opportunity to play detective, to look for clues on what is true and what is a perception.

Think about your audience as well: different stakeholders will have different needs. Segment the data based on the audience for better understanding of their key pain points.

Data is much easier to collect than you realize. This scrappy method is not meant to be statistically significant with thousands of people. This is just to give you (and your team) visibility into what can be proven. When I wore the product manager hat, I constantly had to provide data to back up my product decisions. At first, it felt uncomfortable: I was confident in my decision-making process, and thought I had enough information to move forward. Being forced to gather data was, in hindsight, a gift. It uncovered blind spots I had in solving the problem and resulted in better solutions for my end users and customers.

Implementing Your Measures

With your measures finally prioritized, it's time to put them into action. Collecting data is one thing, but rolling out a meaningful measurement system is another. Meaningful measurements are intentionally planned, living, and in service of change. Here are six things that are necessary for implementing a meaningful measurement system:

- **Clear success criteria:** To create a truly impactful system, define clear success criteria for each measure. Numbers, percentages, and "directions of objects for outcomes" are meaningless without context. Set internal goals or use external benchmarks to track progress and improvement over time.

- **A data collection and analysis plan:** This includes identifying data sources, addressing potential hurdles, and defining the frequency and format of data collection (manual or automated, monthly, or real-time). Standardize data calculation for consistency and reliability and include a plan for analyzing the results to gain valuable insights.

- **Roles and responsibilities:** Clearly define who is responsible for collecting, analyzing, and reporting on each data set. This ensures that everyone understands their role and avoids scrambling later.

- **Communication and reporting:** Before diving into charts, revisit your goals and target audience. Craft a compelling story and tailor the format to your audience's preferences—dashboards, decks, presentations, etc. Every report should answer "So what?" and provide clear takeaways, with an actionable request for your audience.

- **Continuous improvement:** Build a feedback loop to refine your measures over time. Just because you've tracked a measure for a while doesn't mean it's relevant forever. Regularly assess how well your current measures align with your evolving design and DesignOps goals. Encourage regular team reviews and discussions about your data.

- **Continuous learning:** Fostering a culture of learning and improvement within your DesignOps team, and beyond, will ensure that your measurement system remains valuable and impactful.

Once implemented, visualize and publicize your progress! How and to whom you share the value your DesignOps has created is just as important as the value itself. Combining quantitative, qualitative, and visual artifacts tells a holistic story of your DesignOps team's impact (Figure 15.4).

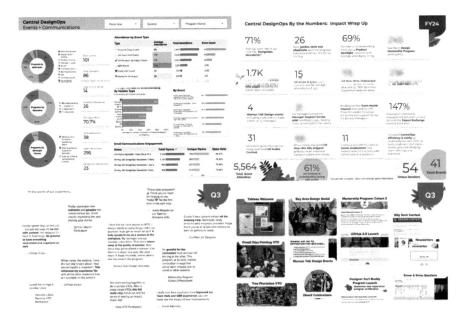

FIGURE 15.4

A variety of ways to share DesignOps value by Rachel Posman, including a dashboard, a one-page summary, a compilation of quotes, and photos of people and artifacts.

Coda: Measure What Matters

We champion the concept of measuring DesignOps' (and design's) value, but caution that "value" extends beyond financial and functional factors. The impact of design goes far beyond the projects that designers directly touch; the products people use, and the broader ecosystem in which they are used, are all in some way influenced by the work that design orgs do. So, it's crucial to make sure a designer's work, and the way it was created, *matters*.

Measures are valuable, too, but only tell part of the story. Design Operations' impact goes deeper than what can merely be quantified—a significant portion of the value DesignOps practitioners provide lies in the emotional impact to individuals. Our discipline's efforts foster a positive emotional landscape; DPMs nurture feelings of confidence, fulfillment, recognition, inspiration, connection, joy, and psychological safety. By positively affecting people's experiences and emotions, DesignOps extends its value beyond what measures can capture. Encompassing both measurable outcomes *and* the human impact on design teams allows DesignOps to make a truly valuable contribution to the organization's success.

A Symphony of Talent
Landing a DesignOps Job

A musical score has a fixed number of parts, and there are only so many chairs in an orchestra. For a musician, having all the talent in the world doesn't guarantee a right to one of those seats—everyone must audition equally and *earn* their place in the performance.

Unsurprisingly, this is true of every job. It's called the *interview*, and it's a vital part of any discipline that requires skilled and experienced talent to fill its ranks. Interviews tend to be framed through the lens of the *interviewee*, but we believe that for DesignOps leaders to assess and hire the right talent, it's critical to understand the practice and process from the *interviewer's perspective*, too. These two sides of the interview experience are difficult in any practice. However, for DesignOps candidates and hiring managers, the complexities and nuances of this discipline—which depends so much on bespoke, organizational context and subtle, iterative work—can make every interview feel like an existential obstacle course. Consider how a DPM candidate might be feeling about how to describe their past experience:

> **Candidate**
>
> In DesignOps, my work feels invisible, but it's a vital conduit powering the backend of my DesignOps team. I'm a multifaceted designer of frameworks, orchestrated collaboration, and detailed spreadsheets. I can choreograph workshops, events, and communications. But these deliverables and my impact are not always tangible or "pretty." Framing and show-casing my operational work can be really hard. How do I illuminate the behind-the-scenes details and bring my contributions to life?

We've been there! We've also been on the other side, too, as hiring managers. If you've never interviewed somebody before—especially for a DesignOps role—consider what the manager might be thinking:

> **Hiring Manager**
>
> The job of interviewing and hiring for these roles can feel daunting. The nuanced aspects of DesignOps expertise are not immediately appar-ent! I need to approach the interview phase with a strategic perspective and a well-defined grasp of the key competencies required. But how can I assess these? Evaluat-ing technical skills, collaborative abilities, and alignment with the organization's design objectives just adds an extra layer of complexity to the hiring process.

Every company has their own unique interview processes and requirements; this chapter covers the most *common* interview elements for DesignOps candidates and hiring managers. We maintain that these common elements are the *interview structure* itself, *standard interview questions* to assess competencies, and the *DesignOps portfolio*. Our position is that by leveraging our sample elements in your interview process (and interviewing *practice*), hiring managers and candidates alike can navigate this moment with greater confidence, effectiveness, and fairness.

The DesignOps Interview Structure

The structure of a successful DesignOps interview should match the structure of its closest partner and peer, the *design* interview. We believe the best structure is the simplest one and recommend the following basic phases (Figure 16.1).

FIGURE 16.1

Four phases of a DesignOps interview.

After submitting a *résumé* that meets the requirements and criteria for the role, applicants and hiring managers will advance to the *screener interview* phase. The initial screening interview, typically conducted by a recruiter, entails a review of the applicant's résumé, and explores how their past experience shows relevancy to the role's prerequisites. Hiring managers should provide the recruiter with questions that specifically dig into how applicants have demonstrated success in the past and how they've demonstrated skill in the DesignOps competencies. For applicants, this phase also serves as an opportunity to ask general questions about the role, compensation, culture, benefits, and the company itself.

CONFRONTING INTERVIEW BIAS

 Let's confront the truth head-on: biases are deeply embedded within us, often lurking unnoticed. And guess what? Those sneaky biases tag along even when we're interviewing candidates for DesignOps roles. It's like an uninvited plus-one crashing the interview party.

Interview bias happens when interviewers evaluate candidates not only on their skills and qualifications, but also on unspoken and subjective criteria, leading to less objective assessments. If we don't actively do something to prevent these biases from informing our hiring decision, then they will.

Recognizing that fact, I aim to take a proactive role in reducing interview bias on my team through these actions:

- **Structured Interview Guide:** I create an interview guide, and we always use competencies to guide the interviews. This structured approach ensures that interviews are grounded in specific skills and qualifications, reducing the influence of personal biases.

- **Diverse Evaluation Voices:** I involve multiple interviewers in the evaluation process. This diversity of perspectives helps balance out individual biases and leads to a more comprehensive assessment of candidates.

- **Training as a Prerequisite:** I require all interview panelists to take the internal training on inclusive hiring before being able to participate in an interview panel.

- **Self-Awareness and Discussion:** I encourage interviewers (including myself) to reflect on their own biases and assumptions before each interview and also afterward. If something comes up, I encourage an honest conversation about it.

Additionally, to increase our circle of qualified candidates, here are some things that I no longer require from DesignOps candidates:

- **Role Labels:** I don't require that specific DesignOps roles and titles appear on their résumé.

- **Specific Pedigree:** I don't require that they have gone to specific schools, companies, or hold certain degrees.

- **Years of Experience:** I don't require a specific number of years of experience in certain kinds of roles. It's not about the time served, but the impact created.

As we talked about in Chapter 7, "Playing Your Part," DesignOps has a responsibility to weave values into everything we do, and interviewing in my opinion, is the best place to start.

The *interview panel* phase should comprise around four one-on-one interviews. This further refines the evaluation process, but it's important not to overdo the interview phase. A Google study found four rounds of interviews were enough to hire a candidate with 86% confidence. After that, confidence only rose by 1% for each new interview round. While the composition and number of interviewers may vary based on the role and level, applicants can anticipate engaging with stakeholders from the full suite of DesignOps performance partners. These may include a DesignOps peer or leader to assess the applicant's grasp of DesignOps practices and responsibilities; a design leader to evaluate adeptness at resolving organizational challenges; a product partner to gauge comprehension of cross-functional collaboration and the delivery process; and a designer to explore the applicant's understanding of the designer's role and challenges.

The final phase in this process is the *portfolio presentation*. Much like designers, DesignOps candidates are increasingly being asked to present a portfolio of their work. This presentation could range from a targeted audience within the DesignOps team, to an expansive audience encompassing the broader design team and its partners. Recognizing that this phase of the interview process can be intimidating, we've put together some insights and best practices later in this chapter to help applicants craft and deliver a compelling DesignOps portfolio.

Candidate
If you're stepping into the DesignOps interview spotlight, knowing these phases can help you prepare. As with any job application, refine your résumé to highlight your pertinent DesignOps skills, experience, and contributions. Address the specific requirements of the role you're pursuing and avoid a one-size-fits-all approach. Pay close attention to the job description in order to tailor your impact stories to the unique needs of the role.

Hiring Manager
If you find yourself hiring for DesignOps roles, the previous interview structure is a great foundation to help you get started. The journey to match a DesignOps practitioner to a specific role requires multiple phases to comprehensively evaluate a candidate's suitability for a position.

DesignOps Interview Questions

In Chapter 4, "It's All About Practice," we discussed the eight DesignOps career competencies, which serve as a framework for evaluating the performance and proficiency of all DesignOps practitioners. These competencies act as a valuable guide during the interview process as well, for candidates and hiring managers alike. In this section, we'll share some tested and trusted questions that help hiring managers (and recruiters) assess how well an applicant has demonstrated these competencies in the past.

Competency 1: Assessing Design and Design Operations

This competency reflects the ability to think like, reason with, and proxy for a designer as a DesignOps practitioner. Here are some questions that can effectively assess this competency's underlying skills:

- "What do you see as the hardest part of the design process for designers and their partners, and how have you helped make it easier?"

- "When considering a proposed design change, how do you frame the pros and cons to encourage objective decision-making by all stakeholders?"

- "How have you used the design process to solve operations problems?"

- "Describe a design project as it progressed from initial ideation through to a finished design solution. Who was involved and what role did you play?"

Competency 2: Assessing Trusted Relationships and Partnerships

This competency is all about building bridges to and between the stakeholders in your DesignOps ecosystem. Here are some questions that can effectively assess this competency's underlying skills:

- "Give an example of working with non-UX stakeholders. How do you help them to understand UX processes and priorities?"

- "Tell me about a situation where it was necessary for you to have the trust of others. What was the situation? How did you know that others perceived you as trustworthy?"

- "Give an example of how you have built diversity, equity, and inclusion into your processes and programs."
- "What, in your opinion, are the key ingredients in creating and maintaining successful working relationships? Give me examples of how you have made these work for you."
- "What steps have you taken to create a work environment where differences are valued, encouraged, and supported?"

DESIGNOPS DECODED

MY FAVORITE DESIGNOPS INTERVIEW QUESTION

Meredith Black, director of DesignOps at Figma and founder of DesignOps Assembly

Top question: "What steps would you take to help the business side of the company understand the value of design?"

Asking this question helps me understand that the candidate can bridge the gap between business and design and speak the language of both sides. It allows me to understand that they have a business acumen that advocates for the designer, while also able to navigate political landmines. It shows me that they build mature relationships and advocate not only for the design needs, but also the business needs.

DESIGNOPS DECODED

MY FAVORITE DESIGNOPS INTERVIEW QUESTION

Patrizia Bertini, DesignOps strategist and leader

Top Question: "What is DesignOps and why does it matter? Can you explain why we should care about it and provide real life examples?"

I try to probe about how much program management versus strategic thinking they apply. I deliberately expect them to sell DesignOps to me with tangible examples or a hypothesis.

Competency 3: Assessing Program Management Proficiency

This competency captures the project and program skills that set design program managers apart from their designer peers. Here are some questions that can effectively assess this competency's underlying skills:

- "Describe a time when you organized and steered a multidiscipline project. What were your primary considerations at the outset?"
- "Tell me about a project that didn't go to plan. How did you handle it and what did you learn?"
- "Tell me about a gap or need you identified and the solution or process you created. How did you gain buy-in, and how did you roll it out?"
- "Describe a design project as it progressed from initial ideation through to a finished design solution. Who was involved and what role did you play?"

Competency 4: Assessing Problem Solving and Resourcefulness

This competency gives shape to the ingenuity DPMs exhibit when confronted with something brand new or without precedent. Here are some questions that can effectively assess this competency's underlying skills:

- "How do you approach solving a problem for which you may have little to no experience? Tell me about techniques that have worked for you in the past."
- "Have you ever had to come to a compromise or make trade-offs with a team you were working with? How did you navigate that interaction, and what was the outcome?"
- "What was the hardest challenge you've had rolling out a new solution or process? How did the conflict impact the effectiveness of the solution? If you could change anything about that experience, what would you do differently?"

DESIGNOPS DECODED

MY FAVORITE DESIGNOPS INTERVIEW QUESTION

Adam Fry-Pierce, UX Leadership, Operations, Google and partner, DesignOps Assembly

Top question: "Can you tell me about a time when your work led to a more effective design organization?"

I'm interested in assessing how they approach this by framing the question around some form of North Star metrics, likely centered on efficiency or efficacy within the broader design organization. I hope to hear them describe a scenario where they successfully facilitated cross-organizational alignment and bonus points if they can connect their efforts to higher-level OKRs (Objectives and Key Results) and/or resource strategy.

DESIGNOPS DECODED

MY FAVORITE DESIGNOPS INTERVIEW QUESTION

Jon Fukuda, co-founder, partner at Limina

Top question: "Can you share a specific example of how you successfully streamlined collaboration between design, product, and engineering teams in your previous role?"

By asking this question, we can assess the candidate's ability to effectively manage the intersection between design and other departments, a critical aspect of DesignOps. It allows the candidate to demonstrate their problem-solving skills, communication abilities, and their understanding of cross-functional dynamics—which we consider *essential qualities for a DesignOps manager.*

Competency 5: Assessing Leadership and Influence

This competency is critical for all DesignOps practitioners, even those not in formal leadership positions. Here are some questions that can effectively assess this competency's underlying skills:

- "How have you brought teams along on a new program journey or initiative? What challenges have you faced and how did you adapt?"
- "Describe a time when you kicked off and led a multiteam project. What were your primary considerations at the outset?"
- "What is your management/leadership style? How do you inspire great work from your teams?"

Competency 6: Assessing Communication and Presentation

This competency is at the heart of all the successful advocacy that DPMs must practice in support of their design teams and new DesignOps programs. Here are some questions that can effectively assess this competency's underlying skills:

- "What was the toughest communication situation you have had to deal with? How did you approach it? What did you say and do? What was the outcome?"
- "How do you successfully present plans or process changes to executive audiences? Provide examples."
- "How have you simplified a complex process or idea in order to explain it to your stakeholders?"

My Favorite DesignOps Interview Question

Adrienne Allnutt, head of Design Operations and Program Management at ServiceNow

Top question: "How do you leverage relationships, tools, and communication methods to influence change?"

This helps me understand how the candidate approaches change management and what they gravitate toward. I look for people who talk about "people" as the center of influence and can share clear examples of how they have moved change (but also talk about how hard and non-linear it can be).

I also really like asking people, "What's an app or product that you think is designed really well?" Although we aren't product/UX designers, I like to hear what people come up with and how they speak to it. It shows me their attention to good UX and their understanding of the design world—which to me, is not critical, but very important when working with creatives.

My Favorite DesignOps Interview Question

Peter Merholz, chief humanist and organizational design consultant

Top question: "Walk me through a DesignOps program you developed, how you knew it was the right thing to build, and what impact it had?"

This question is for when you're establishing Design Operations and building the team. The answer to the question will help me understand how the candidate takes initiative, the data and insights they use to make decisions, the scale and scope of what they're capable of, and their orientation on results and making positive change.

Competency 7: Assessing Company and Business Acumen

This competency enforces DesignOps' role in leveraging their understanding of their company's product or service and how they use this knowledge to influence design decision-making. Here are some questions that can effectively assess this competency's underlying skills:

- "Describe how you stay current with industry design trends. How do you leverage best practices without producing work that's merely derivative?"

- "Tell me about a time you didn't have an answer to a complex question. What did you do to uncover the solution?"

- "Tell me about a time you volunteered to take on a significant assignment outside of your comfort zone in order to expand your capabilities."

- "How would you describe the vision and purpose of the work you do?"

- "Think about a recent decision you had to make that had a broad impact. How would you describe your thought process about how you wanted to make the decision?"

Competency 8: Assessing Values and Culture

This competency reflects a DPM's outsized role in leading with and modeling the values that guide a design org. Here are some questions that can effectively assess this competency's underlying skills:

- "What steps have you taken to create a work environment where differences are valued, encouraged, and supported?"

- "Give an example of how you have built diversity, equity and inclusion into your processes and programs."

- "Tell me about a time when you had to speak up about something that was contrary to someone's views. Did you have to take personal risk to do so?"

- "What's a value that's very important to you? How would others see that expressed in your day to day?"

Interviewing the Interviewers

As a candidate, *asking* questions is as important as answering them during an interview. This demonstrates your genuine interest in the role and provides an opportunity to gain deeper insight into the organization, the team, and the role you're pursuing. Your questions showcase your critical thinking, your ability to assess the company's alignment with your own goals and values, and your curiosity about the DesignOps landscape.

Candidate

Here are some great candidate questions we've received while interviewing:

- "How has your DesignOps team helped to deliver [insert your personal value, such as inclusivity, belonging, joy]?"
- "How does the company support professional growth and development within the DesignOps team?"
- "How is your DesignOps org structured and what opportunities/challenges have you encountered with this org structure?"
- "What is the evolution of the DesignOps organization in your company and how did you arrive at the current composition of your team?"
- "What would be the first and most important challenge you'd want me to solve and why?"
- "What is something DesignOps tried but failed to implement and why?"
- "How will my performance be evaluated and what are the advancement opportunities for DesignOps?"
- "What is something you would change about the product development process at your company if you had a magic wand?"
- "Who are the biggest champions for DesignOps outside of DesignOps?"

Asking questions can be hard. Preparing *great* questions is even harder. And knowing which questions can fairly and accurately assess competencies and company values is hardest of all. We hope applicants and hiring managers alike find value in knowing the questions we trust most to make the interview process meaningful for everyone.

Candidate

As the candidate, use the questions above to gain a deeper understanding of the kinds of topics you may be asked about in your interviews. Identify which examples and stories showcase your unique skills and point of view relevant to each competency. Practice your answers.

Hiring Manager

As the hiring manager, consider how these questions will not only help you understand the candidate better, but also will allow the candidate to better understand what matters most to your organization. Further, anchoring your job requirements in these career competencies (and the underlying skills described in Chapter 4) makes the process more fair all around.

DESIGNOPS DECODED

BUY-IN OR BUST

Kamdyn Moore, head of Design Program Management at Cash App and former head of R&D Enablement and head of Design Operations at Spotify

I was recently interviewing with a company looking for a Design Operations Lead, and I asked this question: "Who else beyond the design organization cares about this role? Who else is invested in this headcount?"

Unfortunately, the hiring manager didn't know. This lack of clarity points to several issues. First, it indicates a misalignment between the design org's needs and broader business needs. Second, it suggests that while this role may benefit individual designers—perhaps all 60 in that particular org—the impact of that role likely won't extend much further without a significant uphill battle. Knowing that operational functions represent a cost to the business, the return on investment on these roles must be well understood beyond the design organization. Without it, DesignOps will consistently fail in the long term.

The DesignOps Portfolio: Preparation

A compelling DesignOps portfolio is more than just a presentation—it's a reflection of an applicant's understanding of design processes and culture. Especially if someone has transitioned from another operational or program management field into UX or design, it's crucial to showcase a grasp of the language, models, and frameworks that shape design as a discipline.

For candidates, your portfolio is a testament to your dedication to research, learning, and the immersion into the world of design and DesignOps. It's also an opportunity to tell your story in a way that resonates with hiring managers.

Here are six candidate tips to prepare and create a great DesignOps portfolio:

1. **Introduce yourself.**

   This is your opportunity to express your personality and what sets you apart. You might choose to discuss your values and which company values resonate with you. Alternatively, you could share a hobby or interest that holds significant meaning for you.

2. **Show your impact.**

   Your portfolio is a canvas to show your impact. Highlight instances where you took the initiative to drive change. Narrate a story of transformation where you didn't just implement a requested process, but also recognized a void, identified the necessity, and proactively filled it. Include case studies that underline your proactive nature and ability to drive change, rather than merely react to it.

3. **Demonstrate your craft.**

   Your portfolio's visual elements aren't just aesthetics—they mirror your ability to simplify complex concepts for diverse audiences. As a DesignOps professional, you'll often find yourself communicating intricate processes and programs to wide-ranging stakeholders. Your portfolio becomes a testament to this skill, where well-crafted visuals harmonize with your narratives, making your ideas tangible and accessible.

4. **Be specific.**

   Whenever possible, include real examples of your work (without violating NDAs or proprietary info). It is much more compelling to show an actual process diagram or a screenshot of your project tracker rather than a bulleted list. Even if you think it's obvious and doesn't require a visual, a specific example of your work demonstrates how you distill, organize, and communicate complex information.

5. **Tell effective stories.**

   Great portfolios share past work in a comprehensive, organized, and concise manner. To this end, structuring your case studies using a "narrative arc" can be very effective (Figure 16.2). This arc starts at context; proceeds through problem, approach, solution, and outcomes; and concludes with impact. These six simple points provide an excellent framework to showcase your experiences in your portfolio.

   1. **Context:** What role did you play? Who is involved? Who are the characters? Where were you? What key context is important to know?

   2. **Problem:** What was going wrong? Why was the current state not working? What was the opportunity?

   3. **Approach:** How did you start to solve the problem? What approach did you decide to take? How did it go? What obstacles did you encounter?

   4. **Solution:** You did it! What was the solution you came up with?

   5. **Outcomes:** What were the outcomes? What are the "fruits of your labor." What did you learn? Remember, even if something doesn't go as planned, that insight is a valuable learning too.

   6. **Impact:** Wrap it up in a bow. What was the impact? What is new and better because of the change you made?

6. **Quality over quantity.**

   Instead of overwhelming your portfolio with a plethora of projects, emphasize quality over quantity. Your portfolio should focus on a narrowed set of exceptional examples. These examples should showcase diverse skills, providing a glimpse into the spectrum of your capabilities. Perhaps one project exemplifies your strategic thinking, while the other demonstrates your operational finesse.

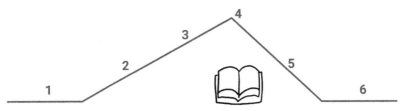

FIGURE 16.2
The narrative arc rises and falls creating momentum that tells an effective story.

DESIGNOPS DECODED

FROM INTIMIDATION TO CREATION: CRAFTING MY FIRST STANDOUT DESIGNOPS PORTFOLIO
Hayley Ng, design program manager at Salesforce

At first I was a little intimidated, because I had no previous DesignOps experience. But I knew my varied interests provided me with the toolkit to succeed in this role. As I was planning my portfolio, I knew that I had what it takes to do the job—I just had to effectively show it. To stand out, I made sure to identify m y transferable skills, like positions of leadership I had in school where I was constantly discovering new ways to simplify complex processes and prioritize trusted relationships. I also connected with the team's purpose and values. I did my research and looked into articles the team had written, and embedded those learnings into my presentation. Lastly, I added my "Hayley" creative flair, and built my portfolio in Figma using the company's brand scheme and colors, to both stand out and show that I was a self-taught Figma experimentalist.

The DesignOps Portfolio: Presentation

The final phase of the DesignOps interview structure is the portfolio presentation. If one-on-one interviewers are satisfied that an applicant has the experience and competencies required for the job, the hiring manager should conclude the interview process with a roundtable portfolio presentation. This is an opportunity for applicants to express themselves and their past work through the lens of their portfolio; it's also an opportunity for stakeholders to observe and engage the applicant in a setting that's more similar to how DesignOps works day-to-day: conversationally, in groups, and working with representatives from multiple functions.

For hiring managers, the portfolio presentation is more than just an opportunity to dig into a candidate's accomplishments. It's a chance to observe how they comport themselves in a workplace setting and to assess DesignOps competencies like communications, presentation, and influence first-hand.

Hiring Manager

Here are three hiring manager tips for navigating this aspect of the portfolio presentation:

- Translating their experiences
- Overcoming setbacks
- Sharing the presentation agenda in advance

Translating Their Experiences

In the portfolio and in the presentation, observe if the candidate can translate their past experiences into a narrative that shows relevance to your business. If a model or framework is shared that solved for a domain-specific problem, inquire how it might be evolved to solve problems in a different context. (That context being your business.) If the portfolio showcases how the applicant helped teams converge on a specific solution, follow up about how much divergent thinking led up to that outcome. What other hypotheses did the applicant have, and what other solutions did they consider? Sometimes, these unexplored options will be the right ones for you, so test how well the candidate can translate these stories in the context of your business.

Overcoming Setbacks

DesignOps is a field where things rarely go as planned. Note if the applicant is sharing stories of their failures—not just their successes. Setbacks aren't admissions of defeat but showcases of growth. Observe if the candidate can illustrate how previous failures spurred them to adapt, improvise, and improve. Recognize, too, that being comfortable talking about failure is a sign of courage, and a DPM applicant who vulnerably talks about their past mistakes is likely to have the resilience to overcome them in the future.

Sharing the Presentation Agenda in Advance

Share with your candidates the specific format you'd like to follow for their portfolio presentation. This allows you to tailor the experience to request case studies that are relevant to your open role; it also provides an equitable experience if multiple candidates are interviewing. If you don't have a portfolio presentation structure on your own team, here's a sample in Figure 16.3 that you can use for a 60-minute presentation (including time for Q&A):

In the end, a DesignOps portfolio is more than a collection of achievements—it's a personal narrative interwoven with expressions of understanding, initiative, growth, and expertise.

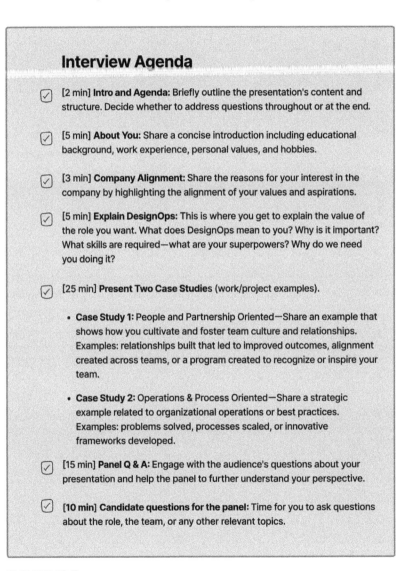

Interview Agenda

- ☑ **[2 min] Intro and Agenda:** Briefly outline the presentation's content and structure. Decide whether to address questions throughout or at the end.

- ☑ **[5 min] About You:** Share a concise introduction including educational background, work experience, personal values, and hobbies.

- ☑ **[3 min] Company Alignment:** Share the reasons for your interest in the company by highlighting the alignment of your values and aspirations.

- ☑ **[5 min] Explain DesignOps:** This is where you get to explain the value of the role you want. What does DesignOps mean to you? Why is it important? What skills are required—what are your superpowers? Why do we need you doing it?

- ☑ **[25 min] Present Two Case Studies** (work/project examples).

  - **Case Study 1:** People and Partnership Oriented—Share an example that shows how you cultivate and foster team culture and relationships. Examples: relationships built that led to improved outcomes, alignment created across teams, or a program created to recognize or inspire your team.

  - **Case Study 2:** Operations & Process Oriented—Share a strategic example related to organizational operations or best practices. Examples: problems solved, processes scaled, or innovative frameworks developed.

- ☑ **[15 min] Panel Q & A:** Engage with the audience's questions about your presentation and help the panel to further understand your perspective.

- ☑ **[10 min] Candidate questions for the panel:** Time for you to ask questions about the role, the team, or any other relevant topics.

FIGURE 16.3

The DesignOps portfolio presentation sample agenda.

Coda: It's Your Turn

Opportunities to join—or hire for—a DesignOps team don't come around very often. Applicants looking to enter the field must do all they can to shine a light on the relevance of their previous work and experience, and to demonstrate how they've made a meaningful impact. The best way to do this is by being prepared for the questions that hiring managers are most likely to ask, and to create a DesignOps portfolio that tells a compelling story, highlights one's skills and strengths, and harmonizes these with the hiring manager's greatest needs.

And for those hiring for these pivotal roles: embrace the concept of asking and answering questions during the interview process. Be fair and equitable in the candidates' experiences. And center the entire process on aligning with the DesignOps career competencies and the company's values. Do these, and hiring managers will certainly find the candidate who will best help them achieve DesignOps success.

CHAPTER 17

Epilogue
An Unfinished Symphony

There is so much more to say about Design Operations. The perspective we provide in this book is informed by our years of experience, but our own careers in this field represent just one possible way to practice DesignOps.

We maintain that the Design Operations fundamentals described in these pages are true and relevant to the supermajority of DesignOps practices out there: the vocabulary of "what we do," the backgrounds and competencies of our practitioners, how DesignOps roles should be leveled and evaluated, and so on. What's different from our perspective and our readers' DesignOps lived experiences, however, is how Design Operations is shaped and contoured by specific businesses and industries. In this discipline, our practices all share a similar architectural blueprint, but for the people living in (or with) DesignOps day-to-day, it's the finishing details that matter most.

We obviously can't capture all the minute but meaningful differences of every DesignOps practice in existence. But in a similar fashion, every "essential field guide" needs to acknowledge the existence of undiscovered species and be content that the most essential collection of "known knowns" has been organized and described. We have tried our best to capture the fundamental state of DesignOps as of this printing but acknowledge that "essential" does not mean "complete." By the time our words are put onto paper, who knows how the world will have changed or what wonders it will have discovered?

Outside of Grammy and Oscar predictions, we're pretty terrible at foreseeing the future. But from where we sit, there do seem to be two major disruptors on the horizon that are likely to impact not just DesignOps practitioners, but the fundamentals of the practice itself. The first is the macro-economic forces that insist on creating complex, negative effects on businesses worldwide. Yes, this is a euphemism for war, climate change, and economic uncertainty—pretty much everything that makes stock markets collectively panic and drives investors to sell. Reader, we are not suggesting that DesignOps needs to anticipate and plan for how a hurricane halfway across the globe will affect design delivery, but we do want to acknowledge that complicated, abstract forces often have very real, tangible effects at a personal level—namely, layoffs and reductions in force.

In the year that we wrote this book, wars have lingered in Europe, the Middle East, and elsewhere. Simultaneously, businesses are laying off tech workers at staggering levels. These two events are related because global currency markets and the investment in digital (and physical) goods operate best when there's macro-economic certainty, and as of this writing, certainty is in short supply. DesignOps is getting particularly hard hit. The team that acts as a force multiplier for design is a ripe target for elimination when the design force itself is reduced. This is creating more competition for scant job openings, and DesignOps practitioners who are still employed are finding that their mission statement is woefully misaligned to the business. *Scale* is out, *optimize* is in, and elements of this book (particularly about growing a DesignOps practice) may seem quaintly out of touch.

On this topic, we want to express that layoffs and job rejections are a reflection of this macro-economic uncertainty and not an indictment of the practice or the practitioner. DesignOps teams are shrinking, yes, but also reforming. For example, DPMs closer to the product are being layered and organized alongside design producers versed in creative and brand marketing. This melting pot is likely to create a new vision for Design Operations, one in which the many expressions of "design" inside a company are collapsed into one, reorienting the DesignOps practice into something collectively focused on delivering top-line business goals and executive design priorities.

The second disruptor is already here—and may have helped us (a bit) in assembling this book. Generative AI, or gen AI, continues to impress us as a technology that's delivering on its potential and promises, despite its enormous hype. Gen AI is "a type of artificial intelligence that has the ability to create new content, such as images, text, or even music, without explicit instructions from a human designer." Yes, gen AI wrote that. And while its utility (among other things) to write sentences, sonnets, and code is well documented, we are just beginning to discover gen AI's role—and potential risks—in the practice of Design Operations.

It's clear that today's demonstrated use cases and capabilities of gen AI barely scratch the surface of what this technology can do. When we started writing this book, gen AI was a novelty that seemed best suited to creating a few laughs: a crude imitation of a Bob Ross painting, or a dinner recipe that "must include 100 lemons—no more, no less." As we finished writing this book, gen AI was creating realistic travel videos of foreign countries and being used by non-coders to develop fully-functional, feature-rich apps for mobile devices. Designers from countless industries have been experimenting with gen AI to understand how it can be used in the design process; meanwhile, DPMs are starting to operationalize and govern gen AI tools in their workflows. Through it all, design and DesignOps have found themselves marveling at the bright lights they've asked gen AI to create, but are just now occasionally squinting at these creations long enough to make out a dark spot on the horizon, and ask: "Is this a technology that might replace us?"

Our prediction is that generative AI will replace a part of us—the mundane, rote, and information gap parts of our roles, to be specific. The adage that knowledge workers "won't be replaced by AI, but rather by someone who knows how to use AI" neatly summarizes this take. We see that gen AI is exceptionally suited to function as a workplace partner—something that can be asked to edit, provide alternative perspectives, to translate and reframe messages, and more. In short, it's something DPMs can delegate to—if they learn how.

Further, we do not believe that gen AI will outperform humans in terms of creativity and craft, especially when it comes to creations that audiences will want to actually own and use. Generative AI seems magical not because it's an artistic genius, but because it produces the most average, middle-of-the-bell-curve responses possible—creations that are engineered to appeal to the broadest range of the audience algorithm. It is exceptionally good at creating average work—we just happen to be asking gen AI to do work that is fantastical and amazing. Assuming that humans will always desire an experience that is better than average, we believe that human creators will likewise be in demand, as will the program managers who partner with them along the way.

Ultimately, DesignOps is a practice that will always be a little unfinished and its future somewhat unknown. But we hope this book has also made Design Operations less mysterious, more approachable, and above all, real as a practice and career path. So long as there is value in making great experiences, there will be value for those who create the experience of making, and in this we see an immense and incredible future ahead.

Encore
Your DesignOps Toolbox

One more thing! This chapter is our DesignOps toolbox, filled with a collection of tools and templates that we find helpful in various applications of the DesignOps role. These tools are simplified versions, to give you a taste of their purpose and format, along with our thoughts and tips for each.

For most of these tools, you can get scrappy and use materials you already have. Got sticky notes and a marker? How about a good old spreadsheet? Good to go. However, to access and implement the more complex tools of design thinking and change management, we recommend going digital. Collaboration tools like Figjam, Miro, and Mural have handy built-in templates for many of these tools.

Additionally, you can explore the capabilities of program management platforms such as Asana, ClickUp, Coda, Airtable, monday.com, and any other tools designed to track, prioritize, and plan work. By harnessing these analog and digital solutions, teams can enhance efficiency, foster collaboration, and elevate the effectiveness of their DesignOps initiatives.

DESIGNOPS DECODED

FORGET THE TOOL, SOLVE THE PROBLEM

Binaebi Akah Calkins, experience architect loving the DesignOps & strategy life

Pivoting from lack of access to the latest hot organizational tool, whether due to lack of interest or funds, is a fascinating design constraint. For the intrepid information architect within, step back and identify the problems you were hoping the tool would solve. Sketch what you need to track and how frequently with your audience(s) in mind, and prove to yourself that you can make a super fancy and beautiful spreadsheet after all. Search engines are your friend here. It's amazing what a well-formed spreadsheet with conditional formatting and clever logic can replicate from tools like Jira, Airtable, etc.

Tools and Templates

Journey Map

The **journey map** is a core design thinking tool used to chart a single user's specific experience. It follows a linear format, detailing the steps a user takes while focusing on their actions, pain points, thoughts, and emotions at each touchpoint. This tool is particularly effective for identifying and fixing specific usability issues, as it optimizes for individual customer interactions and touchpoints, and shorter durations or specific episodes. Good DesignOps use cases for the journey map include mapping a new employee's journey from recruitment to first day, mapping the user journey for onboarding to a new internal tool, or mapping a specific handoff interaction between designer and their engineering partner.

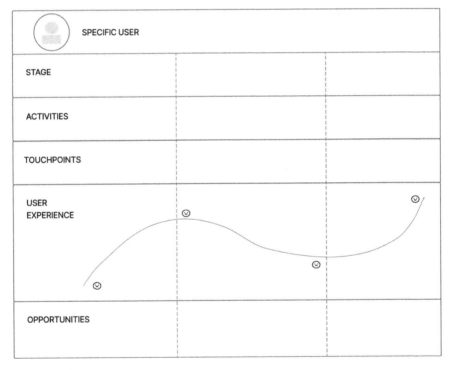

FIGURE 18.1

Journey map.

Experience Map

The **experience map** is similar to the journey map but expresses a more generalized experience for a *group* of users. It takes a broader, holistic view of user interaction that can encompass multiple journeys, emotions, and external factors influencing the overall experience. The experience map helps to understand and improve the entire customer experience looking at bigger trends and opportunities for systemic change.

Some DesignOps use cases for the experience map include outlining how different teams interact with the design system through their product design process, visualizing how designers and cross-functional partners interact during the end-to-end release cycle to pinpoint roadblocks and opportunities for better integration, or mapping the entire employee onboarding journey.

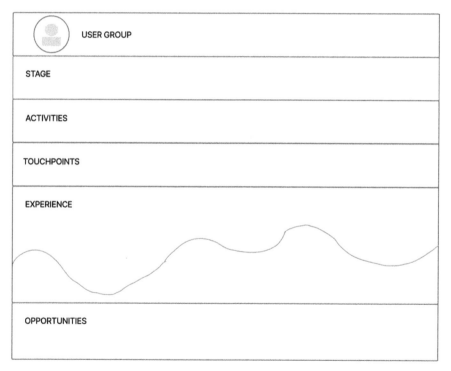

FIGURE 18.2
Experience map.

Service Blueprint

The **service blueprint** is a service design tool used to understand and optimize the customer experience while also improving service efficiency and effectiveness. This tool utilizes the concept of front and backstage. Similar to a stage production, the front-stage activities are what the customer or user sees and interacts with, while the backstage activities encompass all the people and processes required to deliver the service or product to the customer.

Chapter 14, "Tuning Your Instruments," included a real example of how this tool can be used to map the onboarding experience. Another relevant DesignOps application would involve visualizing the event experience for larger-scale, org-wide meetings, such as a Quarterly Business Review or Design Town Halls. This entails mapping the front-stage experience for participants while simultaneously considering all the backstage details crucial for orchestrating a seamless event.

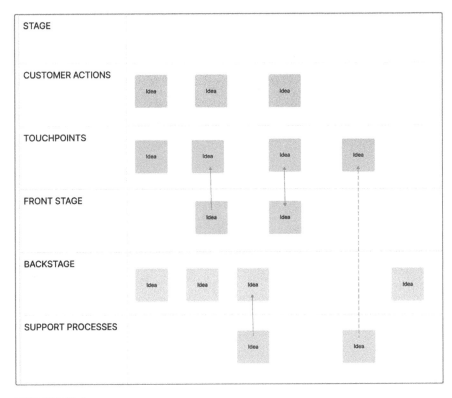

FIGURE 18.3
Service blueprint.

Fashioning Tools and Breaking the Rules

Christina Rodriguez, senior manager, product DesignOps at Zendesk

Tools and fashion have a lot in common. Journey maps, service blueprints, and SWOT (strengths, weaknesses, opportunities, and threats) analyses are like a classic white tee—they provide a foundational starting point. The real fun comes when you accessorize, mix patterns, experiment with silhouettes, and infuse your own personality.

Recently, while working with my design team, I needed to evaluate the effectiveness of our team meetings. Initially, I tried a 2x2 matrix but found it limiting. So, I expanded on it and developed my own rubric tailored to our specific needs.

Alexander McQueen said, "You've got to know the rules to break them. That's what I'm here for, to demolish the rules but to keep the tradition." So, learn and use the basic tools, but then get creative. DesignOps gets to break the rules, too.

Empathy Map

An **empathy map** visually explores users' thoughts, feelings, needs, and pain points, helping DesignOps create solutions that genuinely address user needs. When used alongside the Jobs to Be Done framework, it offers deeper insights into user motivations and behavior. This tool is particularly valuable for understanding diverse user groups. For example, when designing programs for design managers, an empathy map can help you understand their frustrations and desires, leading to more impactful learning and enablement programs. Beyond what they "say, think, do, and feel," you can uncover what motivates and inspires them (gains) and what hinders or frustrates them (pains). In addition to understanding various user groups, empathy maps are also valuable for tailoring communication effectively. By creating empathy maps for different stakeholder groups, DesignOps can craft targeted messaging and engagement strategies that resonate with each audience.

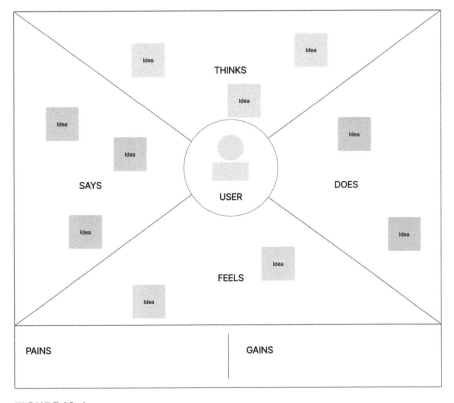

FIGURE 18.4
Empathy map.

Affinity Mapping

Affinity mapping helps DesignOps make sense of large amounts of qualitative data (user research, feedback, ideation) by turning it into meaningful themes and categories. Typically, sticky notes are used to write down ideas and data points and then physically moved around on a wall or board to identify patterns and connections. In DesignOps, this tool can be applied at the outset of prioritization to identify the most crucial themes that need addressing first. Or, when conducting a Design Critique, affinity mapping can be used to collect feedback and pinpoint areas requiring improvement.

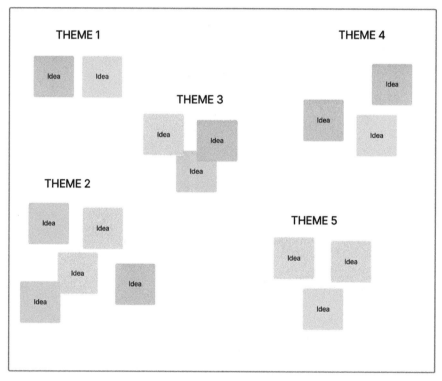

FIGURE 18.5
Affinity mapping.

Mind Map

A **mind map** is a visual tool that radiates from a central topic, branching out into related ideas, concepts, and details. This non-linear format encourages brainstorming and facilitates information organization. In DesignOps, it proves beneficial at the start of a project for organizing all components of the program. Additionally, if an issue arises in how design is functioning, you can use it to document your existing knowledge about the problem and identify areas that require further exploration. It's a good place to start when you are first digging into an ambiguous problem space (which we do pretty often).

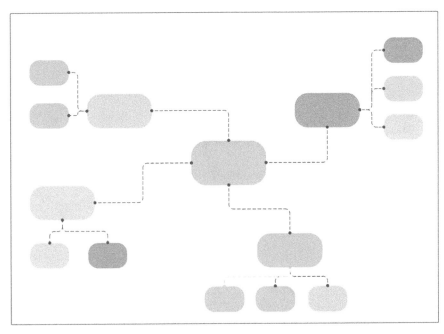

FIGURE 18.6
Mind mapping.

RACI Stakeholder Map

The **RACI stakeholder map** is a tool used in project management and design thinking to clarify the roles and responsibilities of various stakeholders involved in a project. It combines elements of a traditional RACI with a stakeholder map, providing a visual representation of how different individuals and groups contribute to the project's success. First, assign colors to the different types of roles, departments, or area of expertise involved in the program. These can include groups such as DesignOps, UX, leadership, and partners. Then write the name of each stakeholder involved on the corresponding-colored sticky note. Finally place each sticky by their appropriate RACI role. This tool can be used at the start of any DesignOps program to ensure that all stakeholders are aligned.

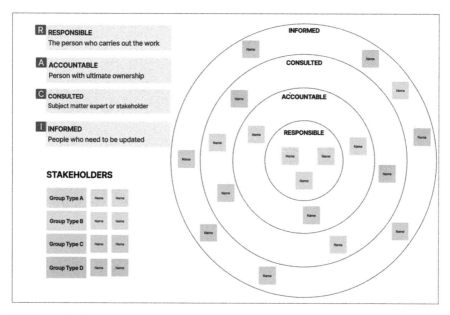

FIGURE 18.7
RACI stakeholder map.

Influence and Interest Stakeholder Map

The **influence and interest stakeholder map** categorizes stakeholders based on their power to influence the project and their level of interest in its outcome. In DesignOps, our stakeholders vary from new hires, to managers, to leaders and executives both inside and outside of design. This version of a stakeholder map is helpful for understanding stakeholder dynamics, prioritizing engagement efforts, and navigating complex relationships. This tool can help prioritize stakeholder engagement based on their potential impact on the project and can help develop targeted communication plans by tailoring messages and communication channels for each stakeholder group. By addressing the specific needs and concerns of each stakeholder group, you can ultimately build stronger relationships. Finally, this tool is helpful in minimizing project risks by proactively managing stakeholders with high power and interest to minimize potential hurdles.

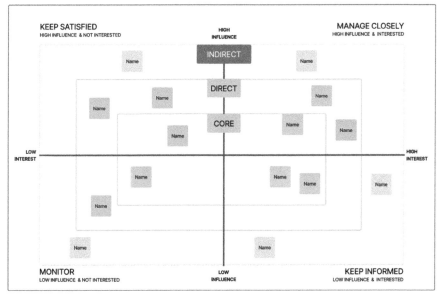

FIGURE 18.8
Influence and interest stakeholder map.

Communications Plan

A **communications plan** is vital for multiple stages of a program. One way to use a comms plan is to outline how you will communicate with your program team and your program stakeholders. Another way to use a comms plan is to plan communications that are included as part of a program rollout. In DesignOps, these are often built into the program plan, but might also live on their own as a communications strategy outlining how the team will manage the multitude of comms that are sent by DesignOps.

COMMUNICATION	PRIORITY	AUDIENCE	DESCRIPTION	FREQUENCY	CHANNEL	OWNER

FIGURE 18.9

Communications plan.

Roadmap

A **roadmap** is a strategic visual representation that outlines the key components, milestones, and timeline of a project or initiative. While the specific elements will vary based on the nature of the project, some common elements of a roadmap include timeline, phases, milestones, tasks, dependencies, deliverables, feedback loops, along with potential blockers and risks. This tool can be used in multiple phases of a DesignOps programs, from the very beginning during setup to defining a program's evolution over time.

ROADMAP

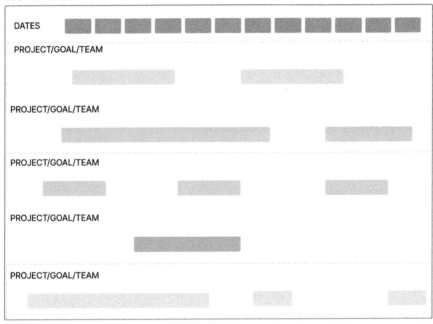

FIGURE 18.10
Roadmap.

Program Plan

A **program plan** acts as a blueprint for successful execution. It lays out the program's scope, objectives, activities, and timelines, offering a clear roadmap from start to finish. But far too often, program plans are used to serve too many purposes: an internal team document and a reference for users and partners. This can be confusing for participants, hindering their experience. **Instead, create two distinct documents:**

1. **Internal Program Headquarters:** This comprehensive document houses all program details for the DesignOps team, including planning, management, and evaluation resources.

2. **Program Participant Guide:** This visually appealing, concise document guides users through the program with clarity and ease, focusing solely on their required steps and interactions.

Another important addition to your program plan should be your purpose and guiding values. Defining the program's reason for being and anchoring it in core DesignOps values provides crucial direction, especially when tackling unfamiliar initiatives. It is your compass, guiding decision-making and keeping you on the right track even in uncertain situations, and it signals priorities to stakeholders.

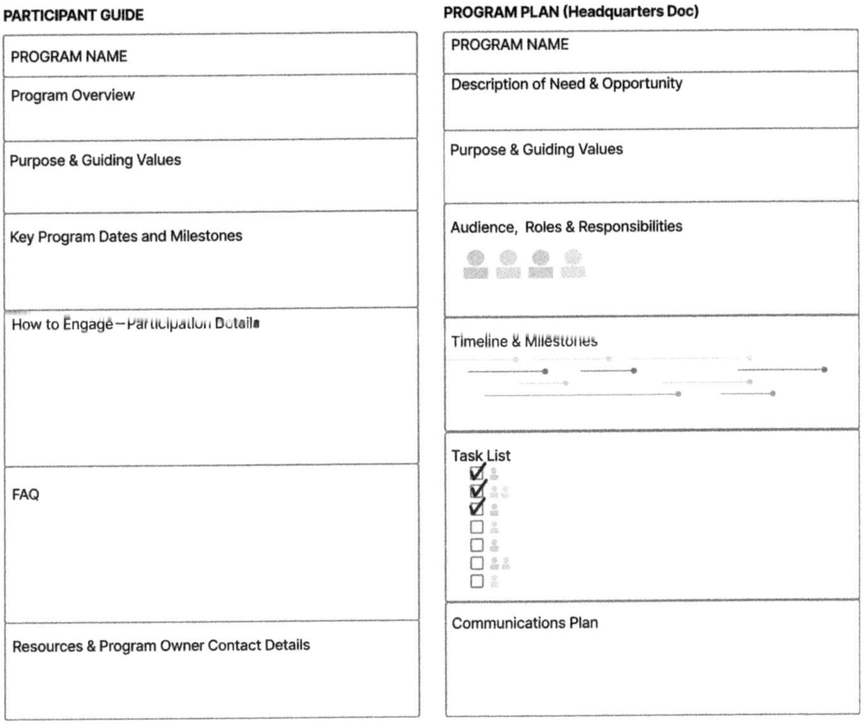

PARTICIPANT GUIDE

PROGRAM NAME
Program Overview
Purpose & Guiding Values
Key Program Dates and Milestones
How to Engage — Participation Details
FAQ
Resources & Program Owner Contact Details

PROGRAM PLAN (Headquarters Doc)

PROGRAM NAME
Description of Need & Opportunity
Purpose & Guiding Values
Audience, Roles & Responsibilities
Timeline & Milestones
Task List
Communications Plan

FIGURE 18.11

Program and participant plans.

Prioritization Matrix

First, a comment on **prioritization**. Rushing into prioritization without a clear understanding of the strategic context can result in misalignment and inefficiencies. Prioritization methods are most effective when aligned with a pre-established strategy, with the tool serving to enhance clarity on scope, sequencing, and strategic alignment to define the path forward. One of the most valuable aspects of these frameworks is their ability to clarify what *not* to do.

That said, the **impact/effort matrix** is a helpful tool that acts as a good indicator of value and helps drive alignment Using it can be as simple as mapping all your tasks or program elements in one of the four quadrants. Going from top left to top right, to bottom left to bottom right, is a smart order to approach your tasks based on priority.

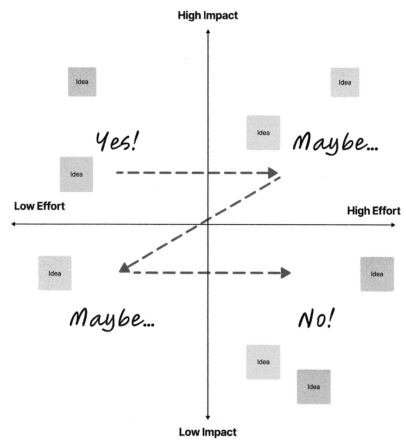

FIGURE 18.12
Impact/effort prioritization matrix.

MoSCoW Prioritization Tool

While the MoSCoW tool was originally designed to prioritize features in product development, it can also be very helpful in prioritizing design or DesignOps tasks. It can assist in prioritizing work for the year ahead or even for a single project or event. MoSCoW is an acronym for the four categories in which you'll place your programs or tasks:

- **Must-Have:** These items are essential for delivery. If any one of them is absent, the initiative cannot be launched, making it the most time-sensitive category.

- **Should-Have:** These requirements are important to deliver, but they're not critical or time sensitive.

- **Could-Have:** These are neither essential nor important to deliver within a timeframe. They're bonuses that would greatly improve customer satisfaction.

- **Won't-Have:** These are the least critical and the first to go when there are resource constraints. They are explicitly excluded from the current scope but will be considered for the future.

We like this tool because of its simplicity. The language used makes priorities crystal clear, eliminating confusion, misinterpretation, and conflict.

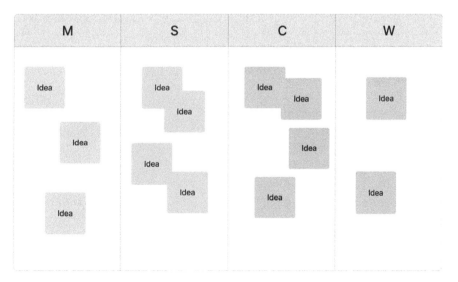

FIGURE 18.13
MoSCoW prioritization tool.

Data-First Design and DesignOps Tools

The templates listed previously are presented at a "ten-thousand foot" view; that is, they are abstracted for the purpose of communicating what the tools look like and suggesting how they can be used. Search these tools by name online for downloadable copies and templates that might be customized for your use cases or check out the "template" features in your favorite collaboration tool (Google Workspace Suite, Figma, Miro, Airtable, and the like).

Recently, DesignOps practitioners have come to understand certain limitations of templates—they are often ephemeral, bespoke, and not truly integrated (in a data sense) into the end-to-end infrastructure that's been built up to deliver great work. This sense that "it's not working" was described in the *2023 DesignOps Benchmarking Report*:

> DesignOps teams are resorting to project management tools to enable design delivery at scale, and it simply isn't working. First, project management tools "fail to support design-specific workflows out of the box." Second, these tools lack DesignOps requirements of "centralization and visibility for stakeholders and decision-makers."[1]

A journey map is a valuable tool to have, but consider: how are its insights connected across your tool stack? Does persona data live only in a research library, which is siloed from where the designers work? Critically, are the various facets of measuring design success—from the objects and directions of the Jobs to Be Done framework, to the actions, outputs, and outcomes from the HEROES framework—traceable throughout your design process?

DesignOps thinkers like Jon Fukuda have seized on this opportunity space and are currently working (as of this writing) on low-code and no-code solutions that take the templated tools described previously and integrate them together into a solution that plugs directly into researchers' and designers' workflows. Imagine user journeys, use cases, Jobs to Be Done, interaction models, and more all as contiguous data that appear in your flow of work. While still in the concept phase, the work being imagined at Fukuda's Limina (www.limina.com) shows promise:

---

1 *2023 DesignOps Benchmarking Report* (DesignOps Assembly, 2023), www.designopsassembly.com/2023report

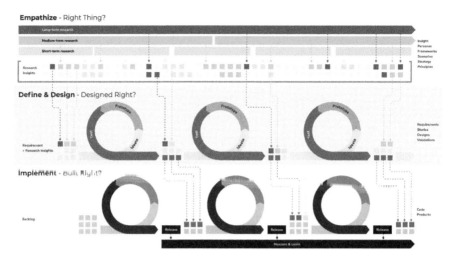

Empathize - Right Thing?

FIGURE 18.14

Limina's tri-track Agile UX methodology.

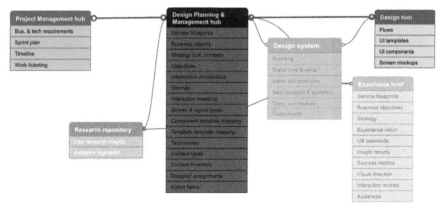

FIGURE 18.15

Design and research data in connected hubs.

A Blank Canvas, Unlimited Opportunities

Lastly, we leave you with the DesignOps Canvas: an activity and worksheet you can use to evaluate your Design Operations maturity, uncover gaps, and identify future opportunities for your DesignOps team and its design partners. This canvas brings together key concepts from this book, allowing you to apply what you've learned to better assess your own DesignOps practice.

The DesignOps Canvas

Evaluate the present. **Uncover** gaps. **Identify** opportunities.

(1) Indicate your personal level of zoom, as well as the size and maturity levels of your design and DesignOps teams.

(2) Review each category and rate how your DesignOps team is performing in each on a scale of 1 to 3 (or N/A, if not applicable).

(3) Identify the solutions you currently have in place for each category (tools, processes, systems).

(4) Identify the measures, metrics, and measurement method for each category.

(5) Review patterns, gaps, and areas of opportunity. Think of ways to refine and improve.

(6) Identify three prioritized updates to implement next.

	PEOPLE						
	Skill Building & Growth	**Team Health & Culture**	**Career Development & Performance**	**Recruiting & Onboarding**	**Retention & Recognition**	**Design Work Tracking**	**Design Delivery Process**
	To what extent are your teams equipped and empowered to excel in their roles? Are there sufficient opportunities to build skills and capabilities and learn from each other?	Does your team have regular rituals for building connections? Are you addressing low employee survey scores? How do you prioritize joy, inspiration, belonging, and psychological safety?	Are there adequate tools, processes, and support for assessing skills and performance? How confident do managers and employees feel about the expectations of the talent review cycle?	How well-prepared are hiring managers and recruiters? Is there a comprehensive and consistent process in place to welcome, educate, and support new team members?	Are recognition and celebration built into your team rhythms and communications? Do team members feel appreciated and seen?	How effective is the system for tracking, scoping, and prioritizing design work? How clear is the visibility for leaders, managers and designers regarding work status and owner?	How aligned is your design team on a delivery method and how well is it utilized? How clear are DoR, DoD and handoff processes? Do your partners integrate design throughout the development cycle?
Rating 1 = struggling 2 = managing 3 = excelling							
Solutions *List the tools, processes, and systems in place for each category.*							
Metrics & Measures *List what metrics you are tracking for each, and how you are collecting data.*							
Ideas & Opportunities • *What is missing?* • *What would make it easier, faster, better?* • *Who can help you?*							

FIGURE 18.16a

The DesignOps Canvas.

Guiding
Values: _____ _____ _____

My DesignOps Zoom

☐ Project ☐ Program ☐ Practice

DesignOps Maturity

☐ Functional ☐ Tactical ☐ Organizational ☐ Strategic

Design Org Size

☐ Small ☐ Medium ☐ Large ☐ Enterprise

Design Maturity

☐ Limited ☐ Emergent ☐ Structured ☐ Integrated

PROCESS			PLATFORM				
Program Management Process	Communication & Documentation	Knowledge & Information Management	Tooling Strategy & Management	Budget Management	Annual and Long Range Planning	Headcount Management	Dashboards & Reporting
How consistent and efficient is your DesignOps team at delivering programs? Do you have templates, trackers and processes of your own?	How strong is your communication strategy? Is it engaging across different audiences and channels, supported by templates and playbooks?	How easily can your teams access the information, assets, resources and files necessary for their work? Are there clear methods and forums for sharing information and showcasing work?	Do you have a well understood suite of design tools (software and hardware)? Are your tools effectively selected, deployed, and managed? Do you have systems in place to optimize and track tool usage?	How efficiently are funds allocated, tracked, and utilized? Do you have processes in place to monitor expenses and optimize financial resources? How well understood are spending guidelines and governance?	How robust are your strategic frameworks and forecasting methods? Do you have mechanisms in place to reassess and adapt to changing circumstances and achieve long-term goals?	How effectively are resources allocated and utilized? Do you have strategies in place to optimize staffing levels and ensure operational efficiency?	To what extent does your team capture, track and visualize key metrics and reporting processes useful and tailored to the needs of stakeholders?

FIGURE 18.16b

The DesignOps Canvas.

INDEX

sustainability, as design org value,
101–103, 110

T

tactical stage of DesignOps driver,
155, 157–158
TeamOps, 10
teams. *See* design teams; DesignOps team
tech fluency, 44
technical program managers (TPMs),
59, 136, 137–139
time horizon, in DesignOps Career
Framework, 70–71
titles and tracks of DesignOps
practitioners, 76–81
toolbox for DesignOps, 285–305
   affinity mapping, 292
   communications plan, 296
   empathy map, 291
   experience map, 288
   influence and interest stakeholder
   map, 295
   journey map, 287, 302
   mind map, 293
   MoSCoW prioritization tool, 301
   prioritization matrix, 300
   program plan, 298–299
   RACI stakeholder map, 294
   roadmap, 297
   service blueprint, 289
tracking of design work, 200, 213
transformative change, 97
Triple Diamond for DesignOps, 220–227,
235–236
Trusted Relationships and Partnerships
   as career competency, 50, 51–52, 59
   interview questions, 266–267

U

uncertainty bias, 228–229
user experience (UX)
   as experience partners, 142–143
   in history of DesignOps, 6
   roles in centralized design org, 117–118

UX Inclusive Meetings & Events Playbook,
106–107
UX operations (UX Ops), defined, 10
UX writing, 144

V

value, defining and measuring, 239–241
"The Value of Design Is Holding You
Back" (Briselli), 240
values
   -driven work, 86
   defined, and value of, 97
   family, 100
Values and Culture
   as career competency, 50, 58, 60
   interview questions, 272
values of design org, 95–110
   core values, role of, 96
   identifying, 98–101
   interpreting and defining, 101–103
   leading with values, 108–110
   operationalizing, 104–107
   value of values, 97
Van Gennep, Arnold, 219
vertical dimensions of DesignOps, 177–179
viability, in design strategy, 218–219
vice president (VP) of DesignOps, 80–81
visibility, 240
vision statement, 173

W

Wachter-Boettcher, Sara, 239
wars, 282–283
Washington, Alana, 87–88, 201
well-being
   of team, 214, 248, 250, 255
   of yourself, 215
work-tracking, 200, 213
workstreams of DesignOps team, 170,
180–185, 190, 254

Z

Zheng, Changying, 55

ACKNOWLEDGMENTS

With So Much Gratitude

Writing the first book dedicated to Design Operations was a daunting experience. Balancing it with full-time jobs and young children was also daunting, but more in a sky-diving-without-a-parachute sort of way. Thankfully, we wrote a book about a practice that attracts the most generous, kind, and supportive people. We couldn't have accomplished this alone and are immensely grateful for the wisdom and encouragement of those who invested their time and energy to help bring this book to life.

First, a thank you to the subject matter experts who gave us feedback, encouraged us to dig deeper, and shared their deep knowledge with us: Adrienne Allnutt, Alana Washington, Jason Kriese, Kamdyn Moore, and Laura Gatewood.

Next, we need to thank all the people who shared their experiences and stories with us. Your journeys, insights, roadblocks, and solutions were an inspiration to us, and—we sincerely hope—everyone who reads this book: Abbey Smalley, Adam Fry-Pierce, Adrienne Allnutt, Alana Washington, Allison Rand, Anel Muller, Binaebi Akah Calkins, Brandon Perry, Brennan Hartich, Cai Charniga, Changying (Z) Zheng, Christina Rodriguez, Courtney Allison Brown, Diane Gregorio, Hayley Ng, Jason Kriese, Jon Fukuda, Jose Coronado, Kamdyn Moore, Kristin Skinner, Kristine Berry, Meredith Black, Michelle Chu, Michelle Morrison, Patrizia Bertini, Peter Merholz, Spencer Stultz, and Victor Corral.

When we wrote our list of dream foreword authors, Kristin Skinner was right at the top. She is a true DesignOps original and a powerful voice in our community. Thank you so much for taking on the immense task of both reading this whole thing and then writing even more about it!

Behind the scenes, this book would not be possible without the work of Lou Rosenfeld, Marta Justak, and Danielle Foster. We also want to especially thank Hayley Ng for our delightful author illustrations.

Finally, much of this book draws upon the research and insights shared in the 2022 and 2023 DesignOps Benchmarking reports. These annual surveys of DesignOps practitioners are what allowed us to ground our point of view in real data, and we'd like to acknowledge those who led to this ground-breaking work: Angelos Arnis, Adam Fry-Pierce, Changying (Z) Zheng, Jules Monza, and Meredith Black.

Rachel would like to thank....

First, my deepest thanks go to John, whose expertise and sharp wit were the yin to my DesignOps yang. I couldn't have wished for a better cowriter. With him, this all somehow felt easier than it should have. And to my fellow DesignOps warriors, the brilliant makers and doers who've shared trenches with me: thank you for doing the good work, fighting the good fight, and for making this work more than just a job. And to my ever-supportive friends and family who still have no idea what I do for a living or what this book is about but will be first in line to buy a copy, I'm eternally grateful. Finally, I owe mountains of gratitude to my husband, Timothy, who steadfastly supported me, fed me, and cheered me on while my mind and time were consumed by every little thing within these pages. And to my two boys, Avi and Isaac, who make every bit of effort worth it.

John would like to thank...

Likewise, I must first thank Rachel for inviting me to join her on this journey. We've worked together professionally for years, and she is a shining example of what can be accomplished when complementary skills join forces. (And she is the real force of nature behind this book!) I also want to thank my wife, Meghan, and our children for giving me the time and grace to accomplish something that required so much extracurricular effort; without their support, I would have never even contributed to the proposal, let alone coauthored this book. Finally, I want to acknowledge everyone I've ever worked with who silently, invisibly supports the greater good of creating amazing experiences: to the producers and program managers in the gaming and software spaces, please know that your tireless efforts are recognized and invaluable to everyone you work with, and those that enjoy the works you create.

 Rosenfeld®

Dear Reader,

Thanks very much for purchasing this book. There's a story behind it and every product we create at Rosenfeld Media.

Since the early 1990s, I've been a User Experience consultant, conference presenter, workshop instructor, and author. (I'm probably best-known for having cowritten *Information Architecture for the Web and Beyond*.) In each of these roles, I've been frustrated by the missed opportunities to apply UX principles and practices.

I started Rosenfeld Media in 2005 with the goal of publishing books whose design and development showed that a publisher could practice what it preached. Since then, we've expanded into producing industry-leading conferences and workshops. In all cases, UX has helped us create better, more successful products—just as you would expect. From employing user research to drive the design of our books and conference programs, to working closely with our conference speakers on their talks, to caring deeply about customer service, we practice what we preach every day.

Please visit rosenfeldmedia.com to learn more about our **conferences**, **workshops**, **free communities**, and **other great resources** that we've made for you. And send your ideas, suggestions, and concerns my way: louis@rosenfeldmedia.com

I'd love to hear from you, and I hope you enjoy the book!

Lou Rosenfeld, Publisher

RECENT TITLES FROM ROSENFELD MEDIA

Get a great discount on a Rosenfeld Media book: visit **rfld.me/deal** to learn more.

SELECTED TITLES FROM ROSENFELD MEDIA

View our full catalog at **rosenfeldmedia.com/books**

ABOUT THE AUTHORS

Rachel Posman is a seasoned Design Operations leader driven by the opportunity to empower teams to deliver customer and business success while achieving personal and professional growth. Currently, Rachel leads the Central DesignOps team for Salesforce's global UX organization, which designs programs, processes, and systems that enable the design of great product *and* employee experiences. Previously, she led design and research operations at Uber Eats, and was a Design Program Management leader for the service and experience design teams at Capital One, Adaptive Path, and others. Rachel draws inspiration from her background in business, design strategy, service design, and a first career as a professional ballet dancer, blending these disciplines into her holistic approach to problem-solving and leadership in DesignOps.

John Calhoun is a designer, writer, and operations leader living in the San Francisco Bay Area. John is currently a leader of Salesforce's Design Operations team, which builds the platform for delivering best-in-class product design solutions and experiences at scale. Previously, John was a producer and game designer for Electronic Arts, with 17 years of experience developing video games and adjacent media. Cultivating a culture of great design through the principles of confidence, clarity, and partnership is what drew John to DesignOps; enabling teams to do great work (and live great lives) will keep him in DesignOps for years to come. John is a frequent speaker on product design and operations topics, and he can be found hiking the open spaces of California and playing bass in his spare time.